WALKING THE PATH OF WISDOM

Lessons from Proverbs for Every Heart

"Ladies Version"

by

Sherri Sullivan

ISBN: **978-1-972565-05-6**

Printed in the United States of America

Walk in the Way of Wisdom

Lessons From Proverbs for Every Heart "Ladies Version"

Published By: SHERRI SULLIVAN INC

www.sherrisullivan.com

THIS BOOK BELONGS TO:

✦✦✦✦✦

DEDICATION

To My Lord and Savior   ✦✦✦✦✦

There are not enough pages in this world to hold what I feel for You. But I will try.

This is for You, the One who found me when I had stopped looking for myself. The One who heard a cry I barely You simply came.

You knew me before I knew my own name. Before I understood what I was capable of, before I had any idea of the road ahead, You already believed in me. You had faith in me when I had none left for myself. That still brings me to my knees.

You reached into the mire, all that mess, all that mud, all that weight I had sunk into, and pulled me out. Not halfway. All the way. And then You did not just set me down and leave. You put my feet on solid ground. You made sure I could stand.

You washed me. Every stain, every scar, everything I was sure could never be undone, You made it white as snow. You gave me a new beginning when I had used up every chance I thought I had. You gave me a new path when I had completely lost my way.

Then You showed me what love actually is. Not the kind that comes and goes, or the kind that keeps score, but the kind that stays. The kind that is patient, gentle, and relentlessly faithful. I did not know love could look like that until I met You.

You gave me a future. A real one. One with purpose and hope and meaning. You took what was broken and You built something out of it that I could never have imagined on my own.

I owe You everything. Every breath I take, every word on these pages, every morning I open my eyes, it all belongs to You. This work is Yours. My life is Yours.

Thank You for not giving up on me.

All of my love, all of my gratitude, all of me.

To You, always.

With gratitude to my family, friends, and especially my beloved husband, who encouraged, prayed for, and believed in me from the beginning.. Special thanks to the person who guided me in life to become more, and for that, I thank you, my sister-in-law, Char. Also, to the members of my faith community, who have ministered God's grace and wisdom in my life.

SHERRI SULLIVAN BIO

Sherri Sullivan is a devoted writer, passionate student of God's Word, and a lifelong seeker of spiritual growth. Known for her heartfelt, approachable style, Sherri's writing resonates with readers seeking encouragement, wisdom, and practical ways to deepen their faith. She has a rare gift for making scripture feel immediate and personal, meeting readers right where they are and gently pointing them toward truth. As the author of the beloved Biblical Devotional Journal, "Walking the Path of Wisdom: Lessons from Proverbs for Every Heart," Sherri brings the timeless truths of scripture to life with warmth, insight, and gentle inspiration. Her work invites readers not just to read but to engage, reflect, and apply Biblical principles to their everyday lives, fostering a deep sense of connection, accountability, and spiritual renewal. Whether someone is new to faith or has walked with God for decades, Sherri's writing creates a welcoming space where every heart can grow.

Sherri's journey to faith was not an easy road. She came to the Lord at sixteen, stepping out of a childhood marked by atheism, abuse, and deep pain. She endured beatings, sexual abuse, and false accusations that landed her in a facility for years. She was forced into a marriage of fifteen years, only to discover it was never legally valid. Along the way, she wrestled with eating disorders, dyslexia, anger, fear, and a shattered sense of self-worth. She was easily manipulated, and by her own honest admission, made choices she deeply regrets. Yet in the middle of all of it, she found a Savior who met her exactly where she was, and coming to Him changed her life in so many beautiful ways.

What God did in Sherri's life did not erase her past; it redeemed it. Every scar became a testimony, every struggle a source of hard-won compassion. It is precisely because she has walked through the darkest of valleys that her writing carries such raw authenticity and grace. She does not write from a place of having it all figured out, but from the place of someone who has clung to God's Word when nothing else held. Sherri's deepest desire is to help others, especially women who feel broken, overlooked, or beyond hope, discover that the same God who restored her is reaching out to them, too.

In addition to her writing, Sherri spent many years leading young ladies' Bible studies, mentoring women in their faith, and serving as a trusted confidant and encourager in her community. She has a deep conviction that life change happens most powerfully in the context of genuine relationships, and she has devoted much of her life to cultivating exactly that. She is passionate about fostering authentic connections, helping others grow in their faith, and creating safe spaces where honest conversation and spiritual discovery can flourish. Sherri believes that every woman, regardless of her background or season of life, deserves a community where she is truly seen and valued. Sherri finds joy in simple pleasures: morning walks that inspire reflection, a hot cup of tea to start the day, painting, and laughter shared with friends and family. Her love of nature and quiet moments fuels her creativity, grounds her spirit, and continually strengthens her sense of gratitude for the life God has given her.

Sherri lives in the Southwest with her husband, a very spoiled cat who often keeps her company during early-morning writing sessions, and her shy little dog. She believes that every heart, no matter its story, struggles, or scars, can find guidance, comfort, and transforming grace in God's Word. That belief is not merely a sentiment; it is the conviction that drives every word she writes. Grateful for the opportunity to walk this journey alongside her readers, Sherri hopes her words will serve as a gentle reminder that no one has to navigate life alone. She hopes to point others to the enduring love and wisdom found in scripture, and to inspire them to seek God wholeheartedly, not just in the easy seasons, but in every season of life.

Table of Contents

READERS ENCOUNTER ...1

PROVERBS OVERVIEW ...2

THE "SIMPLE ONE" IN PROVERBS ...3

THE "FOOL" IN PROVERBS ...4

THE "SCORNER" IN PROVERBS ...6

THE "WISE" IN PROVERBS ...7

ALWAYS BELIEVING IN EVERYONE ...9

THE PROCRASTINATOR ...13

THE FALL ...17

JOURNEY TO UNDERSTANDING ...21

THE ONE THAT WENT ALONG ...25

ALWAYS KNOWING BEST ...29

THE WEIGHT OF HER CROWN ...33

WISDOM IN CONFLICT ...37

THE NEED TO FIT IN ...41

THE QUICK COMEBACK ...45

WOULD NOT LISTEN ...49

WISDOM IN WAITING ...53

THE STRUGGLE TO MANAGE ...57

RISKY RISKY ...61

THE LAUGH THAT COST EVERYTHING ...65

WISDOM IN FINANCES ...69

TAKEN ADVANTAGE OF ...73

THE PROMISE KEEPER ...77

THE TROUBLE CARRIED ...81

WISDOM IN HEALTH ...85

CHATTY LIPS ...89

CENTER OF IT ALL ...93

THE ONE WHO ALREADY KNEW ...97

WISDOM IN FAMILY 101

THE ADVENTURE 105

I'M DOING IT MY WAY 109

THE FIRE OUT OF CONTROL 113

WISDOM IN DECISIONS 117

THE GIVER 121

LAUGHING IT UP 125

THE SEARCH THAT NEVER ARRIVED 129

WISDOM IN REST 133

DON'T WORRY 137

THE THRILL 141

ANSWERED TO NO ONE 145

WISDOM IN LEARNING 149

OVERLY COMMITTED 153

THE NON-PLANNER 157

THE COMPANY KEPT 161

WISDOM IN FORGIVENESS 165

ALWAYS SEEING THE BEST IN PEOPLE 169

THE POT STIRRER 173

BROKEN PEACE 177

SERVING THE POOR 181

KEEPING THE PEACE 185

ON MY OWN TERMS 189

THE LOUDEST VOICE 193

WISDOM IN MARRIAGE 197

BEING LED 201

THE WEIGHT THAT WAS BUILT 209

THE BEGINNING OF WISDOM 213

A PRAYER FOR YOU 217

- Realistic scenarios that mirror contemporary struggles peer influence, financial stewardship, setting healthy boundaries, forgiving others, and navigating social pressures.

- Candid journal entries that model vulnerability and invite readers to reflect on their own choices, mistakes, and victories.

- Accessible Q&A sections that clarify the difference between wisdom and folly and offer concrete steps for growth.

- Prayers that are honest, hope-filled, and relevant to the heart's deepest needs, whether seeking forgiveness, courage, discernment, or a fresh start.

- Application prompts that help readers connect biblical wisdom to personal life, relationships, and community impact.

Walking the Path of Wisdom is not just a book; it is a companion for spiritual formation. It fosters self-examination and spiritual maturity, encouraging readers to move from naivete to discernment, from stubbornness to teachability, and from cynicism to humility. The devotional structure provides space for both guided reflection and personal journaling, making it ideal for individual study, small groups, youth ministries, and family devotions.

Key themes include:

- The journey from simplicity and naivete to wisdom and maturity.

- Overcoming the traps of pride, mockery, and stubbornness through humility and openness to correction.

- The redemptive power of God's love, which meets us in our mistakes and empowers lasting transformation.

- The vital role of community, mentorship, and wise relationships in spiritual growth.

- Practical disciplines for daily life: prayer, accountability, self-control, forgiveness, stewardship, and peacemaking.

- The Journal is intended for self-discovery and self-paced as God tenderly ministers His Grace in their lives.

Whether you are a seeker, a seasoned believer, or someone longing for a fresh start, this book offers encouragement and guidance for every step of the journey. Its pages are filled with grace and truth, meeting readers in their struggles and pointing them toward hope, wholeness, and abundant life.

Let Walking the Path of Wisdom be your guide as you seek to live with clarity, courage, and compassion embracing the wisdom that leads to true freedom, joy, and a legacy of blessing.

PROVERBS OVERVIEW

The Book of Proverbs was written to provide practical wisdom for living a godly, successful, and ethical life. Its primary goal is to instruct readers, especially the young, in moral behavior, wise decision-making, and reverence for God. The proverbs serve as guidance for daily living and interpersonal relationships.

Authorship:

Solomon, the son of King David and the third king of Israel, is traditionally credited as the principal author of Proverbs (see Proverbs 1:1). However, the book also includes sayings from other wise men, such as Agur (Proverbs 30) and King Lemuel (Proverbs 31), as well as anonymous contributors.

Date Written:

Most Proverbs are believed to have been compiled during Solomon's reign (circa 970–931 BCE). Some sections may have been added or edited later, possibly up to the time of King Hezekiah (circa 715–686 BCE), as indicated in Proverbs 25:1.

Theme:

The central theme is the pursuit of wisdom, which begins with *"the fear of the Lord" (Proverbs 1:7)*. The book emphasizes virtues such as honesty, diligence, humility, self-control, and the value of wise counsel. It contrasts wisdom with folly and underscores the consequences of both.

Additional Information:

Proverbs is classified as wisdom literature in the Hebrew Bible.

The book is structured as a collection of short, pithy statements, poems, and discourses.

Its teachings are universal, offering advice for people of all ages and backgrounds.

Many proverbs use vivid imagery and parallelism, a hallmark of Hebrew poetry.

The book addresses a broad range of topics:

- Family
- Friendships
- Work
- Justice
- Speech

THE "SIMPLE ONE" IN PROVERBS

The "Simple One" sometimes translated as "simple," "naive," or "foolish" is a recurring figure in wisdom literature, especially the Book of Proverbs. Unlike the scorner, whose actions are shaped by pride and contempt, the Simple One is marked by inexperience, lack of discernment, and a willingness to be led astray. Their greatest danger is not malice but a lack of vigilance and understanding.

1. Lacks Wisdom and Discernment

- **Proverbs 1:4 (NIV)** – "for giving prudence to those who are simple, knowledge and discretion to the young."
- **Proverbs 7:7 (NIV)** – "I saw among the simple, I noticed among the young men, a youth who had no sense."
- The Simple lack discretion and understanding and are inexperienced.

2. Easily Led Astray and Gullible

- **Proverbs 14:15 (NIV)** – "The simple believe anything, but the prudent give thought to their steps."
- **Proverbs 22:3 (NIV)** – "The prudent see danger and take refuge, but the simple keep going and pay the penalty."
- The Simple are easily deceived and lack caution, accepting things at face value.

3. Prone to Foolishness and Danger

- **Proverbs 1:32 (NIV)** – "For the waywardness of the simple will kill them, and the complacency of fools will destroy them."
- **Proverbs 7:7–23 (NIV)** – "The simple are led into sin and destruction.
- Their lack of discernment leads them into trouble and even ruin.

4. Loves Simplicity and Avoids Wisdom

- **Proverbs 1:22 (NIV)** – "How long will you who are simple love your simple ways? ... fools hate knowledge."
- The Simple are content with their naivete and do not actively seek wisdom.

5. Can Be Instructed and Corrected

- **Proverbs 9:4, 16 (NIV)** – "Let all who are simple come to my house!"
- **Proverbs 8:5 (NIV)** – "You who are simple, gain prudence; you who are foolish, set your hearts on it."
- The Simple are open to being taught and can become wise if they respond to instruction.

6. Vulnerable to Seduction and Evil Influences

- **Proverbs 7:7–23 (NIV)** – "The simple are depicted as easy prey for the adulterous woman, illustrating their susceptibility
- **Proverbs 19:25 (NIV)** – "Flog a mocker, and the simple will learn prudence; rebuke the discerning, and they will gain knowledge."
- They are easily influenced by others, for good or for ill.

7. Needs Protection and Guidance:

- **Proverbs 27:12 Proverbs 27:12 (NIV)** – "The prudent see danger and take refuge, but the simple keep going and pay the penalty."

THE "FOOL" IN PROVERBS

The "fool" is a prominent figure especially the Book of Proverbs. Unlike the Simple One, whose folly is rooted in inexperience and naivete, the fool is characterized by stubbornness, willful ignorance, and a repeated rejection of wisdom. The fool's greatest danger is not lack of knowledge, but a hardened heart that refuses to learn or change.

1. Despises Wisdom and Instruction

- **Proverbs 1:7 (NIV)** – "...but fools despise wisdom and instruction.
- **Proverbs 23:9 (NIV)** – "Do not speak to fools, for they will scorn your prudent words."
- Fools hate learning and refuse to accept guidance.

2. Quick to Anger and Uncontrolled

- **Proverbs 12:16 (NIV)** – "Fools show their annoyance at once, but the prudent overlook an insult."
- **Proverbs 29:11 (NIV)** – "Fools give full vent to their rage, but the wise bring calm in the end."
- Fools react impulsively, lacking self-control

3. Speaks Carelessly and Causes Harm

- **Proverbs 10:18 (NIV)** – "Whoever conceals hatred with lying lips and spreads slander is a fool."
- **Proverbs 15:2 (NIV)** – "...but the mouth of fools gushes folly."
- **Proverbs 18:6-7 (NIV)** – "The lips of fools bring them strife, and their mouths invite a beating.
- The mouths of fools Their words are reckless, contentious, and often destructive.

4. Rejects Correction and Discipline

- **Proverbs 15:5 (NIV)** – "A fool spurns a parent's discipline, but whoever heeds correction shows prudence."
- **Proverbs 12:15 (NIV)** – "The way of fools seems right to them, but the wise listen to advice."
- Fools resent and ignore correction, refusing to change.

5. Trusts in Their Own Way

- **Proverbs 12:15 (NIV)** – "The way of fools seems right to them, but the wise listen to advice."
- **Proverbs 28:26 (NIV)** – "Those who trust in themselves are fools, but those who walk in wisdom are kept safe."
- Fools are self-assured and stubborn, rejecting outside advice.

6. Repeats Foolish Behavior

- **Proverbs 26:11 (NIV)** – "As a dog returns to its vomit, so fools repeat their folly."

- Fools do not learn from their mistakes and continually repeat them.

7. Careless with Money and Work

- **Proverbs 21:20 (NIV)** – "The wise store up choice food and olive oil, but fools gulp theirs down."
- **Proverbs 10:23 (NIV)** – "A fool finds pleasure in wicked schemes, but a person of understanding delights in wisdom."
- Fools are wasteful, lazy, and irresponsible.

8. Brings Grief and Sorrow to Others

- **Proverbs 10:1 (NIV)** – "A wise son brings joy to his father, but a foolish son brings grief to his mother."
- **Proverbs 17:21 (NIV)** – "To have a fool for a child brings grief; there is no joy for the parent of a godless fool. "
- Their foolishness causes pain and distress to family and community.

9. Unreliable and Untrustworthy

- **Proverbs 26:6 (NIV)** – "Sending a message by the hands of a fool is like cutting off one's feet or drinking poison."
- Fools cannot be trusted with responsibility.

10. Mocks at Sin

- **Proverbs 14:9 (NIV)** – "Fools mock at making amends for sin, but goodwill is found among the upright."
- Fools treat wrongdoing and moral failure as trivial.

11. Lacks Understanding and Knowledge

- **Proverbs 18:2 (NIV)** – "Fools find no pleasure in understanding but delight in airing their own opinions."
- Fools are not interested in true understanding, only in expressing themselves.

12. Quarrelsome and Stirs Up Strife

- **Proverbs 20:3 (NIV)** – "It is to one's honor to avoid strife, but every fool is quick to quarrel."
- Fools create conflict and meddle in matters that do not concern them.

THE "SCORNER" IN PROVERBS

he "Scorner" (sometimes translated as "mocker" or "scoffer") is a recurring character in the book of Proverbs in the Bible. This figure embodies pride, contempt, and resistance to wisdom and correction. Here are the key characteristics of the Scorner, based on the Proverbs passages:

1. Prideful and Arrogant

- **Proverbs 21:24 (NIV)** – "The proud and arrogant person—'Mocker' is his name—behaves with insolent fury."
- Scorners are marked by arrogance, pride, and a sense of superiority.

2. Despises Correction

- **Proverbs 9:7–8 (NIV)** – "Whoever corrects a mocker invites insults; whoever rebukes the wicked incurs abuse. Do not rebuke mockers or they will hate you; rebuke the wise and they will love you."
- **Proverbs 13:1 (NIV)** – "A wise son heeds his father's instruction, but a mocker does not respond to rebukes."
- Scorners reject advice, discipline, and correction, often responding with hatred or anger.

3. Mocks at Goodness and Wisdom

- **Proverbs 1:22 (NIV)** – "How long will you who are simple love your simple ways? How long will mockers delight in mockery and fools hate knowledge?"
- **Proverbs 14:6 (NIV)** – "The mocker seeks wisdom and finds none, but knowledge comes easily to the discerning."
- They take pleasure in mocking others and despise true wisdom.

4. Creates Strife and Division

- **Proverbs 22:10 (NIV)** – "Drive out the mocker, and out goes strife; quarrels and insults are ended."
- Their presence brings conflict, quarrels, and dishonor.

5. Unteachable and Stubborn

- **Proverbs 15:12 (NIV)** – "Mockers resent correction, so they avoid the wise."
- Scorners refuse to seek counsel from the wise and avoid those who might correct them.

6. Incur Severe Consequences

- **Proverbs 19:29 (NIV)** – "Penalties are prepared for mockers, and beatings for the backs of fools."
- **Proverbs 3:34 (NIV)** – "He mocks proud mockers but shows favor to the humble and oppressed."
- Scorners face judgment and disgrace.

7. Influence Others Negatively

- **Proverbs 24:9 (NIV)** – "The schemes of folly are sin, and people detest a mocker."
- Their influence is harmful, and they are detested by others.

THE "WISE" IN PROVERBS

Wisdom is one of the central figures in the book of Proverbs, representing the ideal character who lives according to God's wisdom. Proverbs uses this archetype to show what godly wisdom looks like in practice. Here are all the core characteristics of the Wise as described throughout Proverbs, with references and brief explanations:

1. Listens and Learns

- **Proverbs 1:5 (NIV)** – "Let the wise listen and add to their learning, and let the discerning get guidance."

- **Proverbs 9:9 (NIV)** – "Instruct the wise and they will be wiser still; teach the righteous and they will add to their learning."

- The wise are teachable, always seeking to learn and grow.

2. Receives Correction

- **Proverbs 9:8 (NIV)** – "Do not rebuke mockers or they will hate you; rebuke the wise and they will love you."

- **Proverbs 10:8 (NIV)** – "The wise in heart accept commands, but a chattering fool comes to ruin."

- They accept correction and discipline gratefully, using it to improve.

3. Fears the Lord

- **Proverbs 1:7 (NIV)** – "The fear of the Lord is the beginning of knowledge, but fools despise wisdom and instruction."

- **Proverbs 9:10 (NIV)** – "The fear of the Lord is the beginning of wisdom, and knowledge of the Holy One is understanding."

- Reverence for God is foundational to true wisdom.

4. Speaks Carefully and Kindly

- **Proverbs 12:18 (NIV)** – "...but the tongue of the wise brings healing."

- **Proverbs 15:2 (NIV)** – "The tongue of the wise adorns knowledge, but the mouth of the fool gushes folly."

- **Proverbs 16:23 (NIV)** – "The hearts of the wise make their mouths prudent, and their lips promote instruction."

- The wise speak with thoughtfulness, healing, and restraint.

5. Plans Ahead and Acts Prudently

- **Proverbs 14:8 (NIV)** – "The wisdom of the prudent is to give thought to their ways, but the folly of fools is deception."

- **Proverbs 21:20 (NIV)** – "The wise store up choice food and olive oil, but fools gulp theirs down."

- The wise person is prudent, foreseeing danger and preparing accordingly.

6. Associates with the Wise

- **Proverbs 13:20 (NIV)** – "Walk with the wise and become wise, for a companion of fools suffers harm."

- They seek the company and counsel of others who are wise.

7. Wins Souls and Influences Others Positively

- **Proverbs 11:30 (NIV)** – "The fruit of the righteous is a tree of life, and the one who is wise saves lives."

- Their life and actions attract, influence, and benefit others.

8. Demonstrates Humility

- **Proverbs 11:2 (NIV)** – "When pride comes, then comes disgrace, but with humility comes wisdom."

- The wise are characterized by humility, not arrogance.

9. Controls Anger and Emotions

- **Proverbs 29:11 (NIV)** – "Fools give full vent to their rage, but the wise bring calm in the end."

- The wise have self-control and do not react impulsively.

10. Values and Seeks Counsel

- **Proverbs 12:15 (NIV)** – "The way of fools seems right to them, but the wise listen to advice."

- **Proverbs 19:20 (NIV)** – "Listen to advice and accept discipline, and at the end you will be counted among the wise."

- They value advice and seek guidance from others.

11. Builds Up, Not Tears Down

- **Proverbs 14:1 (NIV)** – "The wise woman builds her house, but with her own hands the foolish one tears hers down."

- The wise use their wisdom to constructively build up their lives and the lives of others.

12. Exhibits Diligence

- **Proverbs 10:5 (NIV)** – "He who gathers crops in summer is a prudent son, but he who sleeps during harvest is a disgraceful son."

- They are hardworking and diligent, not lazy.

ALWAYS BELIEVING IN EVERYONE

THE SIMPLE ONE

PROVERBS 27:6 (NIV)

"Wounds from a friend can be trusted but an enemy multiplies kisses."

Emily was the kind of person who found it impossible to say no. She'd offer her seat on a crowded bus, share her last sandwich with a stranger, and always made sure to greet the kids sitting alone at lunch. Teachers appreciated her. Friends depended on her. She didn't spend much time thinking about it. Kindness was part of her, just as playing soccer or drawing came naturally to other kids. She didn't have to try; it was simply who she was, and she figured that was a good thing.

Midway through the semester, a new kid named Mark showed up. He stood in the doorway of homeroom, looking like he'd rather be anywhere else. Emily knew that feeling, sort of. She'd moved schools once in fourth grade and still remembered how long the first week felt. So, she walked over, introduced herself, showed him where the good water fountain was, and told him to sit with her group at lunch. Within a week, they were talking like they'd known each other for years.

A few days in, Mark showed up to class empty-handed. He'd forgotten the math homework, he said, and just needed to peek at her answers real quickly. Emily paused for a second. Something felt a little off. But he looked genuinely stressed, and she told herself it wasn't a big deal. The next week it was English. "I'm so behind," he said, dragging out the words. "You're literally so good at this. Just this once, can I copy?" She noticed he didn't look that stressed this time.

She said yes again. She told herself she was being a good friend, that he was still adjusting, that it was just homework. But then it stopped being a question. He'd nudge her elbow before class or slide a blank worksheet across the desk with a grin like it was already settled. Emily's stomach started doing that thing where it tightens up, and you don't totally know why. She wanted to say something, but she was scared it would come out wrong, like she was accusing him.

Then Mrs. Hernandez kept them both after class. She laid their papers side by side on her desk without saying anything at first. Same wrong answers. Same phrasing. Same everything. Emily's face went hot before Mrs. Hernandez even opened her mouth. Mark stared at the floor. Emily tried to explain. "I was just trying to help him," she said, but even as the words came out, she heard how thin they sounded.

Standing there, Emily understood something she hadn't let herself see before. She hadn't been helping Mark. She'd been making things easier for him in a way that made things harder for both of them. He got to skip the work, and she got to feel useful, and neither of those things was actually good. She'd looked the other way because she didn't want to think badly of him. But wanting to believe the best in someone isn't the same as being wise about them.

Mrs. Hernandez didn't yell. She just said that real friendship doesn't put someone in the position of having to choose between helping a friend and doing what's right. She let Emily redo the assignments on her own. Mark had to meet with the school counselor.

Walking home that afternoon, Emily wasn't sad exactly. She was quieter inside. She replayed the whole thing, every time she'd handed over her paper, every excuse she'd made for him, every moment she'd pushed down that uneasy feeling. She was frustrated with herself. Not because she'd been kind, but because she'd let her kindness run on autopilot.

Over the next few weeks, things shifted. She apologized to Mrs. Hernandez and meant it. She kept being friendly with Mark, but when he nudged her elbow before class, she just shook her head. At first, he looked annoyed.

Eventually, he started doing his own work. It wasn't a dramatic turnaround. It was just quieter and more honest. Emily figured out that caring about someone doesn't mean carrying them. Sometimes it means stepping back and letting them carry themselves. She still saw the good in people. She always would. But she stopped pretending not to notice the rest.

Day 1: Q&A:

Q: How can being too trusting cause problems?
A: When you lead with a wide-open heart and no filter, people with bad intentions will find you. That's just the truth. Being simple-hearted isn't a character flaw. It means you're still in the process of learning how to match your generosity with good judgment, and that's a process most people are still working through well into adulthood. Proverbs 1:4 says wisdom exists "to give prudence to the simple, knowledge and discretion to the young." God isn't trying to make you suspicious of everyone. He's trying to help you get smarter about who you open up to and when. Boundaries aren't about shutting people out. They're about making sure the love you give actually lands somewhere good, rather than being used up by someone who was never really invested in you.

Q: Can Simple Ones learn from their mistakes?
A: Yes, and honestly, that's often how the best growth happens. Not in a classroom, not from a lecture, but from something that went sideways and made you sit with it afterward. Proverbs 9:9 says, "Give instruction to a wise man, and he will be still wiser; teach a righteous man, and he will increase in learning." The keyword there is learning. You have to actually let the lesson in. A lot of people replay their mistakes on a loop but never really examine them. When you take a hard moment to God and ask Him what He's trying to show you through it, something changes. You stop just feeling bad about it and start seeing it differently. Being simple-hearted doesn't have to be a permanent state. It's a starting point. Where you go from here is what matters.

Day 2: Explanation: Proverbs doesn't paint Simple Ones as villains. It describes them as people who haven't yet built up the inner tools to read a situation clearly before stepping into it. That's not a moral failure. It's a gap, and gaps can be filled. Proverbs 22:3 puts it plainly: "The prudent sees danger and hides himself, but the simple go on and suffer for it." The person with wisdom slows down. They pray. They look at the situation from multiple angles before they move. The simple-hearted person just goes, because their instinct is to trust and to help. That instinct isn't wrong. It just needs something steadier underneath it, something that asks a few more questions before the heart takes over completely.

Day 3: Anecdote: A pastor I heard speak once talked about his first few years in ministry. He said he used to treat every request as urgent and genuine, no questions asked. Someone needed rent money, so he gave it. Someone needed a ride at midnight, he went. He thought saying yes to everything was what serving looked like. Then one afternoon, he got a call from someone he'd helped three times already, and he felt something he didn't expect: resentment. That scared him more than anything. He started praying differently after that, not just for the people who came to him, but for the wisdom to know when helping was actually helping. Have you set boundaries in your life by refusing to let others take advantage of your kindness?

Day 4: Warning: A giving spirit is a gift, but left unguarded, it can become a liability. Proverbs 14:15 says it directly: "The simple believes everything, but the prudent gives thought to his steps." Not every hard-luck story is a lie, but not everyone is true either. The people who take advantage of generous folks rarely announce themselves. They show up looking like a friend, or a good cause, or someone who just needs one more chance. Proverbs 2:6 tells us that God gives wisdom to those who ask for it. So, before you hand over your time, your money, your loyalty, or your work, stop and ask. It doesn't take long. It just takes the habit.

Day 5: Encouragement: God isn't looking at your open heart and wishing you were more guarded. He put that warmth in you on purpose. The fact that you want to help people, that you see the good in them before you see the risk, that's not a weakness to fix. Proverbs 3:13 says, "Blessed is the one who finds wisdom, and the one who gets understanding." He's not asking you to become someone colder or more calculating. He's asking you to grow. To bring your whole self, your kindness, and your discernment into the same room. Do you have an open heart to learn and let Him refine the gifts He has already placed in you?

Day 6: God's Love and Redemption: Being taken advantage of hurts. There's no way around that. But it doesn't disqualify you, and it doesn't define you. God sees what happened, and He doesn't hold your openness against you. What he wants is to use that experience to build something in you that wasn't there before. Not bitterness. Not walls. But a deeper, steadier kind of wisdom that comes from having actually lived something. He's good at that, taking the things that knocked us down and turning them into the very ground we stand on. Have you prayed that you truly learn and that God shows you so you don't keep repeating the same life choices?

Day 7: Reflection Questions:

Q: Have you ever helped someone out of kindness, only to realize later that your trust was misused? What did you learn from that experience? Looking back, were there signs early on that something wasn't right, things you noticed but talked yourself out of? How has that moment changed the way you decide who gets your time, your energy, or your help today?

Q: What would it look like to protect your kindness without shutting it down completely? Are there specific people or situations in your life right now where you keep giving more than feels right? And what would happen if you said something honest instead of just going along with it? Would speaking up actually be the more loving thing to do?

Q: When you think about the times you've said yes out of kindness—even when it cost you something—what might change if you paused to ask yourself what you truly wanted in that moment? How would it feel to let yourself be honest about your limits, and how might that honesty change your relationships going forward?

Q: What would it look like to build a small pause into the moments when someone asks something of you? Not a wall, just a breath, a quick prayer, a moment to check in with God before you respond. Is there a verse or practice that could help you make that a real habit rather than just a good intention?

PRAYER JOURNAL

racious Father, Thank you for your compassionate heart. I admit that, sometimes, my kindness and trusting nature have left me vulnerable or open to being taken advantage of. Forgive me for the times I have acted without seeking Your discernment or have failed to set healthy boundaries.

Lord, I ask for wisdom to know when to help and when to pause. Teach me to balance grace with truth, and to love others in ways that honor You and protect my heart. Guide me to seek Your counsel and to learn from both my successes and my mistakes.

Thank You for redeeming my experiences, for never giving up on me, and for always leading me toward greater maturity. May Your love shape how I serve and interact with others.

In Jesus' name, Amen. *Prayer Thoughts for Today:* ✦✦✦✦✦

~ END PRAYER JOURNAL "THE SIMPLE ONE" ~

THE PROCRASTINATOR

THE FOOL

PROVERBS 12:15 (NIV)

"The way of fools seems right to them, but the wise listen to advice."

Jenna had a routine. She'd cram the night before, grab four hours of sleep, walk into class, and somehow pass. It had worked since sixth grade, so why change it? Her friends actually found it impressive. They'd stay up until two in the morning, making color-coded flashcards, while Jenna watched TV and still managed a C-plus. She liked that about herself. She didn't think of it as being lazy, just efficient.

Mr. Reynolds announced the exam on a Tuesday. Two weeks out, which felt like forever. He passed around a four-page study guide, front and back, and told everyone to chip away at it a little each night. The test would cover themes and analysis, not just names and dates. "You'll thank yourself later," he said. Jenna folded the study guide in half and stuffed it in her binder. She whispered to her friend Camille, "He says that every time. Watch, it'll be fine."

The study guide stayed folded in her binder for nine days. She had drama rehearsals on Monday and Wednesday, and on Thursday, Camille got a new dog; they spent two hours at her house just holding it. The weekend came and went. Her mom asked once about the test, and Jenna said she was handling it, which wasn't technically a lie because she did intend to handle it. She saw kids quizzing each other at lunch and thought, I should do that. She did not do that.

Sunday night, she finally opened her textbook. The chapter headings didn't look familiar. She flipped back further. None of it looked familiar. Her phone lit up with a thread from Camille about a show they'd both been meaning to watch, and Jenna told herself she'd just put it on in the background while she read. She didn't read. At midnight, she set her alarm for five-thirty and called it a plan. When five-thirty came, she turned it off without sitting up and slept until her mom knocked on the door at seven-fifteen.

The test had six short-answer questions and one essay. Jenna read the first question twice, still unsure what it wanted. She wrote a sentence, crossed it out, then wrote it again a little differently. The essay prompt asked her to compare two turning points from the unit and explain their long-term effects. She stared at the page for a while. She wrote three paragraphs she knew were mostly off, but at least they looked like paragraphs. She handed it in eight minutes early, figuring sitting there wasn't going to help.

The tests came back on a Friday. Jenna flipped hers over fast, the way you rip off a bandage, and then just sat there looking at the number. Sixty-one. There were comments in the margins in red pen, things like "needs more context" and "unsupported claim." She turned it face down on her desk. Her throat felt tight in a way she wasn't expecting. She thought about texting Camille, but didn't know what she'd even say. By the time she got to the hallway, she'd already decided on her angle. "Mr. Reynolds made that test impossible," she said loudly enough for people to hear. "Who even writes questions like that?" A couple of kids laughed. That helped a little.

At home, she told her parents the whole class bombed it, which wasn't true but wasn't something they could easily check. When Mr. Reynolds pulled her aside and offered to go over her answers with her, she smiled and said, "Sure," but then didn't show up. She told Camille he was one of those teachers who liked making kids feel bad. Camille nodded but didn't say much.

October turned into November. Jenna's history grade hovered at a sixty-four, and her English grade wasn't much better. She watched a girl named Priya move from a C on the first test to a B-plus on the second, and felt something she didn't want to name.

It wasn't exactly jealousy. It was more like being annoyed at someone for making you look bad just by doing well. Jenna made more jokes. Her friends still laughed, but it was getting harder to tell whether they actually thought she was funny or just didn't know what else to do.

Report cards came on Thursday. Her dad looked at hers for a long time without saying anything, which was worse than if he'd just yelled. Her mom asked if something was going on, like maybe something at school was hard or something had happened. Jenna said no and meant to stop there, but then she started crying, something she hadn't planned. She cried for a while. Later, sitting on her bed, she thought about the study guide still folded in her binder. She thought about Mr. Reynolds saying, "You'll thank yourself later." She'd thought he was performing concern. Maybe he wasn't.

She didn't change everything overnight. She just started glancing over her notes before bed, even when she didn't feel like it, even if it was only for fifteen minutes. One morning, she went to Mr. Reynolds before school and asked about the essay she'd missed. He wasn't weird about it; he just explained it. On the next test, she scored a seventy-eight. It wasn't a dramatic turnaround. It was just a seventy-eight. But this time, she actually knew the answers, and that felt different from any C-plus she'd gotten from cramming.
She never became the color-coded flashcard type. That just wasn't her. But she stopped pretending the work didn't matter. She stopped acting for people who weren't really paying attention anyway. Sometimes she thought about the sixty-one, not to feel bad, but to remember what it felt like to sit in that hallway and have to decide who she wanted to be. She'd made the wrong choice that day. Later, she made a different one. That felt like enough to build on.

Day 1: Q&A:
Q: Why did Jenna refuse to take her studies seriously, even after her teacher gave her clear warnings and a detailed study guide?
A: She rejected sound instruction, thinking she knew better and that consequences wouldn't apply to her. Jenna's pride blinded her to the value of preparation, and she mistook her past luck for genuine ability. Rather than heeding her teacher's guidance, she chose entertainment and distraction over discipline. Proverbs 12:15 reminds us, "The way of a fool is right in his own eyes, but a wise man listens to advice."

Q: What happened as a result of Jenna's choices, and how did her response to failure reveal even deeper problems in her character?
A: Jenna faced disappointment and embarrassment, an outcome that often follows those who ignore wise counsel. Rather than accepting responsibility, she deflected blame onto her teacher and made excuses to protect her pride. Her unwillingness to acknowledge her own failure only deepened her struggle and kept her from growing. Proverbs 13:18 says, "Poverty and shame will come to him who ignores instruction, but whoever heeds reproof is honored."

Day 2: Explanation: The Bible says, "Fools make a mock at sin" (Proverbs 14:9). When we ignore warnings and make light of instruction, we set ourselves up for hardship. God's guidance is not meant to restrict joy, but to protect us from unnecessary pain and regret. Like Jenna, we can fall into the trap of believing that wisdom only applies to others, not to us. Proverbs 19:20 urges us, "Listen to advice and accept instruction, that you may gain wisdom in the future." When we humble ourselves to receive correction, we position ourselves for growth, blessing, and a life that honors God.

Day 3: Anecdote: A friend once shared that he always ignored his mechanic's advice to change his car's oil regularly. He thought the warnings were exaggerated and that skipping the maintenance would save him time and money. Eventually, the engine failed completely, costing him far more than regular maintenance ever would have. He learned the hard way that ignoring simple wisdom brings bigger problems, a lesson echoed in Proverbs 5:12-13, "How I hated discipline, and my heart despised reproof! I did not listen to the voice of my teachers or incline my ear to my instructors."

Day 4: Warning: There's a version of Jenna in all of us. The one who keeps brushing things off, figuring we'll deal with it later, until later turns into a report card, a failed relationship, or something harder to recover from. Proverbs 15:32 says, "He that refuses instruction despises his own soul." That's a strong word. But it's honest. Ignoring wisdom long enough doesn't just cost you the test. It costs you the habit of listening.

Day 5: Encouragement: Jenna didn't fix everything at once. She just stopped pretending and started showing up. That's usually how it goes. You don't need a dramatic turning point. You just need one honest moment where you decide to try differently. Proverbs 24:16 says, "For the righteous falls seven times and rises again." Seven times. God isn't surprised when you fall. He's just watching to see if you'll get back up. You still can.

Day 6: God's Love and Redemption: God doesn't walk away when you've made a mess of things. He's seen worse and stayed. Proverbs 3:11-12 says He corrects the ones He loves, the way a father does with a kid he actually cares about. That's not punishment for the sake of it. That's someone invested in where you end up. Whatever you've been avoiding or ignoring, it's not too far gone. Bring it to Him and see what He does with it.

Day 7: Reflection Questions:

Q: Can you recall a time when you dismissed someone's advice or instructions, thinking you knew better? What happened as a result?

Q: Why do you think people sometimes make light of their mistakes instead of learning from them?

Q: What are some practical ways you can begin to accept wisdom and guidance in your daily life?

Q: How does God's promise of forgiveness and new beginnings encourage you when you've acted foolishly?

PRAYER JOURNAL

G racious God, Thank you for your endless patience and loving guidance. I confess that I have often ignored wise advice and laughed off the seriousness of my mistakes. Forgive my pride and stubbornness and help me to recognize the value of instruction from those who care for me. Give me a teachable spirit and the courage to admit when I am wrong. Fill my heart with humility and a desire to grow in wisdom. Thank You for Your mercy and the fresh start You offer every day. Lead me away from the paths of foolishness and into the safety and blessing of Your truth. May I always remember that Your love redeems every failure and Your wisdom lights my way.

In Jesus' name, Amen.

Prayer Thoughts for Today:

✦✦✦✦✦

~ END PRAYER JOURNAL "THE FOOL" ~

THE FALL

THE SCORNER

PROVERBS 21:24 (NIV)

"The proud and arrogant person, 'Mocker' is his name—behaves with insolent fury."

Monica grew up believing she was the most important person in any room. Her childhood in the grand estate her father built on Calder's outskirts was filled with constant reminders of her supposed exceptionalism. Compliments from her father, admiration from tutors for her quick mind, and the respectful distance of household staff all fed her sense of superiority.

As Monica became an adult, her influence in Calder grew, thanks to her family name and wealth. She moved through social circles with determination rather than kindness, often leading charitable boards more for status than for a genuine desire to help. Her presence announced her power, and she seldom saw anyone as her equal.

Inside her family's business, Monica became known for never accepting correction. She brushed off advice from experienced colleagues, trusting only her own untested opinions. When her choices backfired, she blamed outside forces, never herself. This arrogance shaped how she saw the working class, too; servants and laborers were just background in the story she told herself. A few people tried to reach her. Constance, a longtime friend of Monica's late mother, gently warned her about the hardness she was developing. Sometimes, Constance's words sparked a flicker of empathy in Monica and reminded her how lonely her attitude could be. But deep down, Monica still resisted change.

Over time, cracks formed in Monica's carefully built world, like the slow crumbling of a hollow foundation. Poor business decisions, born from her refusal to listen to anyone, started to unravel the financial empire her father had built. Her need to look in control only made things worse, leading to devastating losses.

When people heard about her financial troubles, Calder's once-admiring social world changed overnight. Invitations stopped coming. Acquaintances who once flattered her now made excuses to avoid her. Boards she once led started asking for her resignation. Monica suddenly found herself on the outside of the society she used to rule.
Eventually, Monica left her grand estate for a modest house on a quiet street. She let her staff go, one by one, until she was alone. The silence in her new home was overwhelming. She had always depended on a busy household, and now she had to face the reality of her own solitude.

With no real relationships left, Monica faced the painful truth: her pride had built walls, not bridges, and she had never learned how to be truly loved. The isolation closed in, showing her that she had no real friends. The warning from Proverbs 21:24 echoed in her mind: "The proud and haughty, one who acts with insolent pride, is labeled a scoffer." She had turned her nose up at humility and wisdom, believing she needed no one and could never be wrong, never realizing her pride might be her undoing. Now, standing in the ruins of her old life, Monica felt the weight of her arrogance pressing down on her. Loneliness wrapped around her, a stark contrast to all the praise she used to enjoy. She'd built her life on confidence and pride, only to find it left her with nothing but silence and a deep longing for connection she'd always taken for granted

Alone, Monica started to reflect on her choices and the emptiness they'd brought. In the quiet, a fragile hope grew: maybe she could finally learn to listen, to herself and to the people she'd ignored. It was a painful reckoning, but also a chance to grow, if she could finally accept the humility she'd always resisted. Redemption wouldn't be easy, but for the first time, it felt possible.

Day 1: Q&A

Q: What does Proverbs 21:24 say about a proud and haughty person?
A: Proverbs 21:24 says that a proud and haughty person, one who acts with pride, is called a scoffer, someone who mocks wisdom, despises correction, and refuses to submit to anyone or anything greater than themselves. This means that arrogance is not just a personality flaw but a spiritual condition that God takes seriously, one that closes the heart off from the very guidance and grace it needs most. Left unchecked, pride does not simply make a person difficult to be around; it becomes a barrier between them and the life God intended for them to live.

Q: How did Monica's pride show up in her everyday life?
A: Monica's pride showed up in the way she dismissed the counsel of others, treated people of lower status as invisible, refused to accept blame when things went wrong, and surrounded herself with flattery rather than truth. Her arrogance touched every area of her life, from business to personal relationships.

Day 2: Explanation: Pride, at its core, is the belief that one is superior to others and therefore not accountable to them or to God. In Monica Ashford's story, we see how pride operates quietly at first, fed by praise, privilege, and unchallenged success. Over time, it hardens into something that cannot receive correction, cannot extend grace, and cannot form a genuine connection. The Bible does not treat pride as a minor weakness. It places pride at the root of many other sins because a proud heart closes itself off from the very wisdom and humility that lead to life. Monica was not simply a woman who thought highly of herself. She was a woman who had made herself the center of her own world, and that kind of pride, Scripture tells us, comes before a fall.

Day 3: Anecdote: A pastor in a mid-sized congregation once told his elders he no longer needed their input on major decisions. He had served as shepherd of the church for 20 years. He had seen what worked. When a young deacon raised concerns about the direction of a building campaign, the pastor cut him off mid-sentence in front of the full board. The deacon left quietly. So did three others over the next year. The pastor preached the same sermons with the same confidence, but the room had changed. Families sensed something they could not quite name, a tightness, a closed door behind the pulpit. Attendance dropped slowly, then sharply. When the building campaign collapsed under debt, there was no one left in the inner circle willing to say they had seen it coming. The most painful part was not the financial loss. It was that the pastor genuinely believed, even then, that he had done nothing wrong. Pride does not always roar. Sometimes it simply stops asking questions and calls that wisdom.

Day 4: Warning: Pride is a patient and deceptive enemy. It does not announce itself. It grows in the quiet spaces where praise goes unchecked, and correction is never welcomed. It disguises itself as confidence, as ambition, as high standards, and as a refusal to settle for less. But beneath those masks, pride is always doing the same work. It is building walls between a person and the truth, between a person and a genuine relationship, and between a person and God. The warning of Proverbs 21:24 is not just about behavior. It is about the condition of the heart. A person who has become a scoffer has reached a place where wisdom can no longer find an entrance. Guard your heart against the slow drift toward arrogance. The moment you stop being teachable is the moment your foundation begins to crack.

Day 5: Encouragement: If you recognize any part of Monica Ashford's story in yourself, take heart. The fact that you can see it is already a sign of grace. Pride blinds, but humility opens the eyes. God does not abandon the proud person to their destruction without first sending warning, sending people, and sending moments of quiet conviction. Monica's story ends in isolation and regret, but that need not be your story. Scripture is filled with men and women who walked in pride, hit the wall of consequence, and then turned. Turning is always possible. Humility is not weakness. It is the posture of a person who has decided that truth matters more than image, and that God's approval is worth more than the applause of any room.

Day 6: Why People Become Scorners: People do not usually set out to become scorners. Like Monica, most people who end up in the grip of arrogance were shaped by a combination of unchecked praise, unaddressed insecurity, and an environment that rewarded performance over character. When a person is never taught that they are fallible, they begin to believe they are not. When correction is treated as an attack rather than a gift, the heart hardens against it. When success comes early and easily, it can create a false sense that one's own judgment is always sufficient. Over time, these patterns compound. The person stops growing because they believe they have already arrived. They stop listening because they believe they already know. And they stop connecting because genuine connection requires a vulnerability that pride refuses to allow.

Day 7: Reflection Questions:

Q: In what areas of your life are you most resistant to correction or outside counsel, and what might that resistance be telling you about the condition of your heart?

Q: Think about the people in your life who have tried to speak truth to you. Have you received them with humility, or, like Monica, have you dismissed them with impatience? What would it look like to go back and truly listen?

Q: Monica's pride did not appear overnight. It was built slowly through years of unchecked praise and unchallenged thinking. What habits or practices can you put in place today to keep your heart soft and teachable before God and others?

ather,

We come before You acknowledging that pride is a danger we are all capable of. Forgive us for the times we have dismissed the wisdom of others, treated people as less than they are, and placed our own judgment above Yours. We do not want to be scorners. We want to be men and women who are quick to listen, slow to speak, and willing to be corrected. Soften our hearts, which have grown hard. Restore the relationships that pride has damaged. Teach us that true strength is found not in the image we project to the world, but in the humility, we carry before You.

In the name of Jesus, Amen.

Prayer Thoughts for Today:

~ END PRAYER JOURNAL "THE SCORNER" ~

Journey To Understanding

THE WISE

PROVERBS 13:20 (NIV)

"Walk with the wise and become wise, for a companion of fools suffers harm."

Emma hadn't always been wise. At twenty-three, she made a financial mistake so big that it took her two years to fix. She rarely talked about it, but it lingered, a quiet reminder that confidence without counsel is just costly guessing. As a kid, she saw people move fast and trust their instincts, so she tried to do the same for a while. It didn't work. What changed her wasn't a book or a sermon, though both helped. It was a conversation with her aunt after the money situation fell apart, an honest, uncomfortable conversation where her aunt didn't soften anything. Emma sat with it for days. Then she started asking more questions and making fewer assumptions. Proverbs 13:20 became a guiding principle in her life: "Walk with the wise and become wise, for a companion of fools suffers harm."

When Emma's company started a mentorship program, she signed up right away, partly out of genuine interest, partly because she hadn't forgotten the cost of her earlier mistake. Her mentor, Mr. Kim, was different from what she expected: direct to the point of stinging, always asking follow-up questions that revealed the holes in her thinking. Some days, she left feeling deflated. Still, she kept coming back.

Over time, she noticed a pattern: the choices she discussed with Mr. Kim worked out better. The ones she made quickly, alone, usually didn't. She started slowing down, asking more questions, and assuming less. Her coworkers noticed before she did that she'd become someone people trusted to think things through. She learned that seeking advice wasn't a weakness; it was real wisdom, just as Proverbs 15:22 says: "Plans fail for lack of counsel, but with many advisers they succeed."

Emma's friends noticed a change, even if they couldn't put their finger on it. She wasn't louder or more confident than before. If anything, she was quieter in arguments, less about winning, more about understanding what was really happening.

When a close friend went through a hard divorce, Emma didn't rush in with advice. She just sat with her, asked questions, and said less than she thought she should. Later, her friend told her it was the most helpful thing anyone had done. At first, Emma didn't get it; she was still learning that wisdom isn't always what you say. Sometimes it's what you don't say, or simply being there. When the promotion offer came, Emma's first instinct was to say yes right away. It was a big job in a city she'd always wanted to try, and the offer felt like proof she'd done things right. But she had learned to be careful with big choices. She asked for two weeks to think. She called her parents, talked to Mr. Kim, and sat with the discomfort of uncertainty.

Talking with her mom brought up a worry she'd tried not to think about, the fact that she'd be leaving behind a community she'd spent years building. It didn't change her answer, but it changed how she made her decision. She accepted the job with her eyes open, not just excited, but honest about what it would cost.

The move was harder than she thought. The new city was fine, the job was good, but starting over at thirty-one felt lonely in a way she hadn't expected. She hadn't realized how much her sense of stability came from the people around her. She found a church in her third month, not the first week, and it took even longer to feel like she belonged. But she kept showing up, kept introducing herself, kept asking questions instead of acting like she had it all figured out. Slowly, it started to feel like home.

Day 1: Q&A:

Q: What set Emma apart from others in her journey, and how did her approach to uncertainty shape the direction of her life?
A: She intentionally sought wisdom from mentors, friends, and God, humbly applying their guidance to every area of her life rather than trusting only her own instincts. Emma understood that no person is wise enough on their own to navigate every challenge, and she was willing to remain a learner no matter how much she grew. Her humility opened doors that pride would have kept shut, and her consistency in seeking counsel built a life of stability and purpose. Proverbs 19:20 affirms this approach: "Listen to advice and accept instruction, that you may gain wisdom in the future."

Q: What blessings did Emma experience as a result?
A: Emma avoided pitfalls that derailed many of her peers, built strong and lasting relationships grounded in trust, and found a deep peace in decision-making that comes only from seeking godly counsel. Her willingness to receive wisdom made her a safe and steady presence for everyone around her, and over time, she became a source of guidance for others who were just beginning their own journeys. The blessings in her life multiplied not just inward but outward, as she freely gave what she had freely received. Proverbs 3:13-14 declares, "Blessed are those who find wisdom, those who gain understanding, for she is more profitable than silver and yields better returns than gold."

Day 2: Explanation: Proverbs 3:13-14 declares, "Blessed are those who find wisdom, those who gain understanding, for she is more profitable than silver and yields better returns than gold." Wisdom is not simply knowledge stored in the mind but a way of living that shapes every decision, relationship, and response we make. When we pursue wisdom with sincerity and humility, God honors that pursuit with protection, peace, and rewards that far outlast any material gain. Like Emma, we can experience the compounding blessings of wise living when we choose to seek counsel rather than lean solely on our own understanding. Proverbs 4:7 reinforces this truth: "The beginning of wisdom is this: Get wisdom, and whatever you get, get insight." Wisdom is not a destination but a daily, intentional pursuit that transforms ordinary lives into extraordinary testimonies.

Day 3: Anecdote: A first-year teacher named Dara nearly quit in October. Her third-period class had stopped listening entirely, and she had no idea why. She had a degree, a lesson plan, and a genuine love for her subject, but none of it seemed to matter. For weeks, she closed her classroom door and tried to fix it alone, convinced that asking for help would signal to her colleagues that she didn't belong there. Finally, after a particularly bad Friday, she knocked on the door of a veteran teacher down the hall named Mrs. Okafor. She expected judgment. What she got was a cup of tea and forty-five minutes of the most practical advice she'd ever received, about proximity, about pacing, about which battles weren't worth fighting. By November, things had shifted. Not perfectly, but enough. Dara taught for eleven more years. She kept Mrs. Okafor's number in her phone the whole time. Proverbs 12:15 speaks directly to her experience: "The way of a fool is right in his own eyes, but a wise man listens to advice."

Day 4: Blessing and Rewards: Those who seek and apply wisdom gain far more than knowledge; they receive divine guidance, supernatural protection, and a joy that the world cannot give or take away. Wisdom shapes the way we see challenges, relate to others, and respond to the unexpected turns of life, making us more resilient and more fruitful in every season. Emma's story is a picture of what God promises to those who walk in wisdom, a life marked by strong relationships, clear purpose, and the deep satisfaction of knowing you are on the right path. Proverbs 2:10-11 says, "Wisdom will enter your heart, and knowledge will be pleasant to your soul. Discretion will protect you, and understanding will guard you. These are not distant promises but daily realities available to every person who chooses to pursue wisdom with a sincere and humble heart. God is faithful to reward those who honor His instruction, and no investment in wisdom is ever wasted.

Day 5: Encouragement: You do not have to figure out life alone, and God never intended for you to carry every decision and challenge in isolation. He delights in giving wisdom generously to all who ask, and He has already placed people in your life who carry the experience, perspective, and care you need for the road ahead. Like Emma, you may be standing at a crossroads right now, uncertain and a little afraid, but the wisest thing you can do is humble yourself and reach out for counsel. Every step you take toward wisdom is a step away from unnecessary pain and a step closer to the abundant life God has prepared for you. Proverbs 8:17 offers this beautiful promise from wisdom itself: "I love those who love me, and those who seek me diligently find me." Begin seeking today, and trust that God will honor every sincere step you take toward understanding.

Day 6: God's Love and Redemption: Most of us can look back and name at least one moment when someone offered us wise counsel and we didn't take it, a warning we brushed off, advice we filed away and forgot, a conversation we cut short because we already thought we knew. God is not surprised by any of that. His love is not contingent on how well we have listened in the past. What matters is whether we are willing to listen now. He has not stopped speaking. He speaks through Scripture, through the people He places in our lives, and through the quiet moments when something in us knows we need to slow down and ask. The door is not closed. It has never been closed. Whatever ground was lost through pride or haste or simple inattention, He is faithful to redeem it for those who come back with an open hand.

Day 7: Reflection Questions:

Q: Who in your life offers wise counsel that you can seek out more intentionally?

Q: How has seeking wisdom blessed you in the past?

Q: In what areas do you need to humble yourself and ask for advice or help?

Q: How can you become a source of godly wisdom and encouragement to others?

PRAYER JOURNAL

*L*oving Father,

Thank You for the gift of wisdom and for surrounding me with people who offer guidance, encouragement, and truth. Forgive me for the times I've relied on my own understanding or ignored wise counsel. Please give me a humble heart, eager to learn and quick to listen. Fill me with discernment and courage to seek help when I need it and grant me the grace to share wisdom with others. Thank You for Your Word and for the blessings that come when I walk in Your ways. May my life reflect Your wisdom, peace, and love to everyone around me.

In Jesus' name, Amen.

Prayer Thoughts for Today: ♦♦♦♦♦

~ END PRAYER JOURNAL "THE WISE" ~

THE ONE THAT WENT ALONG

THE SIMPLE ONE

PROVERBS 1:10 (NIV)

"My son, if sinful men entice you, do not give in to them."

Maddie grew up in a quiet town where everyone knew each other, and life moved at an easy, predictable pace. Her days followed a gentle routine: school, chores, evenings on the porch with her parents, and weekends spent fishing at the pond or riding bikes down the main street. In a place where little changed and everyone looked out for one another, Maddie found comfort in blending in. She rarely questioned what she was told, and she'd become used to following the lead of her friends and family.

From a young age, Maddie learned that going along with the crowd was the simplest way to avoid trouble. She was never the loudest or the boldest, but she was always agreeable. Whether it was picking teams for baseball or choosing where to hang out after school, Maddie was content to let others decide. She prided herself on being easy to get along with, and her friends appreciated that she never made a fuss.

One long summer evening, as the sun dipped low behind the rows of maples, Maddie found herself with a group of older teens at the edge of town. They were the kind of kids she'd watched from a distance for years: confident, a little reckless, and always with a story to tell. Excited to be included, Maddie laughed at their jokes and listened as they swapped daring tales. As dusk settled, one of them suggested sneaking into the old abandoned mill on the outskirts of a place rumored to be haunted and off-limits.

Maddie felt a knot of anxiety tighten in her stomach. She'd heard stories about the building: creaking floors, broken windows, and the occasional stray animal. She knew her parents would disapprove, and her gut told her it was a bad idea. But as the other teens nudged each other and swapped grins, Maddie hesitated, caught between her fear and her longing to belong. "Come on, Maddie, don't be such a kid," one of them teased, already hoisting himself over the fence.

Not wanting to be left behind or seem cowardly, Maddie followed. They crept through the shadows, flashlights flickering, their laughter echoing in the hollow halls. The thrill of the forbidden pulsed through her veins, but so did a growing sense of dread. Every sound seemed louder, every movement more suspicious. She tried to steady her breathing, telling herself it would all be over soon, a story to laugh about later.

Suddenly, a sharp beam of a flashlight swept through the darkness, and a stern voice commanded them to freeze. The police had been tipped off about trespassers, and now, caught red-handed, Maddie's heart nearly stopped. The officers escorted them outside, their faces grim. The embarrassment was immediate; neighbors peered out from behind curtains, shaking their heads at the spectacle. The older teens shrugged it off, making jokes and acting tough, but Maddie felt something different: a deep, gnawing shame.

As she sat on the curb waiting for her parents to arrive, Maddie felt exposed and vulnerable. Thoughts raced through her mind: How did I end up here? Why didn't I just say no? The consequences were clear. She would have to explain herself to her family, face the disappointment in their eyes, and perhaps earn back the trust she had carelessly risked.

That night, after a tense and tearful conversation with her parents, Maddie lay awake staring at the ceiling. She realized that her desire to fit in had cost her more than she ever imagined. She had let others decide for her, ignoring her instincts and the values her parents had taught her. If she was honest with herself, this was not the first time she had gone along just to go along, but it was the first time the cost had been so high.

In the days that followed, Maddie withdrew from the group of older teens. It wasn't easy; sometimes she felt lonely, and she missed the excitement of being included. But she started spending more time with friends who respected boundaries and shared her interests. She talked honestly with her parents about what happened, and they encouraged her to trust her own judgment, even when it meant standing alone.

Slowly, Maddie rebuilt her confidence. She learned to pause and consider her choices, to listen to the quiet voice inside that warned her when something did not feel right. She discovered that true belonging did not require betraying her own conscience and that thinking for herself was far more important than following the crowd.

Looking back, Maddie knew the experience had changed her. She couldn't erase the shame of that night, but she could use it as a turning point: a reminder that the person she wanted to be was someone who made decisions with courage and integrity, even in a quiet town where everyone knew her name.

Day 1: Q&A:

Q: Why do Simple Ones often follow the crowd?

A: Simple ones lack the experience and confidence to stand alone. They crave acceptance and sometimes fear missing out more than they fear the consequences. Without a firm foundation of wisdom and self-worth, they become easy targets for peer pressure and poor decisions.

Q: How can someone break this habit?

A: By seeking wisdom through God's Word, prayer, and the counsel of trustworthy mentors, a Simple One can begin to develop the discernment they lack. Learning to pause and consider the outcome before acting is key, because wisdom is not just knowing right from wrong but having the courage to choose it. Over time, these habits build a strong inner foundation that makes it easier to stand firm, even when the crowd pulls in the opposite direction.

Day 2: Explanation: Proverbs call simple ones to move beyond passivity. God wants us to be thoughtful and courageous, not just agreeable. Growing in wisdom means learning to say "no" when it matters. Remember, saying "no" to the wrong thing is saying "yes" to God's best for your life. Have you prayed for courage to stand firm in Christ to say "No" when you need to?

Day 3: Anecdote: A boy named Caleb was thirteen when his cousin talked him into skipping school to hang out at a friend's house across town. He knew it was wrong before he even left the driveway. He went anyway. By noon, the friend's older brother had brought out things Caleb had no business being around, and suddenly skipping school was the least of his problems. He called his mother from the bathroom, voice low, asking her to come get him. She did, no questions until the car ride home. Caleb said later that the hardest part was not the punishment. It was realizing he had known, before any of it started, exactly how it would go. He just did not want to be the one who said no. True kindness does not mean agreeing with everything; sometimes the most loving thing you can do is speak truth with grace. Have you prayed for balance to be kind and yet stand firm in Godly wisdom?

Day 4: Warning: If you always follow others without discernment, you may end up in dangerous or harmful situations. Proverbs 7:7 describes the Simple Ones as "lacking sense" and in need of guidance. Without wisdom, even small compromises can open the door to much greater harm down the road. God calls us to be alert and sober-minded, guarding our hearts and minds against influences that pull us away from His truth. Do you just go with the flow and allow others to lead you?

Day 5: Encouragement: God gives you strength to make wise choices even if it means standing alone. He promises to be with you and to honor your commitment to do what's right. Proverbs 13:20 reminds us that walking with the wise makes us wiser, while the companion of fools will suffer harm. When you surround yourself with people who love God and seek His ways, you create an environment where wisdom flourishes and temptation loses its grip. Ask God to open your eyes to the Godly relationships He has already placed in your life and be intentional about nurturing them. Have you prayed for Godly friends who encourage wisdom and not folly?

Day 6: God's Love and Redemption: God's love meets you in your mistakes. Even if you've followed the wrong crowd, He offers forgiveness and a new path. Proverbs 3:5-6 reminds us to trust in the Lord, and He will direct our paths. No matter how far you've strayed, His grace is greater than your greatest failure, and His mercies are new every morning. He does not define you by your worst moment but by the new creation He is shaping you to become through Christ. As you seek Him daily, His wisdom will replace the confusion of the crowd with the clarity of His perfect will for your life. Every day is a fresh chance to choose wisdom. Have you prayed for wisdom?

Day 7: Reflection Questions:

Q: Can you think of a time when you followed the crowd instead of making your own decision? What was the outcome?

Q: What fears or desires most influence your choices when you're with others? Consider whether it is the fear of rejection, the desire for approval, or something else that tends to drive your decisions in social situations. How might surrendering those fears and desires to God change the way you respond to peer pressure?

Q: Who are some wise mentors or friends you can turn to for advice when you're unsure about a decision? Think about the people in your life who consistently reflect Godly wisdom and integrity. How can you be more intentional about seeking their counsel before making important choices?

Q: What practical steps can you take to pause and consider the consequences before going along with others in the future? Am I too passive?

Prayer Journal

*L*oving God, Thank You for always being near, even when I am tempted to follow the crowd. I confess that my desire to fit in has sometimes led me away from what is wise and true. Forgive me for moments when I have chosen acceptance over obedience to You.

Grant me the courage to stand for what is right, even when it is difficult or lonely. Fill me with Your Spirit, so I can seek wisdom, think for myself, and honor You in every choice. Help me find strength in Your presence and trust that You are with me when I stand alone.

Thank You for Your unfailing love, forgiveness, and the fresh start You offer every day. Lead me in Your ways and make me bold to follow You above all else.

In Jesus' name, Amen.

Prayer Thoughts for Today:

◆◆◆◆◆

ALWAYS KNOWING BEST

THE FOOL

PROVERBS 12:15 (NIV)

"The way of fools seems right to them, but the wise listen to advice."

Kayla always thought she knew best. Even as a child, she was stubbornly independent and fiercely believed in her own judgment. She prided herself on being street-smart and quick-witted, and she never hesitated to tell others when she thought they were wrong, especially her parents. She usually saw their advice as outdated or overprotective, and it often went in one ear and out the other.

As Kayla entered her late teens, her desire for freedom only grew. She found herself drawn to friends who shared her rebellious spirit, and together they chased excitement and adventure, pushing boundaries just for the thrill. Her parents saw the risks and tried to warn her. They asked Kayla to let them know where she was going, to respect curfews, and to be careful about who she spent time with. "You don't know them like I do," Kayla would protest, rolling her eyes and brushing off their concerns. "I can handle myself."

One Friday night, Kayla's friends came up with a plan to sneak into a club that was off-limits to anyone under twenty-one. The temptation to break the rules was too strong. Her parents told her to be home on time and to be careful, but Kayla barely listened, already thinking of what she would say when she came home late. As the group disappeared into the night, Kayla felt a rush of adrenaline and was sure nothing could go wrong.

Inside the club, the music pounded, and the energy was electric. For a while, Kayla felt unstoppable. She was exactly where she wanted to be, doing what she wanted. But the thrill quickly faded. The bouncer caught their nervous glances and checked their IDs. Minutes later, the police arrived. Kayla and her friends were led outside, questioned, and given a stern warning. Embarrassed and angry, Kayla felt the night slip away from her.

When her parents picked her up from the station, Kayla would not meet their eyes. Instead of admitting her mistake, she started ranting. "If you hadn't been so controlling, I wouldn't have had to sneak out! If the police weren't so uptight, none of this would have happened! My friends should have had my back!" She blamed the club, the bouncer, her friends, her parents, anyone but herself.

In the days and weeks that followed, Kayla's frustration only grew. She was grounded, lost privileges, and her parents' trust was shaken. School felt harder, her friends seemed distant, and her sense of isolation deepened. She could not shake the feeling that life was unfair, that things were always going against her. She sulked through dinners, avoided conversations, and spent more time alone in her room, replaying the night in her mind.

But as the weeks went by, something began to change. Kayla's anger gave way to restlessness and doubt. She noticed her parents' worry and disappointment, and she saw how her younger siblings looked at her differently. She wondered why things always seemed to go wrong and why trouble seemed to follow her.

One evening, after a tense argument at home, Kayla sat outside on the back steps, staring up at the sky. For the first time, she let herself replay the choices she had made, not just that night but over the past months. She remembered the warnings, the advice she had ignored, the pride that made her believe she was always right. She realized how quickly she shifted blame, refusing to own up to her actions.

It was a hard truth to accept. Kayla realized that her stubbornness, not her parents or the police or her friends, was at the root of so many of her problems. She saw that ignoring wisdom and refusing to take responsibility had led her to where she was now: isolated, mistrusted, and unhappy.

That realization stung, but it also brought a strange sense of relief. For the first time, Kayla wondered what might happen if she listened, admitted her mistakes, and let go of her need to always be right. She decided, though she felt nervous, to apologize to her parents. The conversation was not easy. Her voice shook, and her pride fought every word. But as she spoke, she saw their faces soften, heard the relief in their voices, and felt the weight on her shoulders lighten.

Kayla knew she still had a lot to learn, but she resolved to change. She began to ask questions, to consider advice before dismissing it, and to take responsibility for her choices. She realized that life wasn't turning against her; she had simply been fighting against the wisdom and support offered by those who cared about her most.

Looking back, Kayla was grateful for the lesson, hard as it was. She understood now that humility, honesty, and a willingness to learn were far greater strengths than stubborn independence. With each new decision, she tried to remember that admitting mistakes wasn't a weakness; it was the first step toward growing wiser and building a life she could truly be proud of.

Day 1: Q&A:

Q: Why did Kayla ignore her parents' warnings?

A: Kayla despised wisdom and instruction, believing she didn't need guidance from anyone, even those who cared about her. Her pride led her to believe that accepting advice was a sign of weakness, so she tuned out her parents, her teachers, and anyone else who tried to steer her in the right direction. Like the fool described in Proverbs, she trusted her own understanding above all else, never stopping to consider that her perspective might be limited or flawed. Sadly, it had real consequences and public embarrassment before she began to see that rejecting wisdom had only made her life harder, not freer.

Q: What was the result of her choices?

A: Kayla's refusal to listen led to shame and trouble, a common outcome for those who reject correction. Every warning she dismissed, and every piece of advice she ignored, became another step down a path that led to broken relationships and lost opportunities. Proverbs 13:18 makes it clear that poverty and shame come to those who ignore discipline, but those who accept correction are honored. Her story is a sobering reminder that pride may feel like strength in the moment, but it ultimately leaves us exposed and without the support we need to recover.

Day 2: Explanation: Proverbs describes the fool not as someone with a low IQ but as someone who has decided, somewhere along the way, that they already know enough. Kayla was not unintelligent. She was perceptive, quick on her feet, and socially sharp. None of that saved her, because the problem was never ability. It was arrogance. A fool in the biblical sense is someone who has closed themselves off to correction, who hears advice and filters it through the question of whether it threatens their sense of control, rather than if it might actually be true. God's Word is not harsh for the sake of it. It names this pattern plainly because the consequences of it are real, and the people who love us are often the first to see what we cannot.

Day 3: Anecdote: A seventeen-year-old named Jordan had been warned three times by his track coach about showing up late to practice. The coach was patient the first two times. The third time, he pulled Jordan from the relay team the day before regionals. Jordan was furious. He had run that leg of the relay all season. He told anyone who would listen that the coach was being unfair, that the punishment did not fit the situation, that the team would suffer for it. What he did not say out loud was that he had also been warned about his attitude, his side comments during drills, and his habit of doing things his way when he thought no one was watching. The team ran without him. They placed second. Jordan sat in the bleachers and watched and had a long time to think. He did not become a different person overnight, but he never forgot what it felt like to watch from the outside because he had refused to listen when it cost him nothing.

Day 4: Warning: One of the quieter dangers of pride is that it does not feel like pride from the inside. It feels like clarity. It feels like knowing yourself. It feels like not letting other people push you around. That is what made Kayla's situation so hard to break out of. She was not sitting around thinking of herself as arrogant. She genuinely believed she was just being real. Proverbs 12:15 says, "The way of a fool is right in his own eyes, but a wise man listens to advice." The word to sit with there is "eyes." The fool is not lying. He truly sees it that way. That is the warning. If you have been dismissing the same correction from more than one person in your life, it is worth slowing down long enough to ask whether the problem is really them.

Day 5: Encouragement: Kayla did not fix everything in one conversation on the back steps. She went back inside, sat across from her parents at the kitchen table, and started talking. It was awkward and slow, and she stumbled over her words more than once. But she started. That is the part worth paying attention to. You do not need to have it all figured out before you take the first step toward change. James 1:5 promises that if any of you lacks wisdom, you should ask God, who gives generously to all without finding fault, and it will be given to you. That generosity is not conditional on how many times you ignored Him before. It is available right now, in whatever room you are sitting in, in whatever situation you are trying to find your way out of. Start there.

Day 6: God's Love and Redemption: There is a moment in Kayla's story that is easy to read past. Her parents came to pick her up from the station. They did not send someone else. They did not make her wait until morning. They came, and when she got in the car and started blaming everyone in sight, they did not throw her out. They drove her home. That is a picture of something. God's pursuit of us does not stop when we are at our worst or our loudest or our most convinced that we are right. He keeps showing up. He keeps offering a way back. The failures we carry do not disqualify us from that. They are often exactly the ground where His redemption does its clearest work.

Day 7: Reflection Questions:

Q: Have you ever ignored advice from someone who cared about you? What was the outcome?

Q: Why do you think it can be difficult to accept corrections or instruction from others?

Q: In what areas of your life do you tend to act impulsively or speak without thinking? How has this affected you or those around you?

Q: How does knowing about God's love and willingness to forgive change the way you view your own mistakes?

PRAYER JOURNAL

Heavenly Father,

Thank You for loving me even when I act foolishly and ignore wise counsel. Forgive me for the times I have rejected correction and chosen my own way, resulting in pain for myself and others. Please give me a humble heart that is willing to listen and learn from those You have placed in my life. Help me to seek Your wisdom above all else and to trust in Your guidance instead of my own understanding. Thank You for Your patience, mercy, and the hope of redemption through Jesus. Teach me to walk in Your ways each day, and restore what has been broken by my past choices. May Your love lead me into a life of wisdom, peace, and purpose.

In Jesus' name, Amen.

Prayer Thoughts for Today: ♦♦♦♦♦

~ END PRAYER JOURNAL "THE FOOL" ~

THE WEIGHT OF HER CROWN

THE SCORNER

PROVERBS 21:24 (NIV)

"The proud and arrogant person—'Mocker' is his name—behaves with insolent fury."

Celeste had always believed that being right was the same thing as being good. She was sharp, quick-thinking, and gifted in ways her family and teachers never let her forget. Every compliment added another layer to the wall she was building around herself, and by the time she became a woman, that wall was thick enough to keep out nearly everything, including the truth.

She built a name for herself in finance, rising through a prestigious firm in Hartwell with a speed that impressed even those who resented her. Her colleagues learned early that disagreeing with Celeste was futile. She heard opposing viewpoints the way a person hears traffic noise from a closed window, aware of it at a distance but completely unmoved. Her haughtiness was not loud or theatrical. It was quiet and constant. She walked into rooms as though they had been waiting for her, signed off on reports without reading her team's concerns, and sat through strategy meetings with the polished patience of someone enduring something beneath them.

Proverbs 21:24 describes the proud and haughty person as one who acts with insolent pride, and that description fit Celeste precisely. Humility, in her estimation, was what people practiced when they lacked confidence. She wore her certainty like a crown, never considering that a crown worn too tightly eventually becomes a trap.

The correction she most despised came from a senior advisor named Ruth, who had navigated the financial world for thirty years. Ruth spoke plainly and without flattery, which made her the person Celeste trusted least. When Ruth raised concerns about a major investment strategy, presenting careful data and measured reasoning, Celeste dismissed them and moved forward as though the concern had never been raised.

Proverbs 13:1 says a mocker does not respond to rebukes, and Celeste had long since closed herself off to rebuke in any form. She responded to the correction not with anger but with something colder, a deliberate silence that left the person who offered it feeling as though they had spoken into empty air. She had surrounded herself with people who confirmed what she already believed and mistaken their agreement for wisdom.

The investment strategy Ruth had warned against began to unravel in the second quarter. What had looked bold on paper revealed itself to be exactly what Ruth had said, an overextension that the market quickly dismantled. The firm absorbed the losses, but the damage to Celeste's standing was harder to recover from, and the quiet authority she had always taken for granted began to feel less certain beneath her feet.

What followed was not a dramatic collapse but a slow diminishment. Projects were quietly reassigned. Meetings were restructured without her at the center. The people she had dismissed did not gloat; they simply went on with their work, and the absence of their deference was more disorienting than any confrontation would have been.

She had never learned how to receive correction because she had spent so long refusing it. She sat in her office one evening, long after everyone else had gone home, and felt the full weight of what she had built. It was not an empire. It was an isolation, a life in which she was always right, always certain, and that life had turned out to be a very small and airless place.

The people who had tried to reach her came back to her mind. Ruth, with her plain and careful words. A mentor who had warned her that the most dangerous thing a gifted person could do was stop listening. A colleague who had offered a different perspective and been met with such cold indifference that she never tried again. Celeste had not seen any of them as gifts. She had seen them as obstacles to be filtered out.

She understood now what the book of Proverbs had known for thousands of years. The proud and haughty woman, the one who acts with insolent pride and stops her ears against correction, is not strong. She is simply alone. And the crown she has worked so hard to keep on her head is the very thing that has kept her from bowing low enough to receive what she actually needed.

Celeste had been right about many things in her life. But she had been wrong about the most important one. Being right had never been the same thing as being good. And it had never, not once, been the same thing as being wise.

Day 1: Q&A
Q: What does Proverbs 21:24 reveal about the character of a proud and haughty person?
A: Proverbs 21:24 reveals that a proud and haughty person, someone who acts with insolent pride, is called a scoffer. This isn't just about bad manners or a difficult personality. It's a deeper issue. The scoffer puts their own judgment above correction, above wisdom, and even above God. Celeste showed this, not through dramatic arrogance, but through the steady, quiet dismissal of anyone who questioned her thinking.

Q: How did Celeste's resentment of correction, as described in Proverbs 13:1 and 15:12, contribute to her downfall?
A: Celeste's resistance to correction meant she kept pushing away the very people who could have helped her. Proverbs 13:1 contrasts those who welcome instruction with those who reject it, while Proverbs 15:12 points out that a scoffer won't seek advice from the wise. Celeste's downfall was the natural result of closing her heart to advice and correction.

Day 2: Explanation: There is a particular kind of blindness that comes with being genuinely gifted. It is not stupidity. It is something closer to overconfidence that has gone unchallenged for too long. Celeste was never a fool in the ordinary sense. She was sharp, capable, and often correct. The problem was that being often correct taught her to believe she was always correct, and that belief slowly closed off every channel through which wisdom could have entered. Proverbs 21:24, 13:1, and 15:12 together describe this progression with uncomfortable precision. The scoffer does not begin as a scoffer. She begins as someone who stopped listening a little too early and never found a reason to start again. By the time the consequences arrived, she had no framework for understanding them as consequences at all. She simply believed the world had failed to recognize what she already knew.

Day 3: Anecdote: A surgeon named Dr. Ellison had been the head of his department for eleven years. He was talented, and he knew it, and for a long time that combination had served him well. But somewhere around year seven, he stopped asking questions in team briefings and started using them to confirm decisions he had already made. A scrub nurse named Patricia had flagged a concern twice in the same week before a scheduled procedure. Both times, she was acknowledged and set aside. The procedure went forward. The complication that followed was serious, and when the review board traced the timeline, Patricia's notes were there in the record, two clear warnings, both ignored. Dr. Ellison did not lose his license. But he lost the department, and he lost the thing that had mattered most to him, which was the trust of the people who worked alongside him every day. He had confused the absence of pushback with the presence of wisdom. They are not the same thing.

Day 4: Warning: Proverbs 21:24 does not describe a villain. It describes a person who was probably capable, probably successful for a stretch, and at some point surrounded by people who tried to reach them. The warning is not aimed at obviously bad people. It is aimed at people who are good at what they do and have started to believe that competence in one area means they do not need correction in any area. That is the specific danger. Not the loud, obvious arrogance that everyone can see, but the quiet, settled kind that feels from the inside like discernment. If the same correction has come to you from more than one direction and your response has been to question the source rather than consider the message, that is worth sitting with honestly before you move on.

Day 5: Encouragement: Celeste's story does not have to be your story, because the same Proverbs that describe the scoffer also describe the path out: Proverbs 11:2 says humility leads to wisdom, and Proverbs 19:20 urges us to listen to counsel and accept instruction so that we may be wise. If you have spent years dismissing correction and surrounding yourself with agreement, the first step is simply to stop defending and let one honest voice speak into your life, because wisdom does not force its way in; it waits at the door that humility opens, and you can open that door today.

Day 6: Why People Become Scorners: Nobody sits down one day and decides to become someone who cannot receive correction. It happens gradually, and it usually begins with something that appears to be a strength. A person is praised early and often. They succeed in environments that reward confidence and penalize hesitation. They learn that certainty gets results and that doubt is a liability. Over time, the habit of projecting confidence becomes indistinguishable from actually feeling it, and the gap between the two closes so quietly that they stop noticing it was ever there. By the time someone tries to offer an honest correction, the person on the receiving end has spent years building a self-image that cannot accommodate it without feeling threatened. That is not a weakness. It is a very human response to a very particular kind of formation. Understanding how people become scorners is not an excuse for staying one. It is simply an honest account of how the door closes, so that those who want to can figure out how to open it again.

Day 7: Reflection Questions:

Q: In what areas of your life do you find it most difficult to receive corrections, and what does that resistance reveal about what you are protecting?

Q: Think of a person who has tried to speak the honest truth into your life and was met with dismissal. What would it look like to go back to that person and genuinely listen?

Q: Celeste surrounded herself with voices that confirmed what she already believed. Who in your life is willing to tell you what you need to hear rather than what you want to hear, and are you truly listening to them?

Q: Proverbs 15:12 says the scoffer will not consult the wise. Who are the wise voices in your life, and what practical steps can you take this week to seek their counsel with an open heart?

PRAYER JOURNAL

Father,

We confess that pride is not always easy to see in ourselves. It hides behind confidence, behind competence, behind the quiet certainty that we know best. Forgive us for the times we have dismissed the correction of those You placed in our lives to help us grow. Forgive us for the moments we chose to be right rather than wise, and for the relationships and opportunities we lost as a result. Soften the places in our hearts that have grown hard. Give us the courage to be corrected, the humility to listen, and the wisdom to know that the voice of truth is a gift, not a threat. We do not want to be scorners. We want to be people who walk in the fear of the Lord, who receive instruction gladly, and who grow wiser with every season of life. Teach us that humility is not weakness but the very foundation on which wisdom is built.

In the name of Jesus, Amen.

Prayer Thoughts for Today: ✦✦✦✦✦

~ END PRAYER JOURNAL "THE SCORNER" ~

WISDOM IN CONFLICT

THE WISE

PROVERBS 15:1 (NIV)

"A gentle answer turns away wrath, but a harsh word stirs up anger."

Mia disliked confrontation and often avoided addressing issues. For most of her life, she preferred to keep the peace, even if it meant swallowing her feelings or ignoring problems that needed attention. The thought of an argument or harsh words made her anxious, so she learned to sidestep conflict whenever possible. As a child, Mia watched arguments tear apart the relationships around her, and she quietly vowed never to let that happen in her own life. She believed that staying silent was the kindest thing she could do, a way of protecting the people she loved from unnecessary pain. What she did not yet understand was that silence, when it covers unresolved wounds, can quietly cause just as much damage as the conflict she feared.

At work, Mia was known for her easygoing nature. Colleagues appreciated her willingness to compromise and her positive attitude. Beneath the surface, though, Mia sometimes felt overlooked or misunderstood. She quietly carried the weight of unresolved frustrations, convincing herself that silence was better than risking a disagreement. There were moments when she wanted to speak up in team meetings, to push back on a decision she felt was wrong, or to simply express how she truly felt. Each time, though, the familiar anxiety would rise in her chest, and she would swallow her words, smile, and move on as if nothing had happened.

One day, a misunderstanding at work threatened a close friendship Mia deeply valued. A project deadline was missed, and Mia's friend Jordan assumed she had failed to deliver her part of the work. Word spread quickly through the team, and soon Mia sensed a change in how Jordan and others treated her.

At first, Mia did what she always did. She told herself time would smooth it over. She smiled at Jordan in the hallway and got a polite smile back, convincing herself that was progress. It was not. Two weeks passed. The distance did not close. One afternoon, she overheard Jordan mention her name in a conversation that stopped the moment she walked in, and she felt the full weight of what avoiding this had cost her. She had spent so long trying to protect the friendship from conflict that she had let the conflict do its damage unchecked.

Mia sat with it for three more days before she did anything. She prayed, but it was not the peaceful kind of prayer she had hoped for. It felt more like an argument with herself that eventually ran out of steam. She opened her Bible and landed on Proverbs 15:1, which reminded her that a gentle answer turns away wrath, and she read it twice because she needed it to be true. She texted Jordan and asked if she wanted to grab lunch. Jordan said yes, and Mia spent the next morning rehearsing what she was going to say. None of it came out the way she practiced. She sat down across from Jordan, opened her mouth, and the first thing she said was that she was sorry, which was not what she planned to lead with but turned out to be the right thing anyway. She stopped talking and let Jordan respond, which was the hardest part.

Jordan had more to say than Mia expected. Some of it stung. There were frustrations that went further back than the missed deadline, things Mia had not known Jordan was carrying. She sat with that and tried not to get defensive, though she did not fully manage. At one point, she started to explain herself, caught Jordan's expression, and stopped. She took a breath and asked Jordan to keep going. By the end of the conversation, they discovered that a technical error had swallowed Mia's submitted work entirely, which neither of them had known. That helped, but what helped more was that they had finally said the things that had been sitting between them. The lunch ran forty minutes longer than either of them planned.

Relieved, Mia and Jordan agreed to work more closely on future projects and to be honest about any concerns upfront. Their restored friendship felt even stronger than before, built on honest conversation and mutual respect.

Mia learned that avoiding confrontation might bring temporary comfort, but true peace required facing issues with wisdom and humility. The experience gave her confidence to address problems directly and trust that God would guide her through challenging conversations.

Over time, Mia's willingness to seek reconciliation and understanding influenced others at work. Her example encouraged colleagues to address conflicts openly and respectfully, creating a more trusting and supportive team environment. Word spread quietly through the office that Mia could be trusted with hard conversations, and people began coming to her for advice when tensions arose. She never claimed to have all the answers, but she always pointed others back to the same source that had helped her: prayer, humility, and a genuine desire to understand before being understood. The team's culture slowly began to shift, and what had once been a place of quiet tension became a place where people felt safe to be honest with one another.

Looking back, Mia was grateful she had not let fear keep her from pursuing wisdom. Her friendship with Jordan became a source of joy and support, and Mia grew in her ability to handle future challenges with grace. Instead of shrinking from conflict, she learned to see it as an opportunity for growth, healing, and deeper connection.

Day 1: Q&A:

Q: How did Mia respond to conflict?
A: She sought wisdom, listened, and addressed the issue humbly. Rather than letting pride or fear drive her actions, Mia turned to God first and allowed His peace to guide her steps. Her willingness to listen before speaking made all the difference in restoring the friendship.

Q: What was the reward?
A: The friendship did not snap back to where it had been overnight. But the distance closed. Jordan stopped going quiet when Mia walked into a room, and Mia stopped rehearsing conversations in her head before they happened. What they built after that lunch was something more honest than what they had before, because it had been tested and had held. The trust that came back was the kind that knows it can survive a hard conversation.

Day 2: Explanation: James 3:17 describes wisdom from above as peace-loving, and it is worth pausing on what that does not mean. It does not mean avoiding conflict. Mia had spent years being peace-loving in the wrong direction, keeping things smooth on the surface while tension built underneath. That is not wisdom. That is management. The wisdom James describes is willing to enter a hard conversation because it cares more about what is true and what is restored than about what is comfortable. It is gentle, but it is not passive. It asks the difficult question, stays in the room when the answer is uncomfortable, and trusts that honesty handled with care is more loving than silence handled with fear.

Day 3: Anecdote: A woman named Renee had not spoken to her sister in four years. The original argument had been about their mother's estate, but by the time Renee came to counseling, she could barely remember the specific details. What she remembered was the feeling of not being heard, and the decision she had made somewhere in year one that she was not going to be the one to reach out first. Her counselor asked her a simple question: What would it cost you to go first, and what is it costing you not to? Renee sat with that for a long time. She called her sister on a Tuesday night with no script and no plan. The call lasted two hours.

They did not resolve everything. But they talked, and that was the thing that four years of silence had not been able to accomplish. Renee said later that the hardest part was dialing. Everything after that was just two people who had missed each other.

Day 4: Blessing and Rewards: There is something that happens to a relationship after it survives an honest conversation that it could not have gotten any other way. Mia and Jordan's friendship after that lunch was not the same as before. It was more careful in some ways and more open in others. They knew something about each other now that they had not before, namely that the friendship could hold weight. Proverbs 11:2 says that with humility comes wisdom, and the reward Mia received was not just a repaired friendship. It was the knowledge that she did not have to keep managing silence to keep people close. That is a freedom that conflict-avoidance never offers, no matter how long you practice it.

Day 5: Encouragement: Mia's prayer before that lunch was not eloquent. It was not even particularly faithful. It was closer to someone admitting out loud that she did not know what she was doing and needed help. James 1:5 says God gives wisdom generously to all without finding fault, and that promise does not have a minimum requirement for how composed you have to be when you ask. If there is a conversation you have been avoiding, a name that comes to mind when you read this, you do not have to have the right words before you reach out. You just have to be willing to go. Clarity tends to come in the middle of the thing, not before.

Day 6: God's Love and Redemption: Four years of silence between two sisters. Weeks of hallway smiles that meant nothing. A friendship that was quietly dissolving because no one wanted to be the one to start. These are not dramatic stories. They are ordinary ones, which is exactly what makes them worth paying attention to. God's reconciling work does not only show up in the spectacular. It shows up in a Tuesday night phone call, in a forty-minute lunch, in an apology that came out in the wrong order but landed exactly right. He is present in the small acts of courage that most people never see, the moment someone decides to go first, to listen longer, to stay in the room. That is where His redemption does some of its quietest and most lasting work.

Day 7: Reflection Questions:

Q: When have you seen wisdom turn conflict to peace?

Q: What makes it hard to approach difficult conversations with wisdom?

Q: How can you listen more deeply to others?

Q: Who do you need to seek peace with today?

PRAYER JOURNAL

*G*racious and Loving Father, thank you for caring deeply about every part of my life and for offering wisdom to guide me through each challenge. I confess that, at times, I have let fear or pride keep me from addressing conflict honestly and humbly. Forgive me for the moments I have avoided difficult conversations, chosen silence over truth, or allowed misunderstanding to build walls between myself and others.

Lord, I ask that You would fill me with wisdom and humility in every situation where disagreement or tension arises. Teach me to listen with an open heart, to speak with kindness, and to seek understanding rather than being quick to defend myself. Help me recognize when I am wrong, apologize sincerely, and extend grace to those who may have hurt me.

Give me the courage to pursue peace, even when it feels uncomfortable or hard. Remind me that reconciliation and truth are worth the effort, and that Your love can restore even the most broken relationships. Where my words or actions have caused pain, bring healing and restoration, and help me to remain patient and gentle as trust is rebuilt.

Thank You for Your patient love that never gives up on me, and for Your example of forgiveness and compassion. Please shape my character to reflect Your wisdom, so that I may be an instrument of peace and unity in my relationships. Guide me to walk in Your ways, to value honesty and openness, and to trust that Your Spirit will lead me into reconciliation and deeper fellowship with others.

Restore what has been damaged by conflict in my life, Lord, and create in me a spirit of gratitude and obedience. May my actions honor You and bring glory to Your name.

In Jesus' name, Amen.

Prayer Thoughts for Today: ✦✦✦✦✦

~ END PRAYER JOURNAL "THE WISE" ~

THE NEED TO FIT IN

THE SIMPLE ONE

PROVERBS 14:15 (NIV)

"The simple believe anything, but the prudent give thought to their steps."

Samantha just wanted to fit in at her new school. She had moved to the city a few weeks ago, leaving her old friends, familiar routines, and the comfort of her former life behind. Everything here felt new and intimidating. The hallways were huge, the faces unfamiliar, and there seemed to be unspoken rules about where to sit and what to wear. Every morning, as she got ready, she practiced what she might say if someone talked to her, hoping she would not say the wrong thing.

On her second Friday at Lincoln Middle School, Samantha finally caught the attention of some kids in her English class. They invited her to lunch, and she felt so relieved. She listened carefully as they talked about teachers, weekend plans, and who was considered popular. Wanting to fit in, Samantha nodded, laughed at their jokes, and tried to join in when she could.

Halfway through lunch, the conversation changed. The kids started whispering about another student, Chloe, a quiet girl who always sat alone by the windows. One person said Chloe had cheated on a math test and that her parents had been called to the principal's office. Someone else said they heard Chloe had been caught stealing snacks from the cafeteria. The rumors went back and forth, getting bigger each time, until they did not sound true anymore.

Samantha felt uncomfortable. She barely knew Chloe and had never noticed anything strange about her. But not wanting to seem different or be left out, Samantha joined in. "I think I saw Chloe acting weird in the hallway yesterday," she said, even though she had not. The group laughed and nodded, and for a moment, Samantha felt like she belonged.

That afternoon, the whispers got louder. Samantha saw Chloe walk past a group of kids, and they snickered behind her back. The next day, Chloe's desk was covered in mean notes that repeated the rumors Samantha and the others had started. Samantha's stomach twisted with guilt. She noticed Chloe's eyes were red, like she had been crying.

The guilt got worse as the week went on. One day, Samantha overheard two teachers talking quietly. "It's really sad about Chloe," one said. "She's been having a hard time since her dad lost his job, but she's always honest and hardworking. Those rumors are so unfair." Samantha's heart sank. In that moment, she realized the stories were not true. The things she had repeated, the comments she made just to fit in, had hurt someone who was already having a rough time.

That night, Samantha could not sleep. She replayed the conversations in her mind and wished she had asked questions instead of believing what she heard. She wished she had thought about Chloe's feelings instead of just wanting to fit in. Tears filled her eyes as she imagined how lonely Chloe must feel, being talked about and laughed at by people who did not know her.

The next day at school, Samantha knew she had to do something, but she did not know how to start. At lunch, when the gossip started again, she started to speak but stopped. The second time someone mentioned Chloe, Samantha quietly said, "I don't think any of that is true." No one replied right away. One kid shrugged. Someone else changed the subject. It was not a big dramatic moment like she had imagined. That afternoon, she wrote a note to Chloe, threw away three drafts, and slid the fourth one through the vent in Chloe's locker. The first time, she did not sign her name. An hour later, she wrote another note and this time signed it.

Chloe did not respond right away. For two days, Samantha wondered if she ever would. Then, on Wednesday, Chloe stopped her in the hallway and said thank you. That was it. No long talk, just those two words. It was enough. Samantha had learned something important: belonging is not worth changing who you are, and the things you say about people when they are not around can follow you home.

Day 1: Q&A:

Q: Why did Samantha join in the gossip?
A: She wanted to belong and didn't stop to consider if what she heard was true, a common trait of the Simple One. The desire for acceptance can be so powerful that it overrides our better judgment, causing us to go along with things we would otherwise question. Proverbs 14:15 reminds us that the simple believe everything, but the prudent pause to weigh their steps before acting.

Q: How can we avoid spreading false information?
A: By seeking the truth before speaking and being slow to pass along what we don't know firsthand, we protect both ourselves and others from the harm that careless words can cause. Proverbs 18:13 warns that answering before listening is both foolish and shameful, reminding us that wisdom always pauses to gather the full picture before responding. When we commit to verifying what we hear before repeating it, we become people of integrity whose words can be trusted.

Day 2: Explanation: Samantha was not a cruel kid. That is the part worth sitting with. She did not walk into that lunch with any intention of hurting anyone. She just wanted to belong, and belonging felt like it required going along. That is exactly the condition Proverbs 14:15 describes when it talks about the Simple Ones who believe everything. It is not about being gullible in an obvious way. It is about the moment when fitting in becomes more important than thinking clearly, when the need for acceptance quietly overrides the habit of asking questions. Most of us have been there. The prudent person is not someone who never feels that pull. They are someone who has learned to pause long enough to ask whether what they are about to say is actually true, and whether the person it is about deserves better than a rumor passed around a lunch table.

Day 3: Anecdote: A boy named Derek was fourteen when he repeated something he heard about a classmate named Marcus at a basketball tryout. He did not know if it was true. He repeated it anyway because the older kid who told him seemed confident, and Derek wanted to seem like he was in the know. The story spread faster than he expected. By the end of the week, Marcus had stopped showing up to practice. Derek found out two months later that the story had been completely made up, started by someone who wanted Marcus off the team. Derek never told anyone he had been part of spreading it. He carried that for years. He later said the worst part was not the guilt, though it was real. It was knowing that he had made a choice in about four seconds that had taken something from someone else that he could not give back.

Day 4: Warning: The thing about gossip is that it rarely feels like a serious decision in the moment. It feels like a conversation. It feels like being included. Derek's four-second choice did not feel like a choice at all. It felt like keeping up. That is what makes Proverbs 11:13 worth reading slowly: a gossip betrays confidence, but a trustworthy person keeps a secret. The word trustworthy is doing a lot of work in that verse. It is not just about keeping secrets. It is about being the kind of person whose words can be relied on, whose account of events is not shaped by what will make them sound connected or in the know. Once people learn that you repeat things without checking them, they stop trusting what you say, even when you are telling the truth. That reputation is hard to rebuild.

Day 5: Encouragement: Samantha wrote four drafts of that note. Derek carried his regret for years before he told anyone. Neither of them got it right the first time, and that is not the point. The point is that the capacity to do better is available to both of them, and to you, not as a reward for getting it right but as a gift offered in the middle of getting it wrong. James 1:5 says God gives wisdom generously to all without finding fault. That generosity covers the lunch table moments, the four-second decisions, and the notes you almost did not sign your name to. If there is someone you have spoken carelessly about, that is a place to start. Not with a grand gesture, but with honesty, the same way Samantha did, one note at a time.

Day 6: God's Love and Redemption: Derek never told Marcus what he had done. He thought about it more than once over the years, but could never find the moment that felt right. He is still carrying that. That is an honest ending to his part of the story, and it is worth noting because not every act of careless speech gets a clean resolution. But the absence of a clean ending is not the absence of grace. God's redemptive work does not require us to have already fixed everything before He shows up. It meets us in the regret, in the four-draft note, in the hallway thank-you that lasted two seconds. First John 1:9 says that if we confess, He is faithful and just to forgive and to cleanse. The cleansing is real, even when the consequences linger. What he offers is not the erasure of what happened but the freedom to stop being defined by it, and the wisdom to choose differently the next time the moment comes.

Day 7: Reflection Questions:

Q: Have you ever repeated something you heard without knowing if it was true? What happened as a result?

Q: Why do you think it can be tempting to believe or spread rumors, especially when trying to fit in?

Q: What habits can you develop to make sure you seek the truth before sharing information with others?

Q: How can you use your words to build others up and reflect God's love, even when those around you are gossiping or spreading negativity? Does sin feel like it's not a big deal?

Prayer Journal

*H*eavenly Father,

Thank You for being the God of truth. I confess that sometimes I have joined in with others or spoken without knowing all the facts. Forgive me for the times I have believed or spread things that were not true, and for not seeking Your wisdom first.

Please grant me discernment and a careful spirit. Help me to pause, ask questions, and seek truth before I speak or act. Strengthen my heart to build others up and to be a source of encouragement, not harm.

Thank You for Your forgiveness and the way You redeem my words and actions. Fill my heart with Your love so I may speak truth with grace and walk in wisdom every day.

In Jesus' name, Amen.

Prayer Thoughts for Today:
♦♦♦♦♦

~ End Prayer Journal "The Simple One" ~

THE QUICK COMEBACK

THE FOOL

PROVERBS 16:18 (NIV)

"Pride goes before destruction, a haughty spirit before a fall."

Madeline always had a quick comeback and a sharp tongue. From a young age, she'd been praised for her wit; teachers chuckled at her jokes in class, and friends admired her ability to roast someone with a single line. Sarcasm became her trademark, a shield she wielded in every social situation. To Madeline, it felt like a superpower: she could make people laugh, turn an awkward moment into a joke, and never risk showing vulnerability. It made her feel clever, confident, and in control.

As she got older, Madeline's sarcasm only sharpened. She was the go-to girl for snappy remarks, the life of any group chat, and the class clown in every setting. But while some friends laughed, others grew uncomfortable. They noticed that Madeline's jokes, once playful, increasingly had a sting to them. When she was bored or annoyed, her comments could cut deeper than she realized. At first, her friends tried to offer gentle advice. One day, after Madeline made a particularly biting joke about a friend's failed math test, she noticed the hurt in her friend's eyes. "Hey, Madeline," the friend said quietly later, "sometimes your jokes go a little far. Maybe just… ease up a bit?" Madeline laughed it off, replying with another sarcastic quip: "Oh, come on. If we can't laugh at ourselves, what's the point?" She brushed off their concerns, convinced they were just being too sensitive or couldn't keep up with her humor.

The more people tried to address it, the more Madeline leaned in, almost as if to prove she couldn't be rattled. Her jokes grew even sharper, her comebacks quicker. She told herself she was just being honest, that people needed to toughen up. But she didn't notice that invitations to hang out became less frequent, or that conversations in group chats often continued without her. The real consequence of her sharp tongue hit home during a family gathering one Sunday afternoon. Relatives had gathered for a barbecue, the backyard filled with laughter and the smell of grilled food. Madeline's younger sister, Lily, who adored her and always tried to include her, wanted to show her a painting she'd been working on for weeks. She handed it to her shyly, her eyes shining with hope.

Madeline glanced at the picture and, without thinking, blurted, "Wow, did you use your left hand or something? This looks like a kindergarten project." The table went quiet. Lily's face fell instantly, the color draining from her cheeks. She mumbled something and slipped away, leaving her painting on the table.

For the rest of the afternoon, Madeline noticed a subtle shift. Family members seemed less interested in chatting with her. Her parents gave her disappointed looks, and her cousins avoided sitting next to her. Even when she tried to make conversation, people seemed distracted or distant.

Later that night, Madeline found Lily curled up in her room, silent tears streaming down her face. She tried to apologize, but Lily wouldn't look at her. "Why are you always so mean?" Lily whispered, clutching her painting. The words stung, lingering long after Madeline had left her room.

Madeline retreated to her own room, confusion and guilt gnawing at her. She replayed her words, realizing for the first time how they must have sounded to Lily. She thought back to the times friends had distanced themselves, the awkward silences after some of her jokes, the invitations that never came. She wondered why people seemed so distant lately, unaware that her reckless speech had been driving others away until now.

As the days passed, Madeline felt increasingly isolated. She tried to reconnect with friends, but conversations felt strained. The laughter that once followed her jokes now sounded forced, if it came at all. At home, Lily avoided her, and her parents encouraged her to think more about her words and their impact.

Eventually, Madeline realized she had to change. She apologized sincerely to Lily, telling her how much her feelings and her art meant to her. She began to listen more and joke less, making a conscious effort to speak with kindness and encouragement. It wasn't easy. Old habits die hard. But over time, people began to warm to her again. Madeline found that true friendship and family closeness were built on trust, respect, and gentle humor, not on tearing others down.

Looking back, Madeline was grateful for the wake-up call, even though it hurt. She learned that words, once spoken, can't be taken back, and that the sharpest wit is never worth the cost of someone's confidence or happiness. With each day, she worked to use her words to lift others up rather than push them away, building stronger relationships and discovering a deeper, more lasting happiness than any joke could bring.

Day 1: Q&A:

Q: Why didn't Madeline listen to her friends' concerns?
A: She rejected correction, thinking her way of communicating was harmless and even funny, never stopping to consider what felt like wit to her felt like a wound to others. Her pride led her to believe that those who were offended were simply too sensitive, making it easy to dismiss their feelings rather than take them seriously. Like the fool described in Proverbs, she could not receive wisdom because she had already decided she didn't need it.

Q: What was the impact of her behavior?
A: Madeline's rash words caused pain and isolation, a common result for those who speak without thinking and refuse to consider how their words land on others. Her sharp tongue pushed away the very people who cared about her most, turning laughter into awkward silence and closeness into distance. Proverbs 12:18 captures it well: "Reckless words pierce like a sword, but the tongue of the wise brings healing."

Day 2: Explanation: Madeline was not a bully in the way most people picture one. She was funny, and for a long time that covered a lot of ground. The problem was that funny and kind are not the same thing, and she had spent years treating them as if they were. Proverbs 18:7 says a fool's mouth is his ruin and his lips are a snare to his soul. The word snare is worth sitting with. A snare is not something you walk into on purpose. It is something that catches you because you were not paying attention to where you were going. Madeline's sharp tongue did not ruin her relationships all at once. It did it slowly, one comment at a time, until the people who cared about her most started keeping a little more distance than they used to. She did not notice until Lily's painting was sitting on a picnic table and the backyard had gone quiet.

Day 3: Anecdote: A woman named Gloria had been best friends with her college roommate, Denise, for almost nine years. They had been through everything together. One night after a long week, Gloria made an offhand comment about Denise's parenting in front of a group of mutual friends. She meant it as a joke. Denise did not take it that way. She went quiet for the rest of the night and did not return Gloria's calls for two weeks. When they finally spoke, Denise told her that it was not the first time; there had been other comments over the years that she had let go, and this one had been one too many. Gloria apologized and meant it. Denise accepted and meant it too. But something had shifted, and both of them knew it. They are still in each other's lives, but the friendship never quite found its way back to what it was. Gloria thinks about that night more than she would like to admit.

Day 4: Warning: Gloria's story does not end in disaster. Neither does Madeline's. But both of them paid a price that did not have to be paid, and that is the point Proverbs 29:11 is making when it says a fool gives full vent to his spirit but a wise man quietly holds it back. The holding back is not about being dishonest or swallowing everything you feel. It is about the pause. The moment between the thought and the words where you ask whether what you are about to say is true, whether it is necessary, and whether this is the right time and place to say it. Most of the damage done by reckless speech happens in moments where that pause was skipped entirely. The comment felt harmless. The joke seemed like it would land. It did not, and now the relationship is carrying something it did not have to carry.

Day 5: Encouragement: Madeline's apology to Lily was not polished. She sat on the edge of Lily's bed and started talking and had to stop twice because she did not know what to say next. What she eventually said was simple: that she was sorry, that the painting was not what she had made it sound like, and that she did not want to be the kind of person who made her sister feel small. Lily did not say much back. But she let Madeline stay in the room, and that was something. Philippians 4:13 says we can do all things through Christ who strengthens us. That includes the apologies we do not know how to start, the habits we have tried to break before and have not managed to yet, and the relationships we are not sure can hold the weight of what we put on them. The strength is available. The question is whether we are willing to sit on the edge of the bed and try.

Day 6: God's Love and Redemption: Gloria's friendship with Denise changed after that night, and it has not fully come back. That is a real and honest thing to say, and it does not mean grace is not present in the story. It means grace does not always undo consequences. What it does is meet us in them. Lamentations 3:22-23 says His mercies are new every morning, and that newness is not a reset button that erases what happened. It is an invitation to show up differently today than you did yesterday. For Madeline it looked like sitting on a bed not knowing what to say. For Gloria it looked like a phone call she almost did not make. For you it might look like something quieter, a word you chose not to say, a pause you took that you would not have taken before. God's redemptive work is often that small and that specific, and it is no less real for it.

Day 7: Reflection Questions:

Q: Have you ever hurt someone with your words, either intentionally or unintentionally? How did it affect your relationship with that person?

Q: What makes it difficult to listen to others when they point out problems with the way we speak or act?

Q: How can you practice self-control and think before you speak, especially in emotionally charged situations?

Q: In what ways does God's forgiveness and grace help you move forward after you've said something you regret?

Prayer Journal

*D*ear Lord,

Thank You for Your grace and patience with me, even when my words have caused pain to others. Forgive me for speaking without thinking, for rejecting correction, and for the times I have hurt those around me with careless or harsh words. Please soften my heart, teach me humility, and help me to listen before I speak. Fill my mouth with words that encourage, heal, and bless instead of wound. When I fail, thank You for the forgiveness and fresh start You offer through Your love. Help me seek reconciliation where I have damaged relationships, and guide me to use my voice for Your glory. Thank You for never giving up on me and for restoring what I have broken.

In Jesus' name, Amen.

Prayer Thoughts for Today: ✦✦✦✦✦

~ End Prayer Journal "The Fool" ~

WOULD NOT LISTEN

THE SCORNER

PROVERBS 1:22 (NIV)

"How long will you who are simple love your simple ways?

How long will mockers delight in mockery and fools hate knowledge?"

Velma didn't care for other people's wisdom. By the time she was an adult, she quietly dismissed the idea that anyone might know something she didn't. She never thought of herself as arrogant. She simply saw herself as realistic. She had learned to trust her own judgment, and that was all she needed.

She built a well-known consultancy in Brenton that changed entire neighborhoods. Her confidence kept bringing results, and each success reinforced the same message: she was right. She didn't think she needed to learn from others. She was the one teaching. Proverbs 1:22 describes people who love their own simplicity and take pleasure in contempt. Velma never thought that verse applied to her. Wisdom, to her, was something she already had, not something she needed to seek.

Her disregard was clearest when people tried to help her. A city planner named Gerald had spent twenty years studying how rapid development affects lower-income communities. He brought research. He brought details. Velma listened as if she had already chosen not to hear, then moved forward without changing anything.

Her board of advisors did no better. She went into meetings with her mind set and left without taking anything from them. Eventually, her advisors stopped offering suggestions, not because they had nothing to say, but because they saw it would go nowhere.

What made it hard to challenge her was how competent she seemed. She never dismissed people rudely. Instead, she responded with a calm, practiced confidence that left others feeling as if they hadn't thought things through. People walked away from conversations feeling smaller. She hadn't argued with them. She just made their concerns seem unimportant.

The turning point was a major redevelopment in one of Brenton's oldest districts. She pushed it through despite objections from advisors, community leaders, and an impact report she barely read. Hundreds of long-time residents were displaced. A community that had lasted for generations fell apart. The backlash drew in city officials and journalists, and the consultancy's reputation quickly unraveled. The only ones not surprised were those who had watched her ignore every warning.

The investigations were thorough. Every dismissed report became part of the record. Every ignored recommendation was read aloud in a crowded room. She kept her usual composed look, but something behind her eyes had changed. The certainty she always had was beginning to fade.

She had built her whole identity on believing her judgment was better than everyone else's. She saw instruction as an obstacle, and those who offered it as less important. Proverbs 1:22 had been speaking to her for years, but she never paused to listen.

The consultancy didn't survive. The board dissolved it quietly, and Velma lost the platform that had defined her for over a decade. In the quiet that followed, the voices she had ignored for years became clear, clearer than she ever allowed them to be when they were right in front of her.

She had rejected wisdom and held good advice in contempt. The life she built on that contempt was just as fragile as the people she dismissed always knew it was.

Day 1: Q&A

Q: What does Proverbs 1:22 reveal about those who show contempt for wisdom and instruction?
A: Proverbs 1:22 is not describing people who never had access to wisdom. It is describing people who chose to stay away from it. They delight in contempt. They turn from righteous counsel on purpose. Velma was that person. Her problem was not that wisdom was unavailable. She had decided long before anyone opened their mouth that she did not need it. That posture had been building in her for years.

Q: How did Velma's contempt for instruction ultimately destroy what she had built?
A: Velma's contempt worked like a filter. Every warning, every experienced voice, got screened out before it could reach her. She was running entirely on her own judgment with nothing to catch what she could not see. The redevelopment was not a random failure. It was years of dismissed counsel finally showing up as public consequence. She had built something, but she had built it without the wisdom that would have made it hold.

Day 2: Explanation: Proverbs 1:22 is not about ignorance. It is about a posture of the heart. The person it describes has met wisdom and chosen contempt. Velma was not unintelligent. She was surrounded by experienced people who wanted to help her build something that would last. Her problem was not access. It was that she had a deep, settled disdain for the idea that she needed anything outside herself. That is what the verse is addressing. The belief that your own understanding is enough and that counsel is something you sit through rather than receive. That posture does not protect you from failure. It walks you straight into it.

Day 3: Anecdote: A highly regarded architect built her career on creativity and vision. As her reputation grew, so did her resistance to outside input. She turned away structural engineers whose recommendations felt limiting. She dismissed safety inspectors as people without imagination. Every external review was an intrusion. Years later, a structural flaw that had been flagged and ignored became a serious safety crisis. The warning had been given. She just chose not to take it. Like Velma, she had mistaken the silencing of counsel for the absence of risk.

Day 4: Warning: Contempt for wisdom does not always look like arrogance. Sometimes it looks like confidence. Decisiveness. Strong leadership. But there is a real difference between a leader who hears counsel and then acts, and one who has already decided before the counsel is offered. Proverbs 1:22 is a warning to anyone who has gotten comfortable dismissing instruction.

The person who scorns wisdom is not just missing good advice. They are pulling out the safeguards that stand between them and destruction. Every dismissed voice is a protection removed. And what gets built without those protections will eventually show it.

Day 5: Encouragement: If Velma's story landed somewhere in you, if you recognize the habit of dismissing counsel, of treating instruction as beneath you, of moving through life certain you already know enough, take it as an invitation, not a condemnation. Proverbs 1:23 follows the warning with an offer. Wisdom calls out to those who turned away and invites them to come back. The door contempt closed is not locked for good. Humility can open it. The first step is not some dramatic overhaul. It is one honest moment of stillness where you ask whether there is a voice you have been dismissing that deserved more than you gave it. Start there. Wisdom is still calling. It did not stop just because it was ignored.

Day 6: Why People Become Scorners: Nobody sets out to become someone who holds wisdom in contempt. It happens slowly, and it usually starts with something that looks like strength. Early success confirms what they already suspected about themselves. Praise for boldness makes caution feel like timidity. One bad piece of counsel becomes the reason to stop listening to all of it. Affirmation becomes the only voice they trust. By the time they have arrived at the place Proverbs 1:22 describes, they do not realize how far they have come. The way out is not shame. It is awareness. The person who can see how they got there has already taken the first step.

Day 7: Reflection Questions:

Q: Where in your life have you gotten into the habit of dismissing instruction before you have really heard it, and what would it actually cost you to open yourself to correction there?

Q: Think of a specific person who has offered you righteous counsel that you dismissed. What was it about their advice that you refused to receive, and is it possible that what they said deserved more consideration than you gave it?

Q: Velma treated wisdom as something she possessed rather than something she needed to pursue. In what ways has your own confidence in your judgment caused you to stop actively seeking wisdom from God and from others?

Q: Proverbs 1:22 describes those who love their own simplicity and delight in contempt. Where in your life do you find it most comfortable to remain in what you already know rather than being stretched by what you have yet to learn?

PRAYER JOURNAL

Father,

We come before You with honesty about the ways we have held wisdom in contempt. We confess the moments we have dismissed counsel without truly hearing it, the times we have treated instruction as an obstacle rather than a gift, and the seasons in which we have trusted our own understanding above Your voice and the voices of those You placed in our lives to guide us. Forgive us for the pride that made us believe we had already arrived. Forgive us for the disdain that caused us to walk away from the very wisdom that could have protected us. We ask You to soften our hearts and open our ears. Teach us to love instruction the way Your Word says the wise love it. Give us the humility to sit with counsel before we dismiss it, the patience to hear correction before we defend against it, and the courage to change direction when wisdom calls us to. We want to be people who build on the foundation of Your wisdom rather than the shifting ground of our own certainty.

In the name of Jesus, Amen.

Prayer Thoughts for Today:

♦♦♦♦♦

~ END PRAYER JOURNAL "THE SCORNER" ~

WISDOM IN WAITING

THE WISE

PROVERBS 3:5-6 (NIV)

5 Trust in the Lord with all your heart and lean not on your own understanding;
6 in all your ways submit to him, and he will make your paths straight.

livia graduated in May with a business degree, a color-coded planner, and a quiet confidence that a job would come quickly. She did everything right: good grades, two internships, and a resume her professor called clean and competitive. She sent out applications the same week she returned her cap and gown, certain she would be working by July.

July came and went, and so did August. She got interviews and even made it to the final rounds a couple of times, but then heard nothing. Or worse, she got the polite email: "We've decided to move forward with another candidate." She started checking LinkedIn less because watching her college friends post first-day photos started to get to her in a way she didn't want to admit.

One night in September, sitting on the floor of her bedroom with rejection number eleven open on her laptop, she just started talking to God. It wasn't a polished prayer, more like venting. She told Him she didn't understand, that she felt like she was doing everything right, and that she was tired. She didn't hear an audible answer, but something in her settled. A thought she couldn't shake: slow down. She didn't love it, but she stayed with it.

She called her old professor, Dr. Renee Carter, who had written her recommendation letters. Dr. Carter told her something she didn't expect: "This gap is not a gap. It's material." She also texted Marcus, a family friend who had worked in HR for twenty years. He told her to keep applying but to stop gripping the timeline so tightly. "You can't force the right door open," he said. "You'll just hurt your hands." She wrote that down.

She signed up for a project management certification she had put off because she thought she wouldn't need it. She started helping with the high school ministry at her church on Wednesday nights, something she had always meant to do but never found time for. Those Wednesday nights became the part of her week she looked forward to most. The kids were funny, honest, and needed someone to show up for them. She could do that.

She started keeping a running note on her phone of things she was actually getting done. She finished the first module, led her first small group discussion, and had a two-hour conversation with a girl in the youth group who reminded her a lot of herself at seventeen. She wasn't where she wanted to be, but she wasn't standing still either.

There were still bad days. Sometimes she refreshed her inbox too many times and then felt embarrassed about it. Sometimes she wondered if she had misread everything, if God was actually silent and she was just telling herself a story. She kept a journal through most of it, not because it came naturally but because Dr. Carter had suggested it. Some entries were just a sentence: "Still waiting. Still okay. I think." That was enough.

In February, almost nine months after graduation, her phone rang with a number she didn't recognize. It was a hiring manager at a nonprofit she had applied to back in October and honestly forgotten about. They had moved slowly, he explained, but they were ready now. The role was in program coordination, which was exactly the kind of work she had been building toward. She interviewed twice, and the second time felt less like a test and more like a conversation.

Two weeks later, she got the call. She sat in her car in a parking lot and cried a little, then called her mom, then texted Dr. Carter and Marcus. When she started the job in March, she noticed something. She wasn't scrambling to figure out who she was in the room. The months of waiting had settled something in her. She knew how to be patient with a process. She knew how to show up when things were slow.

She had learned that from Wednesday nights with teenagers who didn't always want to be there. She told that story at a college ministry event a few months later, not because it had a perfect ending, but because she remembered how lonely that parking lot floor had felt and thought someone else might need to hear that the waiting had a point.

She didn't have a tidy summary for what the waiting had taught her. It was more like a posture she had grown into without fully noticing. She trusted more easily now and rushed less. When younger friends came to her frustrated about timelines that weren't moving, she knew exactly what to say because she had lived it.

Day 1: Q&A:

Q: What did Olivia do during her wait?

A: She called people she trusted and actually listened to what they said. She picked up a certification she had been putting off. She showed up every Wednesday night for a group of teenagers who needed consistency. None of it felt dramatic in the moment. It just kept her moving and kept her connected to something beyond her own frustration. Looking back, those months shaped her in ways a quick hire never would have.

Q: What was the blessing?

A: She got a job that fit her well, but the deeper thing was that she wasn't the same person who had applied for it. The waiting had done something to her. She was less anxious, more grounded, better at sitting with uncertainty without falling apart. She walked into that role ready in ways she couldn't have manufactured on her own.

Day 2: Explanation: Psalm 27:14 says, "Wait for the Lord; be strong and take heart and wait for the Lord." That word wait in the original Hebrew carries the idea of expectant watching, like someone leaning forward, not checked out. Waiting on God is not the same as doing nothing. It is choosing, sometimes daily, to trust that He is at work in the parts of your life you cannot see or control. That is harder than it sounds. But it is also where some of the deepest formation happens.

Day 3: Anecdote: A missionary named Claire trained for two years expecting to be sent overseas right away. Instead, she was placed in a small rural town in the Midwest that she described as "the opposite of where I thought God was sending me." She stayed anyway. She learned the rhythms of the community, built friendships slowly, and sat with people through hard things without having answers. When she eventually did get to serve abroad, she said those years in that small town were the reason she was any good at it. She had learned to be present without an agenda. That, she said, was something you could not shortcut.

Day 4: Blessing and Rewards: James 1:4 says that when patience is allowed to finish its work, we come out complete, not lacking anything. That is a real promise, and it is worth sitting with. Patience is not just a virtue to admire. It produces something. It builds a kind of steadiness in us that cannot be faked or rushed. The people who tend to handle hard things well are usually the people who have had to wait before, and who learned something during it.

Day 5: Encouragement: If you are in a waiting season right now, this is for you: it is not wasted time. It might feel like it. It might look like it from the outside. But Romans 8:28 is not a bumper sticker. It is a promise with weight behind it. God is working in the quiet, in the unanswered, in the doors that haven't moved yet. Olivia's story is not unique. It is the kind of story God keeps writing, and He may be writing one just like it for you.

Day 6: God's Love and Redemption: Isaiah 40:31 promises that those who wait on the Lord will find their strength renewed. Not eventually, not as a reward at the end, but in the waiting itself. That is what love does. It does not abandon you in the hard seasons and shows up for the good ones. It sustains you through the whole thing. If the silence has felt long, that is real. But you are not alone in it. God's love is not waiting for your circumstances to improve before it shows up. It is already there.

Day 7: Reflection Questions:

Q: Are you in a season of waiting, and if so, what are you trusting God with right now?

Q: How can you use this time to grow and prepare, and what is one practical step you can take this week?

Q: What wisdom has God given you while you wait, and how has it changed the way you see your season?

Q: Who can you encourage as they wait? Is there someone in your life right now who needs a reminder that their waiting is not wasted?

PRAYER JOURNAL

*L*oving Father,

Thank You for being with me in every season, including those times of waiting that stretch my patience and test my trust. I confess that I often want answers right away and struggle when doors seem closed or pathways uncertain. Forgive me for the moments I have rushed ahead or doubted Your timing, thinking I know best.

Grant me wisdom as I wait, Lord. Teach me to see this season not as wasted time, but as a gift an opportunity to grow in faith, to deepen my relationship with You, and to prepare my heart for what You have planned. Fill me with hope and contentment as I serve and learn where I am. Help me to notice the lessons and blessings You place along the way.

Give me a spirit of humility, willing to learn from others, to listen to wise counsel, and to accept that Your timing is always perfect. Quiet my anxious thoughts and help me to surrender my plans to You. When I am tempted to compare my journey to others, remind me of Your unique purpose for my life.

Thank You for Your steadfast love and for the peace that comes from trusting You. Lead me to wait with a grateful heart and to encourage others who are also in seasons of waiting. May I honor You in my attitude and actions, knowing that You are always working for my good.

In Jesus' name, Amen.

Prayer Thoughts for Today:

~ END PRAYER JOURNAL "THE WISE" ~

THE STRUGGLE TO MANAGE

THE SIMPLE ONE

PROVERBS 21:20 (NIV)

"The wise store up choice food and olive oil, but fools gulp theirs down."

Theresa had always looked forward to the day she would earn her own money. When she finally landed a part-time job at the local electronics store, she felt a rush of pride and independence. The first time she saw her name on a paycheck, her hands tingled with excitement. She imagined all the things she could finally buy for herself: new headphones, the latest phone, trendy sneakers, and meals out with friends. For once, she'd be able to say yes to the things she wanted, without having to ask her parents for money.

She had no idea how fast money disappears when you're not watching it. The day she cashed that check, her friends wanted to hit the mall. They found her standing in front of a display of wireless earbuds, doing the mental math. "Girl, you just got paid. You deserve it." That was all it took. She swiped her card before she could talk herself out of it, and walked out of the store feeling like she'd finally arrived.

That same weekend, the group chat wouldn't stop. Pizza. Burgers. A movie. Theresa said yes to all of it. She didn't want to be the one who suddenly went quiet after getting paid. So, she covered her share, chipped in for gas, grabbed snacks for the whole crew at the theater. Every time she swiped, it felt fine. More than fine, actually. It felt good to be the one saying yes.

By week three, her bank balance looked wrong. She checked it twice, thinking maybe there was a glitch. There wasn't. Her phone bill was due. She needed a textbook for school. She opened her account again and just sat there. Not enough. The sick feeling that hit her wasn't dramatic. It was just quiet and heavy. She stopped answering the group chat. Made up excuses. She wasn't about to admit to anyone that she'd burned through a whole paycheck in three weeks.

The next few weeks were rough. Bus fare. A charger when hers broke. Lunch, some days. She ended up borrowing from her little sister, which was maybe the most humbling part of all of it. Her sister didn't make a big deal out of it, just handed her the cash. That somehow made it worse. The freedom she'd felt at the start of the month was completely gone.

One night she passed on yet another hangout and just sat at her desk, staring at her wallet. Nothing in it. She thought about her mom, who had tried to talk to her about budgeting before she even started the job. Theresa had half-listened, nodded, figured she'd work it out herself. She hadn't.

She went and knocked on her mom's door. Didn't really explain much, just said she needed help. Her mom didn't say "I told you so." She just grabbed a notebook. They sat at the kitchen table for an hour: bills, expenses, what was actually necessary versus what could wait. It wasn't complicated, but seeing it written down made it feel real in a way it hadn't before.

Next paycheck, she paid her phone bill first. Set aside money for the textbook. Then, and only then, did she let herself think about anything else. She still went out with her friends, just not every time. When she said no, a couple of them gave her a hard time. But one of them, her friend Maya, got quiet and said, "Honestly, I need to start doing that too." Theresa hadn't expected that.

She'd learned the hard way, but she'd learned. And honestly, the pride she felt checking her savings account, even when it was still small, felt nothing like the buzz of buying something she didn't need. That feeling lasted. The earbuds were already scratched...

Day 1: Q&A:

Q: Why did Theresa spend all her money so quickly?
A: Honestly, Theresa just hadn't been taught yet. She wasn't careless because she didn't care. She was careless because nobody had ever walked her through what to actually do with a paycheck. So, she did what felt good in the moment and trusted that the rest would sort itself out. It didn't. Most of us have been Theresa at some point. The sting of an empty wallet has a way of getting our attention when nothing else does.

Q: How can someone gain financial wisdom?
A: You find people who are actually doing it well and you pay attention. You ask questions. You stop pretending you've got it figured out. Proverbs 15:22 says, "Plans fail without good counsel," which is just a timeless way of saying nobody gets wise alone. God designed it that way on purpose. When we're humble enough to say "I don't know what I'm doing," that's usually where real growth starts.

Day 2: Explanation: In Proverbs, the "simple" aren't bad people. They're just inexperienced ones. They haven't been taught, or haven't been paying attention, and so they drift toward whatever feels good right now. That's not a character flaw; it's a starting point. But God doesn't want us to stay there. How we handle money turns out to say a lot about where our trust actually lives. Proverbs 3:9 calls us to honor God with our wealth, not as a financial tip, but as an act of worship. Stewardship is spiritual.

Day 3: Anecdote: A financial advisor I heard speak once said something that stuck with me. He said that in college, he was a disaster with money. Spent everything, ignored every warning, racked up debt, and convinced himself the whole time that he'd figure it out eventually. He didn't figure it out. The debt did it for him. What turned things around wasn't a seminar or a budgeting app. It was Proverbs and a few older men who let him watch how they lived. He said wisdom doesn't usually arrive all at once. It shows up in a hundred small decisions that you almost don't notice you're making.

Day 4: Warning: Here's the hard truth: financial carelessness has consequences that compound over time. Debt doesn't stay small. Opportunities don't wait. Proverbs 21:20 puts it plainly: the wise have something left over, and the foolish consume everything they have. That's not a judgment, it's a pattern. And the earlier you recognize the pattern in your own life, the easier it is to change. This isn't about shame. It's about waking up before the consequences get louder.

Day 5: Encouragement: It's not too late, and you're not too far behind. Seriously. God's wisdom isn't reserved for people who grew up with good financial role models or who never made a mess of their money. It's available right now, to you, today. Ask for it. Find someone who's living it out and ask them to show you. That's it. That's the whole thing.

Day 6: God's Love and Redemption: Whatever you've done with money, however many times you've started over, however much you've wasted or lost or given away for the wrong reasons, God is not standing over you with a scorecard. He's not waiting for you to get it together before He'll help you. He meets you in the mess and says, let's start from here. His Spirit doesn't just offer forgiveness; He offers direction. And the goal was never just your financial stability. It was always so you'd have something to give.

Day 7: Reflection Questions:

Q: Have you ever spent money quickly without thinking about future needs or responsibilities? What was the result?

Q: Who are some trustworthy people you can learn from about wise financial habits?

Q: What practical steps can you take to plan and manage your resources more wisely in the future? **Q:** What practical steps can you take to plan and manage your resources more wisely in the future?

Q: How can seeking God's wisdom help you become a better steward of what He's given you?

aithful God,

Thank you for providing all I need. I admit that sometimes I have made choices with my resources without thinking ahead or seeking Your wisdom. Forgive me for following others' ways rather than asking for Your guidance on how I spend and save.

Please give me a heart of stewardship and teach me to be wise in handling what You have entrusted to me. Help me to resist pressure to conform and instead act with prudence and self-control. Guide me to honor You in every decision, big or small.

Thank you for your patience and for giving me new opportunities to learn and grow. May Your Spirit lead me to generosity, balance, and financial wisdom that brings blessing to myself and those around me.

In Jesus' name, Amen.

Prayer Thoughts for Today: ♦♦♦♦♦

~ END PRAYER JOURNAL "THE SIMPLE ONE" ~

Risky Risky

THE FOOL

Proverbs 14:16 (NIV)

"The wise fear the Lord and shun evil, but a fool is hotheaded and yet feels secure."

Rachel grew up in a house where her mother kept a prayer journal and her father checked the weather before every road trip. She was the kid who climbed the tallest tree in the yard and jumped before anyone could talk her out of it. By the time she was a teenager, that same impulse had grown into something harder to laugh off. She wasn't looking for trouble exactly, but she wasn't avoiding it either.

It started with small things. Sneaking out to parties her parents didn't know about. Riding her bike down the steepest hill in the neighborhood without a helmet, just to feel the wind. But by the time she was in her twenties, the small things weren't doing it anymore. She started skydiving with a group that operated out of a field two hours from home, skipping the safety briefing because she thought it was for people who were scared. She drove fast on back roads with her friends in the car, weaving between lanes while they gripped the door handles and laughed nervously, or didn't laugh at all.

Her dad started texting her when she was out. Just a simple "you good?" at ten, then eleven, then midnight. She usually answered eventually. Her mom stopped asking about her weekends because the answers made her stomach hurt. Rachel knew this, on some level, but she filed it away somewhere she didn't have to look at it. She had seen friends get hurt before. A girl from her high school had broken her collarbone during a stunt that Rachel herself had passed on that day, and Rachel remembered thinking she had just gotten unlucky.

Then one afternoon she clipped a parked car while cutting through a narrow street too fast. Her friend Dani was in the passenger seat and didn't say a word for the rest of the drive home. When Rachel tried to make a joke about it, Dani just looked out the window. That night, Rachel told the story at dinner like it was funny. Her dad set his fork down and her mom got up to refill her water glass even though it was still full. Rachel kept talking.

She genuinely couldn't figure out why people were so worried about her. She was fine. She had always been fine. What she didn't see was that "fine" had started to mean something different to the people around her. It meant she hadn't gotten seriously hurt yet. It meant they were still waiting.

She found a group online, people who posted videos of themselves doing things that had no business being on the internet. She fit right in. They called her fearless in the comments and she screenshot everyone. But somewhere between the posts, in the quiet of a Tuesday afternoon when there was nothing to chase and no one watching, she felt something she didn't have a word for. Not sad exactly. Just hollow. Her younger brother used to call her every Sunday. He had stopped a few months back and she hadn't asked him why.

Then, one evening, her mom called, and somewhere in the middle of the conversation, her voice cracked. She said she was scared. Not frustrated, not disappointed. Scared. Rachel sat with that word for a long time after they hung up. She had spent years convincing herself that the people who worried about her just didn't understand her. But her mom's voice had sounded so tired. For the first time, Rachel let herself wonder if maybe the people who loved her weren't trying to hold her back. Maybe they were just trying to hold on.

But old habits die hard, and Rachel's story was far from over.

Day 1: Q&A:

Q: Why did Rachel ignore warnings about her behavior?

A: She had built her whole identity around the idea that she was different, tougher, more capable than the people handing out warnings. Accepting advice would have meant admitting she didn't have it all figured out, and that felt like too high a price. Pride has a way of making the most dangerous path look like the brave one. Proverbs describes the fool not as someone who lacks intelligence, but as someone who refuses to be taught, and Rachel fit that description not because she was incapable of wisdom, but because she had decided she didn't need it.

Q: What was the outcome of her choices?

A: The people who loved her got tired. Not because of her, but because of the fear. Her friend Dani stopped reaching out. Her brother went quiet. Her parents aged in ways she didn't want to think about. Recklessness has a way of spreading outward, touching everyone close enough to care. Proverbs 13:20 warns that the companion of fools will suffer harm, and Rachel's story is a good example of how true that is. The consequences of her choices didn't stay with her alone.

Day 2: Explanation: Proverbs 14:16 says, "A wise man fears and departs from evil, but a fool rages and is self-confident." That word "rages" is worth sitting with. It's not passive. The fool isn't just drifting into bad decisions; he's charging toward them, chest out, certain he knows better. That kind of self-confidence feels like strength in the moment, but it has a way of leaving a person alone with the wreckage. God doesn't call us to wisdom to shrink our lives. He calls us to it because He can see around corners we can't.

Day 3: Anecdote: A man I know, the kind of person who has an opinion on everything and rarely second-guesses himself, went hiking with a group a few years back. The guide told everyone to stay on the marked trail. He thought that was a suggestion. Two hours in, he had separated from the group and had no cell signal. He spent the better part of an afternoon working his way back, cold and embarrassed, before he finally found a trail marker. He told me later that what stuck with him wasn't the fear, though that was real enough. It was realizing how little it had cost him to listen, and how much it had cost him not to.

Day 4: Warning: There is a particular kind of exhaustion that comes from repeating the same mistakes. You know the cycle. The thrill, the fallout, the brief moment of clarity, and then the slow drift back toward the same choices. Proverbs 26:11 puts it bluntly:

"Like a dog that returns to his vomit is a fool who repeats his folly." It's not a flattering image, but it's an honest one. God's warnings in scripture aren't written to make us feel small. They're written by someone who has watched this pattern play out across generations and loves us enough to say something.

Day 5: Encouragement: If you've lived a version of Rachel's story, even a quieter one, you already know how tiring it gets. The good news is that the door to wisdom doesn't close. It doesn't matter how many times you've walked past it. James 1:5 says that if anyone lacks wisdom, they should ask God, who gives generously without finding fault. That last part matters. He's not keeping score of how long it took you to ask.

Day 6: God's Love and Redemption: The father in Luke 15 didn't wait on the porch. The text says he saw his son "while he was still a great way off" and ran to him. He didn't let the son finish his rehearsed apology. He was already calling for the robe and the ring before the words were out. That's the picture God gives us of Himself. Not someone standing at a distance, arms crossed, waiting to hear a good enough explanation. Someone running. If you've spent time in Rachel's shoes, that image is for you. It doesn't matter how far out you've gone. He already sees you coming back.

Day 7: Reflection Questions:

Q: Have you ever ignored warnings or advice because you thought the rules didn't apply to you? What was the outcome?

Q: Why do you think people are sometimes drawn to risky or reckless behavior, even when they know it could lead to harm?

Q: What are some ways you can seek and apply wisdom before making decisions, especially in situations that seem exciting but risky?

Q: How does knowing that God offers forgiveness and a fresh start encourage you to change course after making reckless choices?

PRAYER JOURNAL

L oving Father,

Thank You for caring about every part of my life and for giving me wise guidance to protect me. Forgive me for the times I have chased after recklessness and ignored the warnings of those who love me. I admit that my desire for excitement and independence has sometimes led me down dangerous paths. Please give me a heart that values wisdom over thrill, and help me to recognize and avoid choices that put myself or others at risk. Thank You for Your grace that welcomes me back, no matter how far I've wandered. Lead me to walk in Your ways, trust Your instructions, and make decisions that honor You. Restore what my foolishness has damaged, and fill me with a spirit of gratitude and obedience.

In Jesus' name, Amen.

Prayer Thoughts for Today: ✦✦✦✦✦

~ END PRAYER JOURNAL "THE FOOL" ~

THE LAUGH THAT COST EVERYTHING

THE SCORNER

PROVERBS 21:24 (NIV):

"The proud and arrogant person—'Mocker' is his name—behaves with insolent fury."

Rose had always found it easy to laugh. Not the kind that pulls people in, but the kind that cuts them down. Back in high school she figured out that a well-timed scoff could flip the whole mood of a room. Could make someone look small before they even finished their sentence. She never lost that instinct.

By her mid-thirties she had a platform, a real one. She talked about culture, politics, and public figures. Her fans said she was the only person willing to say what everyone else was thinking. Her critics had a different word for it. She did not mind either way. The contempt was the point.

Her favorite targets were the ones she called the pious. Pastors, community leaders, anyone who stood up and said that choices have consequences. She had a gift for making their sincerity look ridiculous. Proverbs 14:9 says fools mock at the guilt offering, treating sin like a punchline. That was Rose's whole career.

The platform grew fast. People shared her clips, quoted her lines, showed up every week for more. She gave her audience something they did not know they wanted: permission. Permission to laugh at the things they feared and call it being smart. Proverbs 19:28 talks about a corrupt witness who mocks at justice. That is a harder charge than just being mean. Rose was not only dismissing serious things. She was training her audience to dismiss them too. The teenagers who watched her started carrying her posture into their own lives, rolling their eyes at anything that asked something real of them. She had no idea how far that was reaching.

It started with a story she got wrong. She had spent months going after a community leader, implying her motives were corrupt, her work was theater. Turned out the source Rose had used was garbage. The leader had a long, documented record that said the exact opposite of everything Rose had put out there. When that came out, it did not come out quietly.

Other journalists started pulling threads. A pattern showed up, story after story where Rose had crossed from commentary into something closer to cruelty. People she had mocked came forward. The community leader filed a formal complaint. The platform that had always trained its sharpest lens on everyone else was now the subject.

Rose's first move was to mock the backlash. Of course it was. She called it fragility, called her critics exactly the kind of people she had always warned her audience about. But the bit was not landing the way it used to. What had looked like fearlessness for years was starting to look like someone who only had one move.

Sponsors pulled out. The audience drifted. People who had shown up every week to laugh along with her quietly stopped showing up. Rose sat in a studio that used to hum with energy and felt the silence in a way she was not prepared for. She had been spending something for years without realizing it, and now the bill had come.

She had laughed at guilt and called it honesty. She had scoffed at accountability and called it courage. She had spent years picking apart people who were genuinely trying to live right, and she had called that wisdom. But Proverbs had seen her coming. The one

65

who mocks sin does not get to skip its weight. The one who builds on contempt finds out, eventually, what contempt is actually worth.

The laugh that had always come so easy turned out to have a price she never saw coming

Day 1: Q&A

Q: What are Proverbs 14:9 and 19:28 actually saying about people who make a habit of mocking sin and authority?
A: Proverbs 14:9 says fools mock at the guilt offering. That means they treat sin like a joke, something beneath serious engagement. Proverbs 19:28 goes further and calls the scoffer a corrupt witness, someone who does not just dismiss justice but actively poisons the ground around it. These are not just descriptions of someone with a bad attitude. They describe a person who has made contempt a way of life and uses it to dodge the discomfort of honest self-examination. Rose did exactly that, and she dragged her audience along with her.

Q: How did Rose's mockery come back on her?
A: Because contempt is not a posture you can turn off when it becomes inconvenient. Rose had spent years refusing to take accountability seriously as a concept, so when the moment came that required it from her, she had nothing. Her instinct was to mock the correction, same as she had mocked everything else. And that revealed the whole thing for what it was: not fearlessness, not honesty, just a long habit of avoiding anything that asked her to sit with something hard.

Day 2: Explanation: Proverbs 14:9 and 19:28 are not just talking about someone with a sharp tongue. They are describing a whole orientation toward life, one where sin is not serious, where anyone who treats moral questions with weight is either foolish or putting on a show. That posture can look like sophistication. It can get packaged as courage. But Proverbs names it plainly: foolishness. The fool who mocks the guilt offering is not being brave. They are just unwilling to sit with something uncomfortable. And over time, that unwillingness does not make you sharper. It makes you less capable of thinking clearly about anything that actually matters.

Day 3: Anecdote: There was a comedian, well known for going after religious institutions and anyone she thought was performing virtue. Her crowd loved it. Then a close friend showed up at her door in a real crisis, the kind that does not want a punchline. The comedian did not know what to do. She sat there and realized she had spent so many years training herself to deflect anything serious that she had lost the ability to just be present with it. Her friend eventually found help somewhere else. The comedian did not forget that.

Day 4: Warning: The pleasure of mockery is real. That is the honest thing to say first. There is something that feels good about a well-aimed scoff, about treating a serious thing as absurd and watching others laugh along. But Proverbs does not let that feeling have the last word. The person who mocks sin does not get out from under it. The person who builds their whole identity on contempt will find, sooner or later, that contempt eats through the foundation. Proverbs 14:9 and 19:28 are not just describing bad manners. They are describing a heart that has slowly closed itself off from the kind of honest reckoning that leads anywhere good.

Day 5: Encouragement: If something in Rose's story landed close to home, that is worth paying attention to. Proverbs 9:9 says that if you give instruction to a wise person, they become wiser. The door is always open to move from one posture to the other. That does not mean giving up humor or becoming someone who takes everything too seriously. It means letting laughter be the kind that does not cost someone else something. The life on the other side of contempt is not smaller. It is just more honest.

Day 6: Why People Become Scorners: Most people do not start out as scorners. They get there. Usually because something hurt them first, a religious community that let them down, someone who used moral language as a weapon, a person in authority who abused it. Mockery starts as protection. It makes sense in that context. But Proverbs is honest about where it goes if it stays. What starts as a shield can harden into a posture that causes more damage than the original wound ever did. Getting out of it does not start with shame. It starts with asking what the contempt was originally trying to guard.

Day 7: Reflection Questions:

Q: Think about a person or institution you have consistently mocked or scoffed at. Is it possible that beneath the contempt there is a wound, a fear, or an unexamined assumption that deserves honest attention rather than ridicule?

Q: Rose's mockery spread to her audience, shaping how they engaged with serious things. Who in your life might be absorbing a posture of contempt from you, and what responsibility does that place on you?

Q: Proverbs 14:9 says that fools mock at the guilt offering. Where in your own life have you used laughter or scoffing to avoid the discomfort of genuine moral reckoning, and what would it look like to face that discomfort honestly before God?

Q: In what areas of your life do you use humor or contempt to avoid engaging seriously with matters of sin, authority, or moral accountability, and what might that avoidance be costing you?

PRAYER JOURNAL

Father,

We confess that mockery can feel like strength when it is really a way of hiding. We have used laughter to avoid conviction, contempt to avoid accountability, and scoffing to keep serious things from reaching the places in our hearts where they need to land. Forgive us for the times we have made light of sin, dismissed those who spoke with genuine moral conviction, and built our sense of superiority on the tearing down of others. We ask You to replace the reflex of contempt with the posture of humility. Teach us to take seriously what You take seriously, to honor what You have placed in authority, and to engage with the weight of moral reality rather than laughing it away. Where our mockery has caused harm, give us the courage to make it right. Where it has become a habit, give us the grace to break it. We want to be people whose laughter comes from joy and not from contempt, whose words build up rather than tear down, and whose lives reflect the wisdom that only comes from sitting humbly before You.

In the name of Jesus, Amen.

Prayer Thoughts for Today:

✦✦✦✦✦

~ END PRAYER JOURNAL "THE SCORNER" ~

WISDOM IN FINANCES

THE WISE

PROVERBS 21:5 (NIV)

"The plans of the diligent lead to profit as surely as haste leads to poverty."

ophia had never been great with money. She knew it, too. She just kept doing it anyway. New clothes, dinner out, something she saw online that seemed necessary in the moment. She liked the feeling of buying something, the small lift it gave her, even when she knew she probably should not. She would swipe and not think about it until the overdraft notice showed up and made her think about it.

The bills did not pile up all at once. It was gradual. A statement here, a minimum payment there, a balance she kept meaning to deal with next month. She told herself she would get serious about it after the holidays, then after her birthday, then after things settled down at work. Things never quite settled down. She stopped opening her banking app the way you stop checking a voicemail you already know is bad news. She had intentions to save. She just never got around to starting.

The thing that finally stopped her was maxing out a card and realizing she had no plan. Not a vague plan. No plan at all. She sat with that for a few days, anxious and irritable, buying a coffee she did not need because it was the one thing that still felt manageable. She did not tell anyone. That was the worst part, carrying it quietly and pretending everything was fine. A friend mentioned a stewardship workshop at their church. Sophia almost said no. She went anyway, mostly because she did not have anything better to do that Saturday and because some part of her knew she could not keep going the way she was going. She expected it to be boring. It was not. Someone stood up and talked about money not as a math problem but as a trust issue, about what it means to handle something that was never really yours to begin with. They talked about the anxiety that comes from treating your finances like a secret you are keeping from yourself. Sophia recognized that immediately. She had not expected to. She started tithing, which felt genuinely uncomfortable at first. She ran the numbers twice trying to make it work and was not sure it did. She almost talked herself out of it on the first month. But she did it anyway, and then she waited to see what happened.

What happened was not dramatic. The money did not multiply overnight. There was no moment where everything clicked and became easy. What changed was quieter than that. She stopped feeling like her finances were something chasing her. She made a budget, her first real one, and stuck to it badly for a few weeks and then a little better after that. She started pausing before purchases, not always, but more than before. She put her phone down in the middle of a checkout more than once. That was not nothing.

She asked a friend who seemed to actually have her finances together how she did it. The conversation was a little awkward because money is awkward and Sophia had never been someone who asked for help easily. But her friend did not make her feel judged. She was honest about her own past mistakes, about the years she had spent doing the same things Sophia was doing, and that made it easier to listen. Sophia started making extra payments when she could. She tracked her debt on a notepad she kept in her kitchen drawer. Some months the number barely moved. Some months she could not make the extra payment at all. She kept going anyway.

It took longer than she wanted. There were months that felt like no progress at all, and a few where she slipped back into old habits and had to start again without making it a bigger deal than it was. But the debts did come down. Slowly, then faster. At some point she opened her banking app without bracing herself, and that felt like a bigger deal than it probably sounds. When she had a little margin, she started giving more intentionally. Not out of obligation but because she finally understood what it was for and what it could do. A friend in her small group was going through something hard and Sophia was able to help in a real way, not just with words but with something tangible. That was new. She had never been in a position to do that before, and she did not take it lightly.

She still prays about money. Not because she has it all figured out but because she learned the hard way what it costs to act like she does. The prayer is not always eloquent. Sometimes it is just asking for the discipline to do the thing she already knows she should do.

Her story is not finished. But it is a lot different than where it started, and that is enough.

Day 1: Q&A:

Q: What change did Sophia make with her money?
A: She started tithing, made a real budget, and asked for help from people who knew more than she did. None of it was comfortable at first. But she kept at it, and over time the anxiety that had followed her around started to lift. The change was not just financial. It was the difference between feeling chased by your own decisions and feeling like you are actually the one making them.

Q: How did God bless her?
A: The debt came down. The dread went away. And somewhere in the middle of that process she found that she actually wanted to give, not because she was supposed to but because she had something to give and knew what it could do. That shift, from anxious and stuck to generous and steady, is the blessing. It did not come all at once. It came because she kept showing up.

Day 2: Explanation: Proverbs 21:20 says "The wise store up choice food and olive oil, but fools gulp theirs down." That image is worth sitting with. Not a dramatic moral failure, just someone who consumed everything they had without thinking about tomorrow. That is an easy pattern to fall into, especially when spending feels normal and saving feels like deprivation. The verse is not calling for anxiety about the future. It is calling for enough self-awareness to realize that what you do with what you have today shapes what is available later. Sophia had to learn that the hard way. Most of us do.

Day 3: Anecdote: A couple in a small group once shared that for the first eight years of their marriage they gave almost nothing because there was never enough left over. They were not irresponsible people. They just spent first and gave from whatever remained, which was usually not much. When they finally flipped the order, giving first and building a budget around what was left, things started to change. Slowly. It took a couple of years before they felt it. But eventually they were able to support a missionary family they had known for years and had always wanted to help. The husband said the thing that surprised him most was not the giving itself but how much he stopped worrying about money once it was no longer the first thing he thought about.

Day 4: **Blessing and Rewards:** Proverbs 11:24-25 says one person gives freely and gains even more, while another holds back and ends up with less. That does not make sense on paper. It is not supposed to. The point is that God's economy does not run on the same logic as a spreadsheet. Generosity is not a financial strategy. It is an act of trust. And the blessing that tends to follow is not always material. Sometimes it is the simple, surprising relief of no longer holding everything so tightly. That is worth more than most people expect.

Day 5: Encouragement: Philippians 4:19 says God will supply all your needs according to His riches in glory. That is not a promise that the numbers will always work out the way you want. It is a promise that He is not indifferent to what you are carrying. If your finances feel like a mess right now, that is not a reason to avoid bringing them to God. It is exactly the reason to. You do not have to have a plan first. You just have to show up honest about where you are.

Day 6: God's Love and Redemption: God does not wait until you have your finances sorted to show up. He meets people in the middle of the mess, in the overdraft notices and the maxed out cards and the embarrassment of asking for help. Sophia's story did not start with a breakthrough. It started with a bad Saturday and a workshop she almost skipped. That is usually how it goes. The invitation is not to get it together first. It is to bring what you actually have, including the disorder, and trust that He knows what to do with it.

Day 7: Reflection Questions:

Q: How can you honor God with your finances?

Q: What financial wisdom have others shared with you?

Q: How can you grow in generosity?

Q: Where do you need God's guidance with money?

PRAYER JOURNAL

*G*racious Provider,

Thank You for every good gift and for the resources You have entrusted to me. I confess that I have not always managed my finances with wisdom or discipline. Forgive me for the times I have spent impulsively, neglected to give generously, or failed to seek Your guidance in my decisions. Lord, grant me wisdom as I steward what You've given me. Teach me to seek Your will before I make choices about spending, saving, or giving. Help me to resist the pull of materialism and to find my security in You, not in possessions or bank accounts.

Give me humility to learn from others and courage to ask for help when I need it. Show me how to live simply, to care for those in need, and to honor You with my finances. Thank You for Your faithfulness, and for providing what I need and for giving me opportunities to be a blessing to others. Restore any damage caused by poor choices and help me to walk forward in obedience and gratitude. May my use of money reflect Your generosity and love.

In Jesus' name, Amen.

Prayer Thoughts for Today:

♦♦♦♦♦

Taken Advantage Of

THE SIMPLE ONE

PROVERBS 19:2 (NIV)

"Desire without knowledge is not good—how much more will hasty feet miss the way!"

*D*aisy had been job hunting for months. She wasn't looking for anything fancy, just something real, something with a steady paycheck and maybe a few hours she could count on each week. She applied to coffee shops, bookstores, a sandwich place on the corner of Fifth that smelled like vinegar. Most places never called back. When the café on Maple Street finally did, she was so relieved she said yes before the manager even finished the sentence. She ironed her shirt the night before, packed her bag, and showed up fifteen minutes early.

Her manager, Ms. Ramirez, met her at the back office and handed her a small stack of papers. "Standard stuff," she said, already reaching for her radio. "Contract, schedule, house rules. Sign where it's marked and bring it back before your shift starts." Daisy sat down at the break table and skimmed the first page. The text was dense, the kind of dense that made her eyes slide off the page. She told herself she'd read it properly later. Everyone here seemed friendly and professional, and the last thing she wanted was to be the new hire who asked too many questions on day one. She signed everything and turned it in with a smile.

For a while, things were genuinely good. She got the hang of the espresso machine faster than she expected. She learned which regulars wanted oat milk without being asked, who needed their order called out loudly because they were always on a phone call, and which afternoon hours were slow enough to restock the pastry case without falling behind. She started bringing home a real paycheck and felt something she hadn't felt in a long time: capable. When someone called out sick, she covered without hesitating. She liked being the person they could count on. She wanted them to know she was serious about this.

Then the hours started creeping up. At first it was just one extra shift here and there, easy enough to absorb. But by the third month, she was regularly scheduled for closing shifts on the same nights she had eight o'clock lectures at the community college. She'd eat whatever she could find in the car between work and class, get home past eleven, and lie in bed too tired to sleep properly. She told herself it was temporary, that things would level out, that she just needed to push through a little longer.

One Sunday night she sat down with her calendar to plan out the week and just stared at it. There was no white space anywhere. Her grades were slipping in two classes. She couldn't remember the last time she'd called her mom back, let alone a friend. She felt a low, steady kind of tired that sleep wasn't fixing. That was when she thought about the paperwork. She dug through her folder until she found the contract from her first day, hoping there was something in there that gave her an out, some clause about maximum weekly hours or a notice period she could use.

She read the contract slowly this time. And there it was, right in the middle of page two: she had agreed to be available for extra shifts as needed, evenings and weekends included. She'd never asked what "as needed" actually meant. She'd never mentioned her school schedule. She had just signed.

She sat there for a long time with the contract in her lap. She kept thinking about that first day, how eager she'd been, how she'd sat at that break table and told herself she'd read it later. Later never came. She had wanted so badly to seem capable and agreeable that she'd handed over control of her own schedule without even realizing it. She hadn't wanted to ask dumb questions. But not asking had cost her months of her life.

She asked Ms. Ramirez for a meeting the next morning. She rehearsed what she was going to say on the drive over, but when she sat down across from her, her voice shook a little anyway. She explained everything: the classes, the early lectures, the exhaustion she'd been carrying around for months, and how she'd been too nervous to say anything sooner because she didn't want to seem like a problem. Ms. Ramirez listened without interrupting. "I'm glad you came to me," she said when Daisy finished. "I had no idea. Let's fix the schedule." And they did. It took about twenty minutes. It wasn't complicated at all. It just required Daisy to speak up.

She still thinks about that stack of papers sometimes. How she signed her name four times without really knowing what she was agreeing to, just because she was eager and a little scared and didn't want to slow anyone down. She wonders sometimes what would have happened if she'd just taken five minutes to read it through, or asked one simple question about her availability before handing it back. She knows better now. Not because she became suspicious of people or stopped trusting her instincts, but because she learned that asking questions is part of taking care of yourself. It's not rude to understand what you're agreeing to. It's not slow or difficult or inexperienced. Nobody else was going to read that contract for her. That part was always her job.

Day 1: Q&A:

Q: Why didn't Daisy read the documents?
A: She was new, eager to fit in, and didn't want to seem difficult. She assumed that because the environment felt safe, the details would be too. That's a natural instinct, but it's also where the Simple One gets tripped up. A friendly face isn't the same as a fair agreement. Wisdom asks us to verify, not just trust the feeling in the room.

Q: How can someone avoid this mistake?
A: Slow down. Read it. Ask someone you trust if something doesn't make sense. There's no shame in saying "I need a minute to look this over." Proverbs 19:20 puts it plainly: listen to advice and accept instruction, and in the end you will be wise.

Day 2: Explanation: Proverbs describe the Simple One as someone who moves on feeling rather than understanding. It's not that they're foolish, they just haven't learned yet to stop and ask. God calls us toward discernment because He knows what's waiting on the other side of a hasty yes. A life shaped by His wisdom isn't just smarter. It's steadier.

Day 3: Anecdote: A mentor once told me she spent her twenties signing things she didn't understand. Leases. Agreements. Commitments she nodded along to because she didn't want to look lost. "I was always in a hurry," she said. "And I paid for it slowly." She wasn't warning me away from trust. She was telling me that a few minutes of careful attention can save years of cleanup.

Day 4: Warning: Wanting something badly is not the same as being ready for it. When we rush past the details just to get to the yes, we sometimes end up somewhere we never meant to go. Proverbs 19:2 says it clearly: "Desire without knowledge is not good, and whoever makes haste with his feet misses his way."

Day 5: Encouragement: Asking for help is not a sign that you're behind. It means you're paying attention. God doesn't roll His eyes at honest questions. James 1:5 says He gives wisdom generously to those who ask, without finding fault. So ask. Pause before you sign, before you commit, before you say yes. That pause is not hesitation. It's wisdom doing its work.

Day 6: God's Love and Redemption: Maybe you've already made the hasty decision. Maybe you're already living with the fallout of something you signed, agreed to, or said yes to before you really understood what you were getting into. God is not surprised by that. He doesn't hold your inexperience over you. He takes the mess and works with it. Your mistakes are not the end of your story. They're often where the real growth begins.

Day 7: Reflection Questions:

Q: Have you ever agreed to something without fully understanding what you were committing to? What happened as a result?

Q: Why do you think it's important to ask questions and seek understanding before making decisions or signing agreements?

Q: Who can you turn to for wise advice when you're unsure about a commitment or opportunity?

Q: How can you make it a habit to pause and pray before making choices that could impact your life?

PRAYER JOURNAL

Wise and Loving Father,

Thank you for caring about every detail of my life. I confess that sometimes I have acted quickly, signed up for things, or agreed to commitments without understanding what I was getting into. Forgive me for my haste and for not seeking Your wisdom first.

Please give me patience and a discerning spirit. Help me to slow down, ask questions, and seek understanding before making decisions. Lead me to wise mentors and teach me to listen to Your voice in everyday choices.

Thank You for Your mercy and for turning even my mistakes into lessons. Fill me with confidence in Your guidance, so I may walk in wisdom and peace.

In Jesus' name, Amen.

Prayer Thoughts for Today:

♦♦♦♦♦

~ **END PRAYER JOURNAL "THE SIMPLE ONE"** ~

THE PROMISE KEEPER

THE FOOL

PROVERBS 20:25 (NIV)

"It is a trap to dedicate something rashly and only later to consider one's vows."

Daphne often made promises she couldn't keep. She would say yes to every favor and every plan, never pausing to consider her own limits or the weight of the words leaving her mouth. If a friend asked for help moving, Daphne would enthusiastically agree, even if she had already promised someone else she'd help them that same day. If her coworkers invited her to join a project, she'd sign on without a second thought, eager to be liked and seen as dependable. She was the first to raise her hand at church when volunteers were needed, the first to offer her home for a gathering, the first to promise a home-cooked meal to a neighbor going through a hard time. Daphne got a small thrill from the look of gratitude on people's faces when she said yes, and she genuinely wanted to be the kind of person everyone could count on. The problem was that wanting to be that person and actually being that person were two very different things.

But as the days and weeks went by, Daphne's calendar filled up with overlapping obligations that she had never truly intended to juggle. She frequently double-booked herself, convinced she could somehow do it all if she just tried a little harder or slept a little less. She overcommitted without thinking about the time, energy, or resources her promises would require. When the time came to deliver, Daphne would either show up late, leave early, or cancel altogether, often with a hurried apology or a hastily crafted excuse sent by text minutes before she was supposed to arrive. Sometimes she blamed traffic, an unexpected work emergency, or even other people for her absence or failure to help, hoping to avoid admitting that she was simply stretched too thin.

At first, her friends and colleagues were understanding. The first few times she backed out, they forgave her and accepted her explanations with a sympathetic nod. Everyone had hard weeks. Everyone got overwhelmed. But as Daphne's broken promises piled up, their patience wore thin and their trust quietly eroded. Friends stopped asking her to join outings or help with important tasks. Invitations to parties and group dinners became less frequent, and Daphne would see pictures of events she was never even told about: birthday dinners, weekend hikes, impromptu gatherings that had somehow happened without her. At work, teammates started seeking out other collaborators, knowing they couldn't rely on Daphne's support or participation when a deadline was on the line. Her manager had even pulled her aside once, gently noting that her follow-through needed improvement. Even those closest to her began to keep their distance, unwilling to risk being let down again.

Slowly, the invitations dwindled, and Daphne began to notice that people didn't reach out to her as often. She felt rejected and confused by the distance growing between herself and those she cared about. She wondered why she was always the one left out, why her phone was so quiet on weekends, and why she never seemed to be included in plans anymore. She would sit with the ache of it, scrolling through group chats she had gone silent in, reading messages she had meant to reply to but never did. Despite this, Daphne didn't see how her careless words and lack of follow-through were the root of her loneliness. Instead, she told herself that others were being unfair, or that they simply didn't understand how busy and overwhelmed she was. She replayed excuses in her mind, blaming her schedule, bad luck, or even a lack of appreciation from others for the way things had turned out. It was easier to point outward than to look honestly at herself.

Still, Daphne continued to make promises she couldn't keep, stuck in a cycle of wanting to please others but ultimately letting them, and herself, down. She felt a pang of regret each time she disappointed someone, but the feeling was fleeting, quickly replaced by a new commitment she'd made in an effort to win back their trust. She mistook enthusiasm for integrity and good intentions for reliability, never realizing that the people around her did not need her excitement. They needed her word.

It wasn't until she found herself sitting alone on a Friday night, scrolling through photos of friends gathered at a restaurant she recognized, laughing at a table she hadn't been invited to join, that something finally shifted inside her. She set her phone down and stared at the ceiling. The silence in her apartment felt different that night, not peaceful, but hollow. For the first time, she didn't reach for an excuse. She didn't blame traffic, a packed schedule, or anyone else. She simply sat with the uncomfortable truth that she had spent years saying yes to everyone and, in doing so, had slowly become someone no one could count on.

Daphne thought about all the times she had let people down: the friend whose couch she never helped carry up three flights of stairs, the coworker whose presentation she had promised to review and never opened, the neighbor who had waited for that meal that never came. Each memory landed with a quiet, specific weight. She realized that her words had been cheap currency, spent freely but never backed by anything real. And the people in her life had eventually noticed.

She didn't know exactly how to fix it. But for the first time, she knew she had to try, not by making another grand promise, but by making one small, honest commitment and keeping it. Just one. And then another. The silence was heavy, but underneath it, Daphne felt the faint, fragile stirring of something she hadn't felt in a long time: the desire to actually mean what she said.

Day 1: Q&A:

Q: Why did Daphne keep making empty promises?
A: Honestly? She wanted people to like her. It's that simple and that complicated. Saying yes felt good in the moment. It made her feel needed, generous, like the kind of person everyone could count on. The problem is she was performing that version of herself instead of actually being it. And eventually, the gap between who she said she was and what she actually did became impossible to ignore.

Q: What was the result of her behavior?
A: People stopped counting on her. Not all at once. It happened slowly, quietly. An invite that didn't come. A task that got reassigned without explanation. She kept showing up, kept saying the right things, but somewhere along the way people had just stopped believing her. That's the part that stings most. You don't always get a confrontation. Sometimes trust just slips out the back door.

Day 2: Explanation: Proverbs 10:8 says, "The wise in heart accept commands, but a chattering fool comes to ruin." That word, fool, feels harsh until you sit with it. The fool in this verse isn't stupid. He's just loud. He talks more than he listens, commits more than he can carry, and mistakes enthusiasm for wisdom. Most of us have been that person at some point. The verse isn't meant to shame us. It's meant to slow us down. Wisdom starts with knowing what you can actually deliver before you open your mouth.

Day 3: Anecdote: A youth leader I know used to say yes to everything at work. Every request, every favor, every last-minute ask. She was on it. Or so she said. The truth was she was drowning, and the people around her could tell before she could. What finally got through to her wasn't a bad performance review or a blown deadline. It was a coworker who quietly said, "I never know if you're actually going to come through." That hit different. She started saying no, not less but more honestly, and the relationships she'd been trying so hard to protect actually got stronger.

Day 4: Warning: Proverbs 20:25 puts it plainly: "It is a trap to dedicate something rashly and only later to consider one's vows."

A trap. Not a mistake, not a misstep. A trap. Because that's what an empty promise really is. It feels harmless when it leaves your mouth, but it's waiting for you down the road. Before you say yes to something, try asking yourself one honest question: Do I actually intend to do this, or am I just trying to avoid an uncomfortable moment right now? The answer tells you everything.

Day 5: Encouragement: If you've been Daphne in someone's story, and most of us have, that's not the end of it. Patterns can change. Reputations can be rebuilt. It's slow work, and there's no shortcut. You don't repair broken trust with a big gesture; you repair it with a hundred small ones. One kept promise. Then another. God doesn't ask you to be perfect before He uses you. He just asks you to be honest: with Him, with others, and with yourself about what you can actually carry.

Day 6: God's Love and Redemption: Here's what's worth holding onto: God doesn't operate the way Daphne did. He doesn't overcommit and underdeliver. He doesn't say one thing and do another. Every promise He's made, He's kept. Not because it was easy, but because His word actually means something. And when we blow it, when we've overpromised, let people down, and burned through trust we can't get back, He doesn't write us off. He starts the slow, patient work of making us into something more like Him. That's not a small thing.

Day 7: Reflection Questions:

Q: Think of a time you promised something you didn't follow through on. Not a grand failure, maybe just something small. What was going on inside you when you made that promise?

Q: When you say yes to something you know you probably can't do, what are you really hoping for in that moment?

Q: Is there someone in your life right now who might not fully trust your word? What's one small, specific thing you could do this week to start changing that?

Q: When you think about how consistently God has kept His promises to you, how does that change the way you think about the promises you make to others?

Faithful God,

Thank You for being trustworthy and true in all Your ways. I confess that I have made promises I couldn't keep and spoken without considering the consequences. Forgive me for letting others down and for not valuing my word as You do. Teach me to be thoughtful and sincere in what I commit to, and help me to become a person others can rely on. Give me the wisdom to know my limits and the courage to be honest when I cannot fulfill a promise. Thank You for Your forgiveness and for the chance to rebuild trust. May Your faithfulness inspire me to honor my commitments and reflect Your character in all I do.

In Jesus' name, Amen.

Prayer Thoughts for Today: ♦♦♦♦♦

THE TROUBLE CARRIED

THE SCORNER

PROVERBS 22:10 (ESV)

"Drive out the scoffer, and strife will go out, and quarreling and abuse will cease."

Nora had a way of walking into a room and changing its temperature, not with warmth, but with friction. She was sharp-tongued, quick to take offense, and quicker still to manufacture it where none existed. She had grown up believing that conflict was a form of engagement and that the people who kept the peace simply lacked the courage to say what everyone else was thinking. She had told herself this so long that it had become the foundation of every relationship she entered.

She worked at a mid-sized nonprofit in Dellwood dedicated to youth development. When Nora arrived, the staff was committed and the mission was clear. Within two years, a third of the staff had left, three department heads had resigned, and the board was fielding complaints from donors who sensed something was deeply wrong.

Nora had not destroyed the organization through incompetence; she was skilled at her work. She had destroyed it through the steady cultivation of strife. She whispered doubts about colleagues, reframed neutral decisions as favoritism, and turned ordinary frustrations into grievances that infected every corner of the office.

Proverbs 22:10 says that when the scoffer is driven out, strife goes with her, and quarreling and abuse cease. This verse captures something precise and important about a person like Nora. The strife was not incidental to her presence. It was inseparable from it. Where she went, conflict followed, not because the world around her was uniquely difficult, but because she was uniquely gifted at finding the fault lines in any community and pressing on them until they cracked.

She had a talent for identifying tensions and amplifying them. A mild disagreement became evidence of deeper incompatibility. A manager's routine decision became, in her retelling, a symptom of festering leadership failure. She did not invent conflict. She refined it and distributed it with a consistency that kept the entire organization in a low-grade state of unrest.

What made her difficult to address was that she rarely seemed to be causing the trouble; she seemed to be responding to it. She positioned herself as a truth-teller who refused to pretend everything was fine. Around her gathered a small group who shared her grievances, reinforced her self-image, and together formed a pocket of contention that grew more disruptive with every passing month.

The director, Harriet, had tried mediation, team restructuring, outside facilitators, and private conversations. None of it worked because the problem was not structural; Nora did not want the conflict to end. Conflict was the environment in which she felt most alive. Peace, to Nora, felt like erasure.

The breaking point came during a fundraising campaign eighteen months in the making. The divisions Nora had cultivated made unified effort impossible. Key staff resigned in the weeks leading up to it. The campaign fell far short of its goal, with direct consequences for the young people the organization served.

The board reviewed the pattern and the decision was made. When Nora left, the strife went with her. Staff described the weeks after her departure as the first time in two years they had come to work without bracing themselves. The conflict that had seemed embedded in the culture turned out to be embedded in one person, and when she was gone, the organization began to breathe again

.

Nora moved on, carrying the same habits and the same conviction that the trouble she generated was always someone else's fault. She had never seen herself as the common thread. And because she could not see it, she could not change it. The trouble would travel with her wherever she went.

Day 1: Q&A

Q: What does Proverbs 22:10 reveal about the relationship between a scoffer and the strife that surrounds them?

A: Proverbs 22:10 identifies the scoffer not as a bystander to conflict but as its source and offers a precise remedy: remove her and the strife ceases. Nora's story confirms this. The conflict that plagued the organization was not a workplace issue. It was a feature of Nora, and when she left, it left with her.

Q: How did Nora's role as a troublemaker differ from someone who simply speaks difficult truths?

A: The difference between a truth-teller and a troublemaker is visible in the fruit. Genuine honesty, even when uncomfortable, moves toward peace. Nora's speech consistently produced the opposite: greater division, deeper suspicion, and more entrenched conflict. She was not a truth-teller who made people uncomfortable. She was a troublemaker who used the language of honesty as cover for the cultivation of strife.

Day 2: Explanation: Proverbs 22:10 is one of the most practically precise verses in all of wisdom literature. It does not simply warn against strife in the abstract. It identifies a specific kind of person as the carrier of strife and offers a specific remedy: remove that person and cease the conflict. The scoffer is not simply someone with a difficult personality. She is someone whose presence actively generates contention and whose relationships are defined by the conflict she produces. Nora was not the victim of a difficult environment. She was the creator of one.

Day 3: Anecdote: A community garden that had thrived for eleven years as a model of neighborhood cooperation began to unravel shortly after a new volunteer coordinator joined. She was capable and energetic, but she carried complaints between groups, reframed neutral decisions as evidence of bias, and positioned herself as the only one willing to name the tensions everyone else was ignoring. Within a year, founding members had left, the volunteer base was divided, and leadership was managing disputes instead of tending the garden. When she moved on, the conflicts dissolved and the cooperation returned almost immediately. Like Nora, she had not manufactured conflict out of nothing. She had found the fault lines and made them her home.

Day 4: Warning: The troublemaker rarely announces herself. She arrives with energy and apparent honesty, gifted at naming real problems others have avoided. This is what makes her dangerous. There is a difference between a person who names problems to solve them and one who names them to sustain them. Pay attention to the fruit. If conflict consistently follows her arrivals and peace follows her departures, Proverbs is giving you clear guidance about what you are dealing with.

Day 5: Encouragement: If you are in a community, a workplace, or a family that has been shaped by the presence of a chronic troublemaker, there is genuine hope in the words of Proverbs 22:10. The verse does not describe a situation without remedy. It describes a situation with a very specific remedy, and it promises that the remedy works. When the scoffer is removed, the strife goes with her. This means that the conflict you are experiencing is not the permanent condition of your community. It is the temporary condition of a community that has not yet addressed its source of strife. That is a very different thing, and it carries with it the possibility of genuine restoration. Communities can recover. Organizations can heal. Families can find their way back to peace. The path is not always easy, and the decision to remove or distance from a chronic troublemaker is rarely without cost. But Proverbs is clear that the cost of keeping her is always greater than the cost of letting her go.

Day 6: Why People Become Scorners: Chronic troublemakers rarely set out to cause harm. Most learned early that conflict was the surest way to command attention or feel a sense of control in environments where they otherwise felt powerless. Over time, those patterns solidify into a personality that feels natural and even virtuous to the person living it. Nora genuinely believed she was a truth-teller, unaware that what she called honesty was the habitual cultivation of division. Understanding this does not excuse the damage. But it does reveal that change, if it ever comes, must begin with an honest reckoning with patterns formed long before the current community ever suffered from them.

Day 7: Reflection Questions:

Q: Think honestly about the communities you are part of. Is there a pattern in which conflict seems to follow your presence or increase after your involvement? What might that pattern be telling you about the role you are playing?

Q: Nora positioned herself as a truth-teller while consistently producing division. Is it possible that some of what you have called honesty has actually been the cultivation of strife?

Q: Have you ever experienced the peace that followed the removal of a chronic troublemaker from your community? What did that teach you about the source of the conflict you had been living with?

Q: What habits or patterns in your own life might be contributing to division in your home, your workplace, or your church, and what would it look like to bring those patterns honestly before God and ask Him to change them?

ather,

We ask You to search our hearts and show us honestly whether we have been carriers of strife in the communities You have placed us in. Forgive us for the times we have stirred up conflict and called it courage, for the times we have circulated grievances and called it honesty, and for the times we have cultivated division while telling ourselves we were simply speaking truth. We do not want to be troublemakers. We want to be peacemakers. We want our presence to bring calm rather than contention, to build up rather than tear down, and to leave every room we enter better than we found it. Where we have caused harm, give us the humility to acknowledge it and the courage to make it right. Where we have developed habits of strife, give us the grace to break them. Teach us to love peace the way You love it, to pursue it actively and not merely to avoid conflict passively, and to be the kind of people whose departure is mourned rather than the kind whose departure brings relief.

In the name of Jesus, Amen.

Prayer Thoughts for Today:

♦♦♦♦♦

WISDOM IN HEALTH

THE WISE

PROVERBS 3:7-8 (NIV):

7 Do not be wise in your own eyes; fear the Lord and shun evil.
8 This will bring health to your body and nourishment.

For years, Linda had put everything and everyone before herself. She worked long hours, ate whatever was fast and convenient, and told herself she would start taking better care of her body when things slowed down. They never did. By the time she hit her late thirties, the fatigue had settled in like something permanent. She would wake up already tired, drag herself through the workday on coffee, and collapse on the couch most evenings, too worn out to cook a real meal. She knew things weren't right, but knowing and doing something about it felt like two very different things.

The turning point came on an ordinary Tuesday. Linda had skipped lunch again to meet a deadline, and somewhere around three in the afternoon, the room started to tilt. A coworker noticed her gripping the edge of her desk and insisted she go home. She went to the doctor instead. The numbers weren't good. Her blood pressure was elevated, her iron was low, and her doctor looked at her with the kind of steady concern that doesn't leave room for brushing things off. Linda sat in her car afterward and cried, not out of self-pity, but because she finally admitted to herself that she had been running on empty for a very long time.

That weekend she called Mrs. Thompson, the woman who had been speaking truth into her life since her twenties. They met at a small diner near the church, and Linda talked for a long time before Mrs. Thompson said much of anything. When she finally did speak, she didn't lecture. She just asked Linda one question: "Do you believe God cares about how you treat your body?" It stopped Linda cold. She had never thought about her health as something connected to her faith. Mrs. Thompson opened her Bible to 1 Corinthians and read quietly, then looked up and said, "Taking care of yourself isn't selfish. It's obedience."

Linda drove home that afternoon with a lot to think about. She didn't make any grand declarations or write out a new meal plan. She just prayed, something she hadn't done with much honesty in a while. She asked God to help her want to change, because even wanting it felt hard. That week, she started with two things: she packed her lunch on Monday, and she kept a water bottle on her desk. Small, almost embarrassingly small. But she showed up for both.

A few weeks in, she started taking short walks after dinner. Just around the block at first. She put her phone in her pocket and left her earbuds at home, and somewhere in those fifteen or twenty minutes of quiet, she started to feel like herself again. The walks got longer. She started cooking on Sundays so she wouldn't be caught hungry and exhausted at the end of a long day. She went to bed earlier, not because she had suddenly become disciplined, but because she was finally paying attention to what her body was asking for.

About two months in, Linda noticed she had made it through an entire week without a headache. She wasn't sure when that had stopped being normal for her. Her focus at work sharpened. She cut back to one cup of coffee in the morning and didn't miss the rest. She still had hard days, but they felt survivable in a way they hadn't before.

She also had weeks that fell apart. A stressful stretch at work sent her back to fast food for five days straight. She skipped her walks, stayed up too late, and woke up one morning feeling like she had lost all the ground she'd gained. She called Mrs. Thompson, who told her that starting over wasn't the same as starting from scratch. Linda wrote that down and taped it to her bathroom mirror. She started again the next morning.

By the time Linda went back for her six-month checkup, her numbers had improved enough that her doctor asked what she had changed. Linda listed the things out loud and realized how ordinary they sounded: more sleep, more water, more vegetables, fewer skipped meals. Nothing revolutionary. But her doctor smiled and said, "Whatever you're doing, keep doing it." Linda sat in her car again after that appointment, just like she had the first time, but this time she wasn't crying out of fear. She was quiet for a moment and then said thank you, to no one in the car, and meant it completely.

People around her started to notice. A coworker asked what she was eating for lunch. A friend from church started joining her on evening walks. Linda didn't make a big thing of it. When people asked, she just told them the truth: she had been running herself into the ground, and she finally stopped.

She still has days when she doesn't get it right. But she has stopped waiting for a perfect streak before she calls herself someone who takes care of herself. She is learning, slowly, that caring for her body is not a project to complete. It is a practice to return to, again and again, with grace.

Day 1: Q&A:

Q: How did Linda change her approach to health?
A: Linda sought wisdom by turning to her mentor and prayer, asking God to guide her toward better habits. Rather than overhauling her lifestyle overnight, she made small, gradual changes, such as packing healthy lunches and adding daily walks. Through every setback and success, she trusted God's grace to sustain and strengthen her.

Q: What was the blessing?
A: As Linda embraced healthier habits, her energy returned in ways she hadn't felt in years. She no longer dragged herself through the day but woke up feeling rested and ready. Beyond the physical changes, she noticed a deepening in her spiritual life, as her daily walks and quiet meals became moments of gratitude and prayer. Caring for her body had drawn her heart closer to God, and she treasured that unexpected gift.

Day 2: Explanation: 1 Corinthians 6:19 Your body is a temple; honor God with it.
In this powerful verse, the apostle Paul reminds believers that their bodies are not their own; they are a dwelling place for the Holy Spirit. Because God lives within us, how we treat our bodies is an act of worship, reflecting our reverence for Him. Neglecting our health through poor eating, lack of rest, or harmful habits can be seen as dishonoring the sacred space God has entrusted to us. Just as we would care for a holy place with intention and respect, we are called to nourish, rest, and steward our bodies as an offering of gratitude to God.

Day 3: Anecdote: A pastor friend came to visit and didn't say much at first. He just sat with him. Then he said, "James, God rested on the seventh day. What makes you think you don't have to?" It was a simple thing, but it landed. Pastor James started protecting one full day a week as Sabbath. He began walking in the mornings. He started eating real meals instead of whatever was leftover from church potlucks. It took months before he felt like himself again, but when he stood in the pulpit the following spring, something had returned. He told his congregation that learning to care for himself had taught him more about God's grace than almost anything else.

Day 4: Blessing and Rewards: Wise self-care brings vitality and joy.

When we begin to treat our bodies as something worth caring for, the effects reach further than we expect. Energy returns. Patience grows. We show up differently for the people we love. These are not coincidences. They are the quiet fruit of honoring what God has entrusted to us.

Day 5: Encouragement: Every small step in wisdom is blessed by God.

You do not have to overhaul your life to begin. The smallest honest step still counts. A glass of water. A short walk. Going to bed thirty minutes earlier. God sees the effort behind the small things, and He meets us there, in the ordinary and the imperfect, just as much as anywhere else.

Day 6: God's Love and Redemption: He cares about your whole being body, mind, and spirit.

God is not only concerned with where your soul is going. He is concerned with how you are doing right now, in your body, in your mind, in your daily life. When you take a step toward caring for yourself, you are not being selfish. You are responding to a God who made you whole and wants you to live that way.

Day 7: Reflection Questions:

Q: How can you care for yourself wisely?

Q: Who models wise self-care for you?

Q: What changes is God prompting you to make?

Q: How does self-care help you serve others?

PRAYER JOURNAL

*H*eavenly Father,

Thank You for the gift of my body and for Your loving care over every part of my life. I confess that I have sometimes neglected my health, overworked myself, or ignored wise advice about rest and self-care. Forgive me for taking my body for granted or for making choices that do not honor You. Please grant me wisdom as I care for myself. Show me how to nourish my body, mind, and spirit in ways that bring You glory. Help me to listen to the signals You've built into my body and to recognize when I need rest, exercise, or healing. Give me humility to seek help and support when I struggle, and help me to resist unhealthy habits or attitudes. Guide my choices each day so that I may have the energy, strength, and clarity to serve You and others well. Thank You for Your sustaining grace and for Your compassion when I fall short. Restore my health, which has been damaged, and give me a spirit of gratitude for every breath and every new day. May I honor You by caring for myself as Your beloved creation.

In Jesus' name, Amen.

Prayer Thoughts for Today: ♦♦♦♦♦

~ END PRAYER JOURNAL "THE WISE" ~

CHATTY LIPS

THE SIMPLE ONE

PROVERBS 14:15 (ESV)

"The simple believes every word, but the prudent gives thought to his steps."

Ruby didn't know a single person at her new church. The move had worn her down more than she expected. She'd underestimated how much starting over would cost her, not just the logistics of it, but the loneliness that came after the boxes were unpacked and life was supposed to feel normal again. On Sunday mornings she'd sit near the back, watching people hug and catch up like they'd known each other for years. She prayed for one real friend. Just one. So when a group of young adults caught her in the parking lot after service and asked if she wanted to grab lunch, she said yes before they even finished the sentence.

They squeezed around a long table at a café down the street, and Ruby barely got a word in for the first twenty minutes. She didn't mind. She was just glad to be there, glad to have somewhere to be. The conversation moved fast and loud and she mostly just listened and laughed when everyone else laughed. By the end of lunch they were already texting her about game night on Thursday. She saved the group chat notification and stared at it for a second before putting her phone down. It felt like something.

The first few weeks, Ruby was too relieved to notice much. But somewhere around week three, she started paying closer attention. The conversations had a way of sliding. Someone would complain about a coworker, and that would open a door. Then it was the woman who sang too loud in worship. Then something someone heard about the youth leader's personal life. Ruby noticed that nobody ever said anything outright cruel. It was always framed as concern, or just venting, or just funny. But the target was always a person, and once the laughter died down, the next person was never far behind.

Ruby knew it felt off. She just didn't say so. Once, when they made fun of a guy who stumbled through a prayer during small group, Ruby laughed too. Not a big laugh. Just enough. She told herself it was nothing. People blow off steam. She didn't want to be the one who made things weird.

A month in, Ruby caught herself doing it on her own. She was on the phone with her mom and heard herself say something sharp about a guy from church she'd never even spoken to, just repeating something from the group chat like it was fact. Her mom didn't say anything, but there was a pause, the kind that meant she noticed. Ruby moved on quickly, changed the subject, talked about work. But it sat with her the rest of the night.

After one lunch that left her feeling flat and tired, Ruby drove home and just sat in her car for a while. She couldn't explain exactly why she felt so drained. The food was fine. The conversation was lively. But something about it left her hollow. She thought about her old church, a guy named Marcus who used to pray for people by name, who'd remember weeks later how something turned out. Nobody in this group prayed for anyone. That night she opened her Bible and landed on Ephesians 4:29. "Do not let any unwholesome talk come out of your mouths, but only what is helpful for building others up." She read it twice.

She hadn't been building anyone up. She'd been tearing people down to stay warm, and the worst part was how easy it had become.

She stopped responding to the group chat as much. It felt awkward, and she second-guessed herself more than once, wondering if she was being too sensitive or too serious. But she started showing up early to help set up chairs before service, and that's how she met a few people who were different. A girl named Priya who worked in the children's ministry and remembered her name the second time they met. A guy who always had his Bible marked up with notes and never made Ruby feel behind for asking basic questions. Quiet people. The kind who didn't need an audience. It was slower going, but it felt clean.

Months later, Ruby noticed she wasn't as tired after church anymore. She was actually looking forward to Sunday mornings in a way she hadn't since before the move. She still saw the old group around. They'd wave, maybe exchange a few words. It wasn't hostile. It was just over, and that was okay. She didn't regret pulling back. She'd learned something she couldn't unlearn: the people you sit with shape what comes out of your mouth. And eventually, what's in your heart.

Day 1: Q&A:

Q: What can you do to protect your heart in new situations?

A: Pay attention to how you feel after spending time with people. Not just in the moment, but a few hours later. Are you more hopeful or more critical? More generous or more cynical? Ask God for the wisdom to notice those patterns early, before they settle in. Setting limits on certain relationships isn't about judging anyone. It's about knowing yourself well enough to protect what matters.

Q: How did Ruby get pulled into gossip and negativity?

A: She wanted to belong, and that want was louder than her instincts. The group didn't pressure her directly. They just made negativity feel normal, even funny. By the time she noticed the shift in herself, it had already been happening for weeks. Wanting acceptance can quietly override a lot of things we think are fixed about ourselves.

Day 2: Explanation: Proverbs warn that bad company corrupts good character, and it's not usually dramatic when it happens. Simple Ones are especially vulnerable because their longing to belong is real and strong. They're not naive in a careless way. They just haven't yet learned to trust the quiet unease that shows up when something is off. So they talk themselves out of it. They stay. And over time, what felt uncomfortable starts to feel normal, which is exactly how character gets slowly reshaped without anyone noticing.

Day 3: Anecdote: A young woman once said her faith didn't collapse in college. It just got quieter and quieter until she couldn't hear it anymore. Her friends weren't cruel or anti-God. They just didn't think about any of that. Church fell off first. Then prayer. Then the version of herself she'd been. She came back eventually, older and a little embarrassed, but mostly grateful. She said the hardest part wasn't the leaving. It was realizing how gradual it had been.

Day 4: Warning: The people you spend the most time with will shape you. That's not a threat, just how it works. Water shapes stone slowly, and you don't notice until the stone is different. Proverbs 13:20 says, "Whoever walks with the wise becomes wise, but the companion of fools will suffer harm." That word suffer is worth sitting with. It's not abstract. The wrong company costs something real, and the bill usually arrives long after the damage is done.

Day 5: Encouragement: You don't have to stay in rooms that make you smaller. God has people out there who will tell you the truth, sit with you in hard moments, and remind you who you are when you forget. They may not show up loudly or all at once. Sometimes it's one person setting up chairs before service. But they're there. Seek God first, and He'll make sure you find them.

Day 6: God's Love and Redemption: If you've drifted, you're not disqualified. God is not surprised by where you ended up or how you got there. His love doesn't require you to have it figured out before He meets you. He restores. He brings back what was lost. And often, He does it through a single person who shows up at the right time and reminds you of who you actually are.

Day 7: Reflection Questions:

Q: Have you ever found yourself slowly picking up habits, attitudes, or ways of speaking from a group of friends that didn't truly reflect your values or who you wanted to be? Reflect on what that experience was like, how it affected you, and what it revealed about the importance of the company you keep.

Q: How do you determine whether the people you spend time with are a positive influence on your life and faith, and what signs do you look for when deciding whether a relationship is drawing you closer to God or quietly pulling you away?

Q: What boundaries might you need to set to protect your heart and character in new relationships or environments, and how can you hold firmly to those boundaries even when the pressure to compromise feels strong or the fear of rejection makes it difficult?

Q: In what ways can you actively seek God for discernment and guidance when choosing friends or communities to be part of, and how might prayer, Scripture, and the counsel of trusted mentors help you make decisions that align with who He is calling you to become?

PRAYER JOURNAL

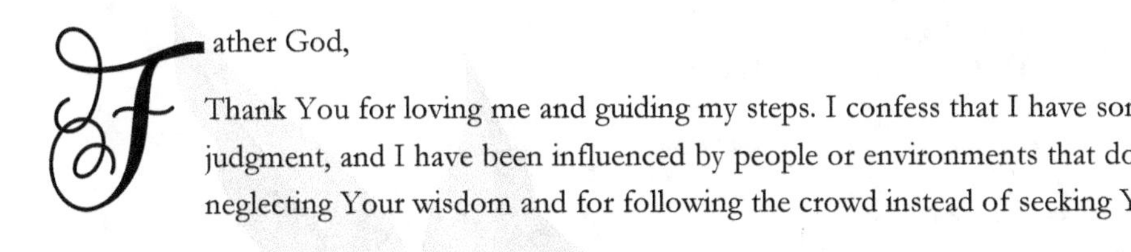

ather God,

Thank You for loving me and guiding my steps. I confess that I have sometimes let the desires of my heart cloud my judgment, and I have been influenced by people or environments that do not draw me closer to You. Forgive me for neglecting Your wisdom and for following the crowd instead of seeking Your will.

Help me choose friends and communities wisely. Give me discernment to recognize influences that are not good for my heart and courage to set healthy boundaries. Lead me to relationships that honor You and help me grow in faith and character.

Thank You for never letting me go, even when I wander. Surround me with Your love and fill me with a desire to walk with the wise, so I may become more like Christ each day.

In Jesus' name, Amen.

Prayer Thoughts for Today: ✦✦✦✦✦

~ END PRAYER JOURNAL "THE SIMPLE ONE" ~

Center of it All

THE FOOL

Proverbs 12:15 (NIV)

"The way of a fool is right in his own eyes, but a wise man listens to advice."

Samantha was the kind of person who filled a room before she even said anything. She'd grown up the oldest of three, which meant she was used to being heard, used to having the answer, used to being the one everyone looked to. And for a long time, that worked out fine. She was sharp, she was funny, and she genuinely worked hard. The problem wasn't that she was wrong all the time. The problem was that she'd stopped being able to tell when she was.

Talking with her could wear you out. She'd cut in before you finished your sentence, not out of meanness, just because she already knew what she wanted to say and saw no reason to wait. Someone else's story would somehow become a story about something that had happened to her. Someone's problem would get solved in thirty seconds flat, whether they wanted a solution or just wanted to be heard. Her friends noticed. Some of them laughed it off. Others quietly stopped telling her things.

She announced her wins the way some people check the weather, casually, like it was just information. A good grade, a compliment from a teacher she respected, a moment where she'd been right about something. She'd stretch a detail here and there if it made the story land better. She didn't think of it as exaggerating. She thought of it as emphasis. Some people found it charming at first. Charm has a shelf life though, and hers was running shorter than she realized.

She didn't take feedback well, but she'd never have described it that way. In her mind, she just thought things through more carefully than most people. When a friend offered a suggestion, she'd hear it out, nod, and then calmly explain why she'd already considered that and why her approach still made more sense. She never raised her voice. She never got visibly upset. She just made it clear, in a very reasonable way, that you were missing something. After a while, people stopped offering.

The history project was where it all came to a head. She showed up to the first group meeting with a color-coded outline, roles already assigned, timeline already mapped. She presented it like it was already decided, which it basically was. A girl named Priya suggested a different angle for the presentation. Samantha listened, nodded, and explained why her original direction was stronger. Priya didn't push back. Nobody did after that. They just went along with it, and Samantha took their silence as agreement.

As the deadline got closer, things started slipping. She'd taken on most of the work herself because she didn't trust anyone else to do it the way she envisioned, and she hadn't built in any room for error. When her own section ran long, there was nobody ready to pick up the slack. She'd sidelined them too early for that. The last two nights before it was due, she stayed up redoing pieces her teammates had already submitted, quietly convinced they'd gotten it wrong. She didn't tell them. She just fixed it and moved on.

When Priya texted the group chat asking if they should meet again before the due date, Samantha replied that she had it handled. She believed that, even when it stopped being true, because admitting otherwise would have meant admitting she'd mismanaged the whole thing from the start.

They got a C minus. Samantha stared at it for a long time. Then she went through the list in her head: Priya had turned her section in late, Marcus hadn't proofread his part, Jordan had gone off the outline. She had a reason for every person on that team. She went through the whole list and didn't put herself on it once.

After the project, something shifted. Priya stopped sitting near her in class. The group chat went quiet. Invitations to things she used to be included in started coming less often, and when she asked why, nobody gave her a straight answer. She noticed all of it. She told herself they were being sensitive, or that they were jealous, or that they just couldn't handle someone with high standards. It was easier to believe that than the alternative.

The same thing had been happening at home and she hadn't connected it until now. Her younger brother had started going to their dad instead of her when he needed help with something. Her mom had stopped asking for her opinion the way she used to. Small shifts, easy to explain away one at a time. Harder to ignore when you lined them all up.

Her English teacher, Mrs. Okafor, was the one who finally said something. She kept Samantha after class one afternoon, waited until the room cleared out, and asked one question: "Do you think your classmates feel like you actually hear them?"

Samantha said yes without thinking. It was a reflex.

Mrs. Okafor didn't argue. She just nodded and said, "I want you to sit with that tonight. Really sit with it."

Samantha almost brushed it off on the walk home. But the question kept coming back. That night she replayed the project meetings in her head, the moment Priya offered her idea, and Samantha had talked right past it. She replayed it more honestly than she had the first time. She didn't like what she found.

She didn't change overnight. But something had shifted and she knew it. She started catching herself mid-interruption and stopping. She started asking follow-up questions when her instinct was to give an answer. She found Priya in the hallway before class one morning and apologized, not in a big way, just directly. Priya looked a little surprised. Then she said thanks.

It was awkward at first, the waiting, the listening, the not always being the one who drove things. But slowly it started to feel like something she recognized from a long time ago, something she'd had before she'd learned to perform, and was only now starting to find her way back to.

Day 1: Q&A:

Q: Why did Samantha ignore her teammates' input?
A: Mostly because she'd built her whole identity around being the one who had it together. When someone offered a different idea, it didn't just feel like a different idea. It felt like a challenge. And she wasn't going to lose.

Q: What was the outcome?
A: She ended up alone in most of the ways that mattered. Not dramatically, just quietly. The people around her stopped bringing their real selves to conversations with her because it wasn't worth it. The grade suffered. The friendships thinned. She got what she said she wanted, to be in charge, and found out it didn't feel the way she thought it would.

Day 2: Explanation: *Proverbs 12:15 says, "The way of a fool is right in his own eyes, but a wise man listens to advice."* That's a hard verse to sit with because most of us don't think of ourselves as the fool in the story. We think of ourselves as the reasonable one, the one who's just being direct, or efficient, or confident. But the verse doesn't ask how you see yourself. It asks whether you're actually listening. There's a real difference between hearing someone and waiting for your turn to talk. Wisdom starts in that gap.

Day 3: Anecdote: I knew someone in leadership once who was sharp and capable and almost universally hard to work with. He had an answer for everything before you finished asking the question. His team learned to stop bringing him problems because the conversation always ended the same way: with him explaining why he'd already thought of that. A mentor eventually told him directly that his team had stopped trusting him, not because he was incompetent, but because he made people feel invisible. He didn't take it well at first. But it stuck. He told me later that was the most useful thing anyone had said to him in years.

Day 4: Warning: Proverbs 26:12 is blunt about this: "Do you see a man who is wise in his own eyes? There is more hope for a fool than for him." That's striking because it's saying overconfidence in your own judgment is actually worse than plain foolishness. A fool might stumble into correction. Someone convinced they're always right won't even look for it. The people around you will figure this out before you do. And by the time you notice them pulling away, they've usually been pulling away for a while.

Day 5: Encouragement: Humility isn't about thinking less of yourself. It's about being secure enough that you don't need to protect your image every time someone pushes back. That kind of security is hard to build on your own, but it's exactly what God offers. Samantha's shift didn't come from trying harder. It came from a single honest question that she actually sat with. You don't need a dramatic turning point. You just need to be willing to ask yourself the same kind of question and not rush past the answer.

Day 6: God's Love and Redemption: One of the things that stands out about how God deals with pride is that He doesn't usually shout. He tends to work through a quiet moment, a question that lingers, a conversation that gets under your skin. He's patient about it in a way that's almost uncomfortable, because it means there's no excuse for not hearing Him. If you've been holding tightly to being right, He's not waiting for you to be perfect before He moves. He just needs you to loosen your grip a little.

Day 7: Reflection Questions:

Q: Have you ever dismissed advice because you were sure you already knew better? What happened? And looking back, were there signs earlier that you were wrong that you chose not to sit with?

Q: Is there someone in your life whose feedback you've been brushing off? What would it actually cost you to take it seriously?

Q: Think about a relationship or situation where things feel stuck. Is there any chance that your need to be right is part of what's keeping it that way?

Q: When was the last time you felt like God was trying to get your attention about something and you kept moving past it? What would it look like to actually stop and listen this week?

Prayer Journal

Heavenly Father,

Thank You for Your loving patience and the wisdom You so generously offer. I confess that pride and self-centeredness have sometimes kept me from listening to others and accepting corrections. Forgive me for insisting on my own way and missing opportunities to learn and grow. Please fill me with humility and a teachable spirit. Help me to value the voices and perspectives of those around me, and to seek wisdom from You above all. Thank You for restoring what pride has damaged and for inviting me into true community. May Your love shape my interactions so I can build others up and reflect Christ in my relationships.

In Jesus' name, Amen.

Prayer Thoughts for Today: ✦✦✦✦✦

~ End Prayer Journal "The Fool" ~

THE ONE WHO ALREADY KNEW

THE SCORNER

PROVERBS 9:7–8 (ESV)

"Whoever corrects a scoffer gets himself abuse, and he who reproves a wicked man incurs injury. Do not reprove a scoffer, or he will hate you; reprove a wise man, and he will love you."

Sylvia had never needed anyone to teach her anything. She had formed her opinions early, defended them fiercely, and carried them forward without allowing new experiences to change a single thing. She was not a stupid woman. But her intelligence had long since been placed entirely in the service of confirming what she already thought, never turned toward the possibility that she might be wrong.

She spent nineteen years as a senior instructor at a training institute that prepared young professionals for careers in public administration. In those years, the field had changed considerably, with new research, new methodologies, and a shifting landscape. None of this had reached her. Not because it was unavailable, but because she had decided that what she knew was sufficient and that anything challenging it was simply noise from people who hadn't yet caught up.

Her colleagues had tried, in the early years, to engage her, sharing articles, inviting her to conferences, and gently questioning whether her approaches had been superseded. She received it all with a smile that communicated tolerance rather than openness. Over time, they stopped trying. They had learned what Proverbs 9:7–8 describes: that correcting a scoffer earns insult, and rebuking her invites contempt.

Her students received an education that was confident, thorough, and increasingly disconnected from the field's realities. She taught with authority because she felt it, and she felt it because she had never allowed anything to disturb it. When students raised questions reflecting newer thinking, she redirected them. When a young colleague offered a differing perspective, she acknowledged it with the patience one extends to someone who simply doesn't know better yet.

The institute eventually underwent an external review. After three days of observations and interviews, the report was thorough, professional, and, for Sylvia, devastating. Her curriculum was significantly outdated. Her methods were effective for their era but misaligned with current best practices. Students reported feeling underprepared. The evaluators recommended a substantial revision and a structured professional development process.

The director presented the findings with care and respect. Sylvia received the report the way she received everything that challenged her: as a document produced by people who didn't understand her approach, who had applied debatable criteria, who had given too much weight to inexperienced students. She did not argue. She simply disagreed, thoroughly and privately, and continued teaching exactly as before.

The consequences unfolded slowly but without mercy. Enrollment declined. Junior colleagues stopped seeking her guidance. The institute eventually restructured her role, reducing her teaching load and moving her to administration. She interpreted this as politics, as the result of forces that had never appreciated her. She did not, even then, consider that the evaluation had been correct.

Proverbs 9:7–8 do not describe a person incapable of learning. They describe a person who has made themselves impossible to teach. Sylvia had not lost the ability to grow. She had simply closed every door through which growth might have entered, so thoroughly, and for so long, that she could no longer see the doors at all. The life she built on that unteachability was smaller, more isolated, and less fruitful than it had any reason to be.

She had known so much for so long. The tragedy was not that she had been wrong. The tragedy was that she had never found out.

Day 1: Q&A

Q: What do Proverbs 9:7 and 9:8 reveal about the unteachable person and those who try to correct them?

A: Proverbs 9:7–8 reveal that correcting a scoffer does not produce growth but hostility. Unteachability is not passive; it is active. The unteachable person pushes back against correction, making the experience costly enough that wise people eventually stop trying. Sylvia's colleagues withdrew one by one, not out of indifference, but because they had learned what Proverbs already knew.

Q: How did Sylvia's unteachability harm not only herself but the students she was responsible for teaching?

A: Sylvia's unteachability created a closed loop: her unchallenged assumptions became the content of her students' education. They entered careers underprepared, not because she lacked intelligence, but because her refusal to be taught had made her incapable of genuinely teaching. Unteachability is never a private matter. It always costs the people in the orbit of the one who refuses to learn.

Day 2: Explanation: Proverbs 9:7–8 address a condition more serious than it first appears. The scoffer is not someone who simply disagrees with advice. She is someone for whom correction itself has become an offense. The practical wisdom is clear: do not rebuke a scoffer, because you will only earn her contempt. This is not despair; it is discernment. It recognizes that unteachability has reached a point where the normal tools of growth cannot penetrate. Sylvia's story shows how each rejected correction makes the next one easier to reject, until unteachability becomes complete.

Day 3: Anecdote: A nurse with twenty-two years in the same unit had developed genuine expertise and a growing resistance to the training sessions her hospital required. She sat through them with visible impatience and returned to her routines unchanged, quietly correcting younger nurses whose updated methods differed from her familiar ones. A near-miss incident prompted a formal review. It confirmed what her colleagues had known for years: she had not kept pace, and patients had been receiving care based on standards revised long ago. She had not set out to cause harm. She had simply decided she already knew enough.

Day 4: Warning: Unteachability is dangerous precisely because it feels so much like confidence. The refusal to be corrected can feel like integrity, like the principled maintenance of hard-won convictions. But Proverbs draws a clear line between the person who weighs instruction carefully and the person who has closed herself off to weighing altogether. The warning is simple: if you have not been genuinely taught anything in a long time, if the people around you have stopped offering honest feedback, it is worth asking whether you have become unteachable. The discomfort of that question is far less costly than the life built without it.

Day 5: Encouragement: Sylvia's story is a cautionary tale, but it need not be yours. Proverbs 9:9 promises that instruction given to a wise person makes her wiser still. The door that unteachability closes, humility can reopen, at any point, regardless of how long it has been shut. The first step is simply sitting with a correction without immediately preparing a defense. Letting an honest word land. Considering, without contempt, that the person offering it might have something worth hearing. That posture, practiced consistently, is the beginning of wisdom.

Day 6: Why People Become Scorners: No one becomes unteachable in a single moment. The journey is gradual, paved with experiences that seemed to justify the growing resistance. Harsh public correction teaches that instruction is humiliation. Dismissed insights breed defensive certainty. Years of hard-won expertise make it painful to admit that the expertise needs updating. Sylvia's unteachability did not begin with arrogance. It began with investment. But what began as self-protection had hardened, over time, into a wall that kept out not only the things that threatened her but also the things that could have made her genuinely great.

Day 7: Reflection Questions:

Q: When was the last time a correction genuinely reached you? Not just one you heard and nodded at, but one that actually moved something. What does the distance between that moment and today tell you?

Q: Name the people in your life who used to speak honestly to you and no longer do. Something taught them to stop. Is it worth sitting with the possibility that you were the one who taught them?

Q: Sylvia never intended to harm anyone. She simply stopped growing, and the people in her care absorbed the cost. Who is absorbing yours? A student, a child, a colleague who deserves more than a version of you that stopped updating years ago?

Q: Proverbs 9:8 says a wise person will love you for rebuking her. There is probably someone who tried. You may have made it cost them something. What would it take to go back to that person, not to explain yourself, but simply to receive what they offered and say thank you?

*F*ather,

We confess that we are far more resistant to instruction than we like to believe. We have received correction with contempt when we should have received it with gratitude. We have defended our existing opinions with energy that should have been spent examining them. We have made ourselves difficult to teach and then wondered why we stopped growing. Forgive us for the pride that disguised itself as confidence and the stubbornness that disguised itself as conviction. We ask You to make us genuinely teachable, not just willing to hear instruction in theory but actually open to receiving it in practice, from You, from Your Word, and from the people You have placed in our lives to help us grow. Soften the places in us that have grown hard. Restore the curiosity and humility that learning requires. Help us to love correction the way the wise love it, as a gift rather than a threat, as an opportunity rather than an offense. We want to be people who grow wiser with every season of life, and we know that is only possible for those who remain willing to be taught.

In Jesus' name, Amen.

Prayer Thoughts for Today: ✦✦✦✦

~ END PRAYER JOURNAL "THE SCORNER" ~

WISDOM IN FAMILY

THE WISE

PROVERBS 15:1 (NIV)

"A gentle answer turns away wrath, but a harsh word stirs up anger."

Daniela and her siblings fought about everything. Whose turn it was to do the dishes. Who grabbed the last clean towel. Who changed the channel without asking. There were three of them crammed into a house that felt smaller every year, and the little things had a way of turning into big things fast. It was never really about any of those things, but in the moment, it always felt like it was. She'd go to bed some nights still stewing, replaying arguments in her head, convinced she'd been right and that nobody cared enough to admit it. She'd wake up the next morning and nothing would be resolved. They'd just move on until the next thing set someone off.

Her parents tried stepping in, but that usually made things worse. Her mom would try to mediate and end up in the middle of it. Her dad mostly stayed quiet, which Daniela used to read as him not caring. Daniela would get defensive, her siblings would disappear into their rooms, and dinner would pass with just the sound of forks on plates and the TV on too loud in the background. She wanted things to be different. She was tired of the tension and tired of feeling like her own home was a place she had to brace herself for. She just didn't know how to start.

One evening, after a blowup over whose week it was to take out the trash, things got loud enough that her dad finally stepped in. He didn't raise his voice. He just looked at Daniela and said, quietly, "Come sit with me for a minute." She followed him to the kitchen, still irritated, arms crossed. She expected a lecture about respect or setting an example. Instead, he pulled his Bible off the counter, the one with the cracked spine he'd had for years, and slid it across the table. He pointed to a verse in Proverbs: "A gentle answer turns away wrath, but a harsh word stirs up anger." He didn't say much after that. Just let it sit there between them. Daniela nodded like she understood and went back to her room. She rolled her eyes a little on the inside. She wasn't the problem, she told herself. Her siblings were louder, more dramatic, quicker to escalate. But the verse kept coming back to her later that night when she was trying to fall asleep. She thought about how exhausted she felt after every fight, how her chest felt tight for hours afterward, how nothing ever actually got resolved. They just got quieter until the next time. Maybe there was something to it.

A few days later, her younger sister started in on her about leaving dishes in the sink again. It was the kind of comment that usually kicked things off. Daniela felt the familiar heat rise up and the words forming before she'd even thought them through. But she stopped herself. She took a breath and actually listened instead of loading up her response. Her sister wasn't just annoyed about the dishes. She was tired. She felt like she was the only one who ever noticed when things needed to be done, and she'd been carrying that feeling for a while. Daniela said, "I hear you. That's not fair to you." Her sister blinked. She looked almost caught off guard, like she'd been ready for a fight and suddenly didn't need to be. The argument didn't happen. They split up the chores and that was that.

She didn't always get it right. There were still moments she snapped, still nights she said something sharp and immediately wished she hadn't. But she started saying sorry faster. That part was hard. Admitting she was wrong felt like losing something. Over time, though, she noticed that a real apology did more than any argument ever had.

Things shifted slowly, and not in any dramatic way. There was no big moment where everyone hugged and decided to be different. It was smaller than that. Her brother started asking her opinion on things instead of just arguing with her. Her sister started texting her funny things during the day, inside jokes that wouldn't have existed six months earlier. Dinners got louder again, but in a good way, more talking, more laughing, less of that heavy silence. Her mom commented on it once, just quietly, while they were cleaning up together after everyone else had left the table. She said she'd noticed things were better. She didn't make a big deal of it. She just said it. That meant a lot. Daniela realized somewhere along the way that the goal was never to win. It was to stay connected to the people she actually loved, even when they drove her crazy.

She still thought about that night in the kitchen with her dad. One verse. Not a long speech, not a list of rules. Just a verse and some quiet. That was enough to start something.

When friends vented to her about their own family drama, she didn't hand them a list of tips or quote verses at them. She just told them what her dad showed her, and what she'd had to learn the hard way herself. That a gentle answer really can stop a fight before it starts. That saying sorry first isn't weakness, it's just choosing the relationship over being right. That peace at home doesn't come from everyone agreeing or never getting on each other's nerves. It comes from choosing, over and over again, to actually hear each other. That's it. That's the whole thing.

Day 1: Q&A:

Q: What did Daniela change in her family interactions?
A: She practiced gentleness and quick forgiveness. Instead of reacting with anger, she learned to pause, listen, and respond with calm, kind words. She also began apologizing more readily when she was wrong, which helped restore peace and trust within her family.

Q: What was the blessing?
A: The blessing was greater family harmony and deeper relationships within the family. As Daniela practiced gentleness and forgiveness, the tension in the home gave way to laughter, real conversation, and a genuine sense of closeness. Her siblings began to open up and support one another through everyday challenges, strengthening their bonds. What had once been a house filled with conflict became a home rooted in trust, love, and mutual respect.

Day 2: Explanation: *Proverbs 15:1 "A gentle answer turns away wrath."* Wisdom brings peace at home.
Proverbs 15:1 reminds us that "a gentle answer turns away wrath," showing that the words we choose can either ignite conflict or bring calm. When we respond with wisdom rather than emotion, we create an environment where family members feel heard, valued, and safe. This kind of wisdom does not come naturally; it requires practice, humility, and a willingness to put others before our own pride. Over time, a home shaped by gentle words and patient listening becomes a place of true peace, where relationships grow stronger, and love runs deeper.

Day 3: Anecdote: A friend shared how family devotions and wise words healed old wounds.
A close friend once shared how her family had carried years of unspoken hurt and misunderstandings that had quietly driven them apart. Everything began to shift when they committed to regular family devotions, gathering each morning to read Scripture and pray together before the day pulled them in different directions. Through those simple, consistent moments, wise and healing words began to replace old patterns of criticism and silence. Old wounds that had seemed impossible to mend were gradually healed as each family member felt seen, loved, and anchored in God's truth.

Day 4: Blessing and Rewards: Wisdom in families brings unity and lasting love.
When wisdom takes root in a family, it produces something far greater than the absence of conflict: a deep, lasting unity that holds the family together through every season of life. Each wise word spoken, each act of patience and forgiveness, lays another brick in the foundation of a home built on love. Over time, family members grow not just as individuals but as a unit, bound by

shared values and a genuine care for one another. This is the reward of wisdom: not a perfect family, but a loving one, where unity is chosen daily and love endures.

Day 5: Encouragement: God delights in blessing homes filled with wisdom. God does not merely tolerate wisdom in the home; He takes great delight in it, and He is faithful to pour out His blessing on families who seek to honor Him through the way they speak and love one another. Scripture tells us that the fear of the Lord is the beginning of wisdom, and when a family anchors itself in that truth, God's presence and favor become evident in their daily life. He brings healing where there was hurt, restoration where there was division, and joy where there was once only strife. Trust that as you pursue wisdom in your home, God sees your effort and is already at work blessing what you are building.

Day 6: God's Love and Redemption: He heals families and guides us to love well.
God's love is not distant or passive; He is actively at work in every family that calls on His name, bringing healing to broken relationships and restoring what sin and pride have damaged. He does not just mend what is broken; He transforms hearts, giving us the capacity to love one another the way He first loved us. His guidance through Scripture and the Holy Spirit shows us how to forgive deeply, speak truthfully, and serve one another with humility. As we surrender our family life to Him, He becomes the foundation from which all lasting love and healing flow.

Day 7: Reflection Questions:

Q: How do you respond to conflicts at home? Pause and consider whether your first reaction in a disagreement brings calm or adds fuel to the fire. Ask God to give you the wisdom to respond with gentleness rather than pride.

Q: What wise habits could bless your family? Reflect on the daily rhythms of your home and consider whether they are drawing your family together or pulling you apart. Simple habits like praying together, speaking words of affirmation, or sharing a meal without distractions can quietly build a culture of love and trust. Ask God to show you one habit to begin this week and commit to it faithfully.

Q: Who in your family needs encouragement? Think of the family member who may be quietly struggling, carrying a burden they haven't yet put into words. A simple note, a kind word, or a moment of genuine attention can mean more than you know. Ask God to show you who needs to be seen today, and then take that small, faithful step.

Q: How can you foster peace? Consider where conflict most often arises in your relationships and ask yourself whether your words have been gentle or reactive. Practice pausing before responding, listening fully before speaking, and offering forgiveness quickly when tensions rise. Over time, these small, intentional habits can transform the atmosphere of your home and draw your family closer together.

aithful God,

Thank you for the gift of family and for placing me in relationships where I can learn, grow, and love. I confess that I have not always acted with wisdom at home sometimes letting anger, impatience, or pride get in the way of peace and unity. Please forgive me for harsh words, selfish actions, or missed opportunities to build others up. Lord, fill me with Your wisdom as I relate to my family. Teach me to listen well, to speak with gentleness, and to seek understanding, even when it is hard. Help me to forgive quickly and to let go of grudges, just as You have forgiven me. Give me a humble heart, willing to apologize and to learn from my mistakes. Show me how to encourage, serve, and love my family in ways that reflect Your grace. Thank You for Your patience and for the healing You bring to broken relationships. Restore what has been damaged by conflict and draw us closer together as we seek to honor You. May my family be a place of wisdom, peace, and joy.

In Jesus' name, Amen.

Prayer Thoughts for Today: ✦✦✦✦✦

~ END PRAYER JOURNAL "THE WISE" ~

THE ADVENTURE

THE SIMPLE ONE

PROVERBS 22:3 (NIV)

"The prudent see danger and take refuge, but the simple keep going and pay the penalty."

ella loved adventure and was always up for something new. Since she was a child, curiosity and excitement seemed to pulse through her veins. She was the first to climb the tallest tree in the neighborhood, the one to suggest exploring the woods behind the school, and the ringleader when it came to organizing a game of midnight hide-and-seek. Her friends admired her daring spirit and looked to her whenever they wanted to break out of their routines.

One bright Saturday afternoon, Bella was hanging out with her friends after soccer practice. The air was thick with the energy of youth, and the kids were eager to make the most of the day. As they wandered through the neighborhood, they saw a cluster of orange cones and fencing blocking off a construction site. Behind the fence, enormous piles of dirt, scattered tools, and the skeleton of a new building beckoned like a secret playground.

"Let's cut through there, it'll get us home faster," one of Bella's friends suggested, eyeing the construction site with a grin. The others nodded, eager for a shortcut and the promise of a little mischief. Without hesitation, Bella agreed, thinking only of the thrill and the story they'd have to tell later. After all, what was the harm? It was just a quick detour, and she was sure they'd be in and out before anyone noticed.

The group slipped through a gap in the fence, laughing as they ducked under caution tape and navigated around muddy puddles. Bella led the way, feeling a rush of excitement as her shoes squished in the soft earth and the unfinished walls towered above. The kids dared each other to climb piles of gravel and balance along beams, their laughter echoing through the empty site.

But the fun ended abruptly when one of Bella's friends, Zack, tried to leap from one stack of boards to another. His foot slipped, and he tumbled to the ground with a sickening thud. The laughter stopped instantly. Zack groaned, clutching his ankle and blinking back tears. The kids crowded around him, panic rising as they realized he couldn't stand.

Bella's heart pounded as reality crashed down. She hadn't considered what could go wrong, not the danger of unstable ground, the sharp nails scattered everywhere, or the rules meant to keep people safe. Nobody had. They'd all just followed each other in, laughing, not one of them stopping to ask whether it was actually a good idea. In that moment, the thrill was completely gone. They managed to help Zack hobble out of the site, one arm around Bella's shoulder, his face tight with pain, while one of the other kids sprinted to get a parent for help.

Later, sitting on the curb outside Zack's house and waiting for news, Bella replayed the afternoon in her mind. She felt responsible, not just because she'd gone along with the plan, but because she'd encouraged it, never stopping to weigh the risks. When Zack's mom emerged from the house, worry etched on her face, Bella's stomach twisted. Zack had a sprained ankle and would be on crutches for weeks.

Bella apologized again, but the words felt small. Nothing could erase the image of Zack hitting the ground. That night, she lay awake staring at the ceiling, thinking about how close they'd come to something much worse. A nail through a shoe. A fall from a higher beam. She realized she'd always prided herself on being spontaneous and fearless, but there was a difference between real courage and just not thinking. She wondered how many times she'd acted first and thought later, trusting that things would work out simply because they always had. This time they almost didn't.

The lesson was painful, but it stuck. Bella promised herself that from then on, she would pause before plunging into the next thrill, taking a moment to consider the consequences, not just for herself, but for those around her. She understood now that true courage sometimes meant saying no to a bad idea, even when everyone else was on board.

In the weeks that followed, Bella's friends teased her a little about being the "voice of caution," but she didn't mind. She still sought adventure, but she learned to balance curiosity with responsibility, excitement with wisdom. Looking back, Bella was grateful for the hard lesson. She realized that thinking before acting didn't make her any less adventurous, just made her a better friend and a wiser leader.

Day 1: Q&A:

Q: Why did Bella go along with the risky idea?
A: She wasn't thinking about what could go wrong. The construction site looked like fun, not a hazard, and nobody in the group stopped to question it. When everyone around you is already moving, it's easy to just move with them.

Q: How do you get better at recognizing when something is actually a bad idea?
A: You start by slowing down just a little before you say yes. When everyone around you is hyped up and moving fast, that's exactly when your own judgment gets the loudest static. A quick prayer, even just a few seconds of asking God if this is actually a good idea, can cut through that noise. It doesn't have to be complicated. Just long enough to ask yourself what happens if this goes sideways.

Day 2: Explanation: Most people don't make reckless choices because they want things to go wrong. They just never built the habit of stopping to think before they act. Proverbs 4:7 says wisdom is the main thing, and that word "main" matters. It doesn't come automatically. It takes practice and some intention. The more you work at it, the more clearly you start to see what's actually in front of you, and the better your instincts get at protecting yourself and the people with you.

Day 3: Anecdote: A youth camp leader once shared how he broke his arm jumping off a roof on a dare as a teen, simply because his friends egged him on and he didn't want to look afraid. He laughed about it years later, but admitted the injury and the weeks of recovery gave him plenty of time to reflect on how one impulsive moment can carry very real consequences. From that point on, he made it a personal rule to think twice before following a crowd into risky territory, no matter how much pressure he felt in the moment.

Day 4: Warning: Bella didn't set out to hurt anyone. But Zack ended up on crutches anyway. That's the thing about impulsive decisions. They don't just affect you. Proverbs 22:3 puts it plainly: "The prudent sees danger and hides himself, but the simple ones go on and suffer for it." God puts warning signs in front of us all the time. When we blow past them because we're excited or don't want to look scared, we don't just risk the moment. We risk weeks or months of consequences that didn't have to happen.

Day 5: Encouragement: God isn't trying to take the fun out of your life. He made you curious and energetic and drawn to new things. That's not an accident. What He wants is to be part of it with you. Not as a referee waiting to call a foul, but as someone who actually knows what's ahead and wants you to make it through okay. When you bring Him into your decisions, even the quick ones, even the ones that feel too small to pray about, you stop navigating everything on your own. That changes things. You can still be bold. You can still take risks. You just stop doing it blind.

Day 6: God's Love and Redemption: If you've made a call that hurt you or someone else, God isn't standing there waiting to remind you of it. That's not how He works. He's more interested in what comes next than in replaying what went wrong. He doesn't need you to have it all figured out before He'll help you. He just asks you to come to Him, be honest about what happened, and let Him help you move forward. His wisdom is there for the asking. You don't have to keep facing hard moments alone.

Day 7: Reflection Questions:

Q: Think of a time you went along with something risky without really thinking it through. What pulled you in? Did anything go wrong? What warning signs did you miss, and what did you take away from it?

Q: What usually pulls you toward a risky decision, excitement, not wanting to look scared, not wanting to be left out? How does knowing that about yourself help you slow down the next time you feel that pull?

Q: What would it look like for you to pause and pray before saying yes to something, especially when everyone around you is already moving? What's one practical thing you can do to stay grounded when the pressure is on?

Q: What's one habit you could build that would help you catch a bad idea before it goes too far? How might that change things, not just for you, but for the people around you?

PRAYER JOURNAL

*H*eavenly Father,

Thank you for giving me a spirit of adventure and curiosity. I confess that sometimes I have rushed into things or followed others without thinking about the consequences. Forgive me for acting impulsively and for not seeking Your wisdom before making decisions.

Please help me pause and pray before I act. Teach me to consider the risks and to seek guidance from You and wise people around me. Give me the courage to say no when something isn't right, and the discernment to see danger before it comes.

Thank you for protecting me, even when I've made mistakes. Lead me in paths of safety and wisdom, and let my choices honor You and bring blessing to myself and others.

In Jesus' name, Amen.

Prayer Thoughts for Today:

✦✦✦✦✦

~ **END PRAYER JOURNAL "THE SIMPLE ONE"** ~

I'm Doing It My Way

THE FOOL

PROVERBS 19:3 (NIV)

"A person's own folly leads to their ruin, yet their heart rages against the Lord."

Trinity doctor had been telling her the same thing for three years. Eat better. Move more. The warnings were always polite, always gentle, and Trinity always nodded like she was taking them seriously. She wasn't. She'd walk out of the office, stop at the drive-through on the way home, and tell herself she'd start fresh on Monday. Monday came and went every week without much changing.

Her husband tried. He started buying different groceries, suggesting they cook together, and mentioned a nearby walking trail their neighbors used on weekends. Trinity appreciated none of it. She'd grumble, reach for the chips, and change the subject. Her friends eventually stopped asking her to join their morning walks. It was easier than hearing the excuses.

Trinity's unhealthy habits became part of her daily routine. She started most mornings with sugary pastries and coffee loaded with cream. Lunches and dinners were often heavy and processed, and they were often eaten in front of the television. Exercise was rare, and even short walks left her winded and frustrated.

The signs were there. She got winded walking up a single flight of stairs. Heartburn kept her up some nights. Her knees ached in the morning before she'd even gotten out of bed. But Trinity had an explanation for everything. Stress. Getting older. Bad weather. Anything but the obvious. "I feel fine," she'd tell her husband when he brought it up. "You worry too much."
As the months went by, Trinity's energy levels dropped. She found herself struggling to keep up at work, often feeling sluggish and irritable. Her sleep became restless, and she woke up most mornings already tired. Still, she clung to the belief that she was just getting older, not that her choices were to blame.

One afternoon, Trinity felt a tightness in her chest that wouldn't go away. Then the pain sharpened, and her breathing got short, and her husband called 911. At the hospital, after the tests came back, a doctor sat down with her and explained what was happening. It was the same condition her own doctor had flagged years ago. Trinity sat there in the hospital bed listening, and instead of feeling relieved that they'd caught it, she felt furious.

In the hospital, Trinity lashed out at the medical staff, frustrated by the constant monitoring and restrictions. She complained about the food, the tests, and the endless warnings, insisting that no one understood what she was going through. Her family tried to comfort her, but Trinity's anger made it difficult for them to reach her.

She blamed her genetics, the stress at work, and even the doctors themselves for not doing more. She couldn't see how her stubbornness and refusal to listen had led her to this point. The idea that her suffering could have been avoided was too painful for her to accept.

As her hospital stay stretched on, visitors came less often. It was hard to sit with someone who met every kind word with a sharp one. The nurses kept showing up anyway, patient in a way Trinity didn't feel she deserved. One afternoon, she watched a man down the hall doing slow laps with a walker, determined and steady, and something about it got to her. She didn't say anything to anyone. But that night she lay there in the quiet and let herself think, for the first time, about the years of warnings she had ignored and what might have been different if she hadn't.

Recovery was harder than she expected. There were days she wanted to quit the new diet, skip the physical therapy, pretend none of it had happened. Her husband showed up every single day. He didn't lecture her. He just showed up. Slowly, Trinity started showing up for herself, too.

Looking back, what hurt most wasn't the hospital stay or the recovery. It was thinking about all the times someone who loved her had tried to help and she'd pushed them away. She couldn't get those years back. But she could decide what to do with the ones she had left.

Day 1: Q&A:

Q: Why did Trinity disregard medical advice?
A: She was convinced the warnings didn't apply to her. Doctors worry too much, she figured. Her family was being dramatic. It's easy to dismiss advice when nothing has gone visibly wrong yet, and Trinity had gotten good at finding reasons not to listen.

Q: What was the result?
A: She ended up in the hospital with a condition her own doctor had warned her about for years. The hard part wasn't the diagnosis. It was knowing it didn't have to happen. Small ignored choices had added up over time into something she couldn't talk her way out of.

Day 2: Explanation: Proverbs 19:3 says, *"A person's own folly leads to their ruin, yet their heart rages against the Lord."* That's Trinity in a single verse. She made the choices, but when things fell apart she pointed at everyone else. Her doctors. Her genes. Her stress. It's a pattern that's easy to recognize in someone else's story and harder to spot in your own. When we ignore wisdom long enough, we don't just suffer the consequences. We usually find someone else to blame for them.

Day 3: Anecdote: A neighbor once shared how he refused to wear a seatbelt for years, convinced it was an unnecessary precaution that didn't apply to someone like him. Then one afternoon, a minor fender-bender jolted him forward hard enough to crack his dashboard, and he sat there shaking, realizing how differently that moment could have ended. From that day on, he never got behind the wheel without buckling up first.

Day 4: Warning: Trinity didn't make one big terrible decision. She made a hundred small ones. More chips. Skip the walk. Dismiss the doctor. None of them felt serious in the moment. That's how it usually works. Proverbs 13:18 puts it plainly:

"Whoever disregards discipline comes to poverty and shame, but whoever heeds correction is honored." The encouraging part of that verse is the second half. It's not too late to be the person who heeds correction. But it's worth asking how long you want to wait.

Day 5: Encouragement: Trinity's recovery wasn't fast or clean. It was slow and frustrating, full of days when she wanted to give up. But she got there. Proverbs 4:22 says God's wisdom brings "life to those who find them and health to one's whole body." That's not a metaphor. It's practical. The choices we make about our bodies, our habits, and our willingness to listen matter to God. He's not indifferent to whether you're well. When you stop fighting the wisdom He's placed around you and actually receive it, things start to change. Not always quickly. But they change.

Day 6: God's Love and Redemption: Trinity spent years brushing off the people God put in her life to help her. And God kept sending them anyway. That's what Lamentations 3:22-23 is getting at when it says His mercies are new every morning. Not that mistakes don't matter, but that they don't have the final word. No matter how many times you've ignored the right thing to do, you haven't used up His patience. He meets you where you actually are, not where you should have been. That's the kind of grace worth receiving.

Day 7: Reflection Questions:

Q: Have you ever ignored important advice about your health or well-being? What happened as a result?

Q: Why do you think people resist making changes even when they know it's for their own good?

Q: What is one practical step you can take this week to be more open to correction or wise counsel?

Q: How does knowing that God's mercies are new every morning change the way you approach the areas of your life where you've been resistant to change?

PRAYER JOURNAL

*G*racious God,

Thank You for caring about my well-being and for placing wise counsel in my life. I confess that I have sometimes ignored important advice and chosen my own way, leading to trouble and regret. Forgive my stubbornness and open my heart to receive instruction with humility. Help me to take responsibility for my choices and to make changes that honor You and care for the life You've given me. Thank You for Your patience and for offering me a fresh start, no matter how many times I've failed. Guide me in wisdom and help me to trust You more each day.

In Jesus' name, Amen.

Prayer Thoughts for Today:

~ END PRAYER JOURNAL" THE FOOL" ~

THE FIRE OUT OF CONTROL

THE SCORNER

PROVERBS 21:24 (NIV)

"The proud and arrogant person—'Mocker' is his name—behaves with insolent fury."

Lorraine had always believed that her anger was a sign of her passion. She had been told this so many times, by so many people trying to find something generous to say about a quality that made her difficult to be around, that she had eventually accepted it as fact. Her anger, she believed, was proof that she cared deeply, that she had standards, that she refused to be treated as less than she deserved. She had never stopped to ask whether the fire she carried was protecting her or burning everything within reach.

She had built a career in corporate training, moving from company to company with a reputation split almost perfectly down the middle. Half the people who had worked with her described her as brilliant, driven, and capable of producing results that other consultants could not match. The other half went quiet when her name came up. She had a gift for developing training programs that worked. She also had a temper that made the process nearly unbearable for anyone who worked alongside her.

The anger was not constant, which was part of what made it so disorienting. There were stretches, sometimes weeks, in which Lorraine was engaged, collaborative, and even generous. But those stretches never held. A challenge to one of her ideas, a question about her methodology, a suggestion that something might be done differently could trigger a response so disproportionate to the moment that it left people shaken and uncertain about what they had done wrong.

Proverbs 21:24 describes the proud and haughty person as one who acts with proud wrath, and that phrase captures precisely what Lorraine's anger was. It was not the anger of someone genuinely wronged. It was the anger of a person whose pride had been touched. A challenge to her work was not intellectual disagreement to her; it was a personal assault. A question was not curiosity; it was an accusation. She responded with a force entirely out of proportion to what had actually occurred.

She had worked on a project team at a large financial services firm for several months, developing a leadership curriculum the firm had invested significant resources in. The team included four other professionals, each with relevant expertise and genuine enthusiasm. In the early weeks the collaboration had been productive, ideas shared freely, the work moving forward. Then came the first real disagreement. One of her colleagues, a calm and experienced woman named Patricia, raised a concern about a module Lorraine had developed, suggesting the approach might not land well with the firm's audience and offering a specific alternative.

Lorraine's response was immediate. She did not engage with the substance of Patricia's concern or consider the alternative offered. She reacted as though the concern itself were an act of aggression, and her wrath left the rest of the team silent and Patricia visibly shaken. The meeting ended without resolution. The damage done in those minutes took weeks to begin to repair. Patricia was not the last colleague to raise a concern, but she was one of the last to raise one directly. After that meeting, the team developed a quiet strategy of working around Lorraine's anger rather than through it. They routed feedback through the project manager, softened their language until concerns were barely recognizable, and timed their questions for moments when Lorraine seemed most settled. The project was completed, but in an atmosphere of such sustained tension that three members of the team declined to work with her again when the firm offered a follow-up contract.

The firm's decision not to renew her contract was communicated professionally, without explanation. Lorraine received it as confirmation of what she had always suspected: that the people around her were threatened by her capabilities and unwilling to work with someone who held high standards. She did not connect the decision to her anger. She never connected any consequence to her anger. The story she told herself was always the same. It was justified. It was passionate. It was the natural response of a person of conviction to a world that consistently failed to meet her standards.

What she could not see, and what Proverbs 21:24 makes plain, is that proud wrath is not a sign of high standards. It is a sign of pride that has been threatened. The person who reacts with wrath when challenged is not protecting something valuable. She is protecting her ego at the expense of every relationship and every opportunity that requires trust, and wrath destroys trust. Lorraine's fire was real. But it had never warmed anyone. It had only ever driven them away.

She moved on to the next contract, and the next, carrying the fire with her. She never understood that the pattern of departure and disappointment she kept encountering was not the world's failure to recognize her worth. It was the harvest of the proud wrath she had never been willing to lay down.

Day 1: Q&A

Q: What does Proverbs 21:24 mean when it describes the scoffer as acting with proud wrath?
A: Proverbs 21:24 identifies an anger rooted not in genuine injustice but in wounded pride. "Proud wrath" is the reaction of a person who experiences correction or disagreement as a personal attack, demanding a forceful response, the defensive anger of someone who has decided her judgment is beyond challenge.

Q: How did Lorraine's proud wrath damage the people and opportunities around her, even when she believed she was simply holding high standards?
A: Lorraine's proud wrath created an atmosphere in which honest engagement became too costly to attempt. Her colleagues stopped raising concerns, routed feedback around her, and eventually declined to work with her again. The collaboration did not survive it. And the standards she believed she was protecting were never actually met, because no one was willing to tell her the truth anymore.

Day 2: Explanation: Proverbs 21:24 describes a person whose anger has become an expression of pride, a reflexive response to anything that threatens their elevated view of themselves. Proud wrath disguises itself as passion, as the righteous indignation of someone who refuses to compromise. But there is a reliable way to tell the difference. Righteous anger responds to genuine injustice. Proud wrath responds when someone questions you. Lorraine was not angry because something unjust was happening. She was angry because her ideas were being questioned, and to her, that felt like the same thing. Left unchecked, that confusion destroys every relationship that requires the humility to be challenged.

Day 3: Anecdote: A gifted chef opened a restaurant that quickly earned a devoted following. But in the kitchen, her temper was a constant presence. Any suggestion from her sous chef, any question from a line cook, any deviation from her specifications was met with an anger that went far beyond correcting a mistake. Every imperfection felt like a challenge to her authority.

Experienced cooks left. The sous chef eventually resigned, citing the impossibility of working in constant tension. The restaurant closed within three years. The chef's talent had never been the question. Her proud wrath had answered it for her.

Day 4: Warning: Proud wrath is deceptive because it feels, from the inside, like strength. The person in its grip feels justified, even righteous, and that justification makes it very difficult to examine honestly. If you consistently react with anger when your ideas are challenged, the problem is not the people challenging you. It is pride that has made the challenge feel intolerable. Proud wrath does not protect you. Over time, people stop pushing back. They go quiet, work around you, or leave. What feels like respect is usually just distance.

Day 5: Encouragement: If this is your pattern, there is a path forward. Scripture's invitation is not to become passive but to become humble. Proverbs 16:32 says that one who rules her spirit is better than one who takes a city. That strength begins with acknowledging that your anger has been serving your pride rather than the truth, and it grows through pausing before reacting, asking whether what you feel is righteous or simply wounded, and choosing the response that builds rather than burns.

Day 6: Why People Become Scorners: People who develop a proud, wrathful disposition rarely set out to frighten others. Most developed it in environments where anger was the only form of power available to them. Over time, that survival strategy becomes a default setting that feels natural and even necessary, until it becomes the very thing blocking what the person was always after. Lorraine did not want to be feared. She wanted to be valued. Proud wrath made sure she never got there.

Day 7: Reflection Questions:

Q: When you are challenged, questioned, or corrected, what is your first internal response?

Q: Think about a specific moment when your anger was disproportionate to what happened.

Q: Who in your life has gone quiet around you? Is it possible that their silence is not agreement but self-protection?

Q: In what specific situations do you struggle to govern your anger, and what practical steps can you take?

PRAYER JOURNAL

*F*ather,

We come before You and confess that our anger has not always been righteous. We have reacted with proud wrath when our pride was touched, and we have called it passion. We have silenced people with our anger and called it holding standards. We have driven away the very voices that could have helped us grow, and we have told ourselves that we were simply refusing to be disrespected. Forgive us for the relationships damaged by our wrath, for the opportunities lost because people chose not to return to a tense atmosphere, and for the ways our anger has served our ego rather than Your truth. We ask You to teach us to be slow to anger and rich in grace. Give us the self-awareness to recognize the difference between righteous anger and proud wrath, and give us the courage to choose humility in the moments when pride wants to choose fire. Help us to become people whose presence brings safety rather than fear, whose correction comes with gentleness rather than force, and whose passion is governed by the Spirit rather than driven by pride.

In the name of Jesus, Amen.

Prayer Thoughts for Today: ◆◆◆◆◆

~ END PRAYER JOURNAL" THE SCORNER" ~

WISDOM IN DECISIONS

THE WISE

PROVERBS 3:5–6 (NIV)

"Trust in the Lord with all your heart, and do not lean on your own understanding. In all your ways acknowledge Him, and He will make straight your paths."

Jade had been staring at the same offer letter for three days. Her company wanted her in their regional office, nearly eight hundred miles away, in a city where she knew almost no one. The promotion was real and the role was one she had worked toward for years. But every time she imagined packing up her apartment, saying goodbye to her church, and starting over, her chest tightened.

She filled pages with pros and cons, crossing things out and rewriting them as if the right arrangement of words might finally produce an answer. At night, she lay awake running the same questions in a loop. Was this the right move? What if she failed? What if she left and regretted it? She was exhausted by her own thinking.

Eventually, Jade stopped trying to figure it out alone. She called her pastor, a former boss, and two close friends who knew her well. Each one listened without rushing her toward an answer. Her pastor said something that stuck: big decisions rarely feel comfortable, but discomfort alone is not a reason to stay still. Her former boss, who had relocated across the country years earlier, told her the fear never fully goes away. You just learn to move while carrying it.

One friend suggested she fast and pray before deciding anything. Jade had never done that before, not for a decision like this. But she was tired of the noise in her own head, so she said yes. She set aside three days, put her phone down more than usual, and tried to simply listen.

She started writing in a journal again, something she had not done in years. She wrote out her fears without editing them. She wrote about the people she would miss, the things she was afraid to want, and the parts of herself she was not sure she trusted. The silence was uncomfortable at first. Then, slowly, it wasn't. A passage of Scripture she had read a dozen times landed differently. A sermon on a Sunday morning felt like it was written for her week.

By the end of the week, something had shifted. Jade was no less uncertain about the logistics, but she felt less frantic about needing to know right now. The checklists lost their grip. She stopped demanding a sign and started noticing what was already there. She realized the process itself had been changing her, not just informing her.

When the deadline arrived, Jade called her boss and said yes. She was not fearless. But she was at peace, and that felt like enough. Her family and friends showed up in the weeks that followed, helping her pack, making her laugh, and sending her off well. The first few weeks in the new city were hard. She missed Sunday dinners with her family, the familiar faces at her home church, and the kind of friendships that do not need explaining. There were nights she questioned herself. But she kept praying, kept reaching out, and eventually found a church where she felt at home. She introduced herself to neighbors. She showed up. Slowly, a new community began to form around her.

Looking back, Jade could see how different this had been from decisions she had made out of fear or impatience. She had not gotten a clear sign or a guaranteed outcome, and she was okay with that. What she had gotten was a process that steadied her. She learned that peace was not the absence of difficulty. It was the quiet assurance that she was not navigating it alone.

When friends came to her later, stuck in their own crossroads, Jade did not hand them a formula. She told them what had helped her: slow down, talk to people you trust, and bring the whole mess of it before God. She had learned that wisdom rarely arrives all at once. More often it comes quietly, in the middle of the waiting.

Day 1: Q&A:

Q: What steps did Jade take in decision-making?
A: She sought counsel from trusted friends and mentors, bringing each concern before God in prayer. Then she waited, allowing peace rather than pressure to guide her final decision.

Q: What was the blessing?
A: After seeking counsel and spending time in prayer, Jade accepted the promotion with a sense of calm assurance rather than anxious uncertainty. The peace she felt was not the result of having all the answers, but of trusting that God was guiding each step of the way.

Day 2: Explanation: Proverbs 3:5–6 reminds us to lean not on our own understanding but to acknowledge God in all our ways, surrendering our plans and fears to His greater wisdom. When we do, He promises to direct our paths, bringing clarity and purpose to even the most uncertain seasons of life.

Day 3: Anecdote: A missionary serving in Southeast Asia once felt pressured to partner with a local organization that promised rapid growth for his ministry. Before committing, he sought counsel from experienced mentors who raised serious concerns about the organization's financial integrity, ultimately saving his ministry from a damaging and costly entanglement. He later credited that moment of humble, patient wisdom as one of the most important decisions of his life.

Day 4: Blessing and Rewards: When we pursue wisdom through prayer, counsel, and patience, God rewards us with a peace that surpasses our own understanding, freeing us from the paralysis of fear and doubt. That peace becomes the foundation for confident, Spirit-led decisions that align with His purpose for our lives. The blessing is not just the outcome of the choice, but the deeper faith and trust in God that grows through the process of seeking Him.

Day 5: Encouragement: God is not distant or indifferent. He cares deeply about every detail of your life, from the biggest crossroads to the smallest daily choices. James 1:5 promises that if anyone lacks wisdom, they should ask God, who gives generously without finding fault. No decision is too small or too overwhelming to bring before Him, so take heart and ask boldly.

Day 6: God's Love and Redemption: In the middle of life's most uncertain moments, God does not leave us to navigate the fog alone; His love compels Him to step in and bring order to our confusion. He takes the tangled threads of our doubt, fear, and indecision and weaves them into a clear and purposeful direction that we could not have found on our own. Isaiah 30:21 promises that we will hear a voice behind us saying, "This is the way, walk in it," whenever we are tempted to turn aside. That redemptive guidance is not reserved for the spiritually mature or the extraordinarily faithful; it is available to anyone who humbly turns to Him. No matter how lost or overwhelmed you feel, God's love is always at work leading you toward clarity, peace, and His perfect plan.

Day 7: Reflection Questions:

Q: What decision are you facing now? Take a moment to name it honestly, whether it involves your career, relationships, finances, or a personal crossroads you have been avoiding. What fears or uncertainties have made it difficult to move forward, and have you brought it fully before God in prayer?

Q: Who can offer wise counsel? Consider the trusted people in your life, whether a pastor, mentor, or close friend, who have demonstrated godly wisdom and genuine care for your well-being. What makes them someone you can turn to, and have you been intentional about seeking their input when facing important decisions?

Q: How do you sense God's leading? Reflect on a moment when you felt a quiet nudge or inner clarity that seemed to come from beyond your own reasoning. Was it through Scripture, prayer, the counsel of others, or simply a settled peace that pointed you in a direction?

Q: What brings you peace in choices? Think about a time when you felt confident and settled after making a difficult decision. What was it about that process, whether prayer, wise counsel, or simply waiting, that allowed peace to replace uncertainty?

PRAYER JOURNAL

*S*overeign Lord,

Thank You that You care about every choice I face big and small. I confess that I have sometimes made decisions quickly or out of fear, without seeking Your wisdom or counsel. Forgive me for relying on my own understanding or for letting worry guide my steps. Grant me wisdom as I make decisions today and in the future. Help me to pause, pray, and listen for Your voice. Surround me with wise advisors and give me discernment to recognize good counsel. Teach me to trust Your timing, even when the way forward is unclear. Give me the humility to admit when I am wrong and the courage to change direction if needed. Thank You for your faithfulness in leading and guiding me. Restore my peace where anxiety or regret has taken hold, and help me to move forward with confidence, knowing that You are with me. May every choice I make bring honor to You and reflect Your love to others.

In Jesus' name, Amen.

Prayer Thoughts for Today:

✦✦✦✦✦

~ END PRAYER JOURNAL "THE WISE" ~

THE GIVER

THE SIMPLE ONE

PROVERBS 14:15 (NIV)

"The simple believe in anything, but the prudent gives thought to their steps."

Olivia had always been the type of person eager to help wherever she could. Her teachers often described her as compassionate and enthusiastic, always the first to volunteer for school drives or community clean-ups. Whether it was collecting canned goods for the food bank, tutoring younger students, or raising money for animal shelters, Olivia loved the feeling of pitching in and making a difference. She took pride in being dependable and supportive, a friend you could always count on.

One afternoon, as Olivia was leaving her literature class, her friend Maya caught up with her in the hallway. Maya's face was animated, her arms full of flyers. "Hey, Olivia! Some of us are going to the protest downtown after school. Will you come? We could really use more voices. It'll be fun, and it's for a good cause!" Olivia glanced at the flyer, which mentioned standing up for justice and making change, but it was vague about the details. Still, she trusted Maya and wanted to be part of something meaningful. She smiled and nodded, "Sure, I'm in!"

After school, Olivia joined Maya and the group as they marched toward the city square, their voices rising with chants and their signs waving in the air. The energy was infectious; Olivia felt swept up in the crowd's enthusiasm. She took a sign from someone and marched, chanting along, though she still wasn't clear on the specifics of the protest. "It's about making things better," she reasoned, "and that's always good, right?"

As the afternoon wore on, Olivia started to notice details that made her uneasy. She overheard heated arguments between protestors and bystanders. Some of the chants grew more aggressive, and the signs, Olivia realized, carried messages she didn't fully understand or agree with. She saw a group confronting a passerby who tried to ask questions, and their harsh words left Olivia unsettled. The more she listened, the more she realized the group's central message wasn't what she had assumed. In fact, some of their demands and rhetoric went against her own values and beliefs.

A wave of embarrassment washed over her. Olivia felt out of place, holding a sign that didn't reflect her own heart. She slipped quietly to the edge of the crowd, her cheeks burning. How had she ended up here, supporting something she didn't even agree with? Why hadn't she asked more questions before jumping in?

That evening, Olivia sat on her bed, replaying the day's events. She felt guilty and confused, not just for having participated, but for having done so blindly. She worried about what her parents would think if they found out, or how she would explain it if someone asked her why she'd joined. Most of all, she felt disappointed in herself for not living up to her own standards of thoughtfulness and honesty.

The next day, Olivia called Maya and explained her feelings. "I'm sorry, Maya, but I didn't really understand what the protest was about, and I don't think it's something I can support." Maya was surprised, but she appreciated Olivia's honesty. The conversation was awkward, but it was also a relief. Olivia knew she had to be true to herself, even if it meant risking discomfort or disappointing a friend.

From that experience, Olivia learned the importance of asking questions and understanding a cause before lending her support. She realized that being helpful didn't mean saying yes to everything and everyone, especially when it meant compromising her own values. Olivia decided that from now on, she would take time to research and reflect before getting involved. She wanted her actions to be driven not just by eagerness, but by wisdom and conviction.

Looking back, Olivia was grateful for the lesson. She still wanted to help wherever she could, but now she knew that true service required both a willing heart and a discerning mind. She promised herself she would never again join a cause, no matter how well-intentioned, without first understanding what she was standing for.

Day 1: Q&A:

Q: What led Olivia to get involved without knowing the facts?
A: Honestly? She wanted to help. That's not a bad thing. But wanting to help without stopping to ask questions is how a lot of us end up somewhere we never meant to be. She said yes before she understood what she was saying yes to.

Q: How can you make wise choices about involvement?
A: Slow down before you sign up. Ask what this is really about, who's behind it, and whether it actually lines up with what you believe. And don't be afraid to say no. Saying no is not a failure; sometimes it's exactly what God is asking of you.

Day 2: Explanation: Most of us have been there: you hear about something, it sounds good, and before you've thought it through, you're already in. That eagerness isn't wrong. But enthusiasm without discernment can take you places you didn't intend to go. Proverbs 4:5 puts it plainly: "get wisdom, get understanding." That's not a suggestion; it's a charge. Before you commit, pause. Pray. Ask a hard question or two. Your time and your name are worth protecting.

Day 3: Anecdote: I knew a woman, sharp and kind, the kind of person who showed up before you even asked. In her younger years, that meant she said yes to everything. Every committee, every project, every cause that sounded remotely good. She told me once, "I thought showing up was the same as doing right." But a few of those situations left her feeling used, confused, and far from where she thought she was headed. One group she'd joined turned out to hold views that embarrassed her. Another drained her completely and left her with nothing to give her own family. It wasn't until a mentor sat her down and asked, "Do you actually believe in what you're doing?" that she realized she'd never stopped to ask herself that. These days, she prays before she commits. She asks questions. And she says no more than she used to, and means it every time.

Day 4: Warning: Here's the hard truth: once you're in, getting out isn't always easy. People remember who showed up. They take pictures. They tag you. And when something goes sideways, your name is already attached to it. That's not meant to scare you, but it is meant to make you think. Misaligned commitments don't just cost you time. They can cost you peace, relationships, and your sense of who you are. Proverbs 14:15 doesn't mince words: "The simple believe anything, but the prudent give thought to their steps." Be the person who thinks before they step.

Day 5: Encouragement: Let me say this clearly: you are not required to say yes to everything. Not to every request, every group, every person who needs a warm body and spots you first. God did not design you to be available to everyone for everything. He designed you with a purpose, and that purpose has a shape. Not everything fits it. James 1:5 says if you need wisdom, ask God, and He won't make you feel bad for asking. So bring it to Him. Sit with it. You'll know the difference between a door He opened and one you're forcing. Trust that feeling.

Day 6: God's Love and Redemption: Maybe you're reading this and thinking about a time you got it wrong. You jumped in too fast, trusted too easily, and ended up somewhere that cost you. That's okay. I mean that; it is genuinely okay. God is not sitting back disappointed that you wanted to do good. He knows your heart. What He offers isn't a lecture. It's a hand. Romans 8:28 is real: He takes the mess and works it. Not around it, but through it. The uncomfortable experience, the embarrassing mistake, the group you wish you'd never joined: He uses all of it. You're not behind. You're not broken. You're just someone who's learning, and He's the best teacher there is.

Day 7: Reflection Questions:

Q: Have you ever said yes to something and later thought, wait, what did I just agree to? What happened, and what did it cost you? Don't rush past this one. Sometimes the experiences we'd rather forget are the ones that taught us the most.

Q: Why do you think asking questions feels hard sometimes? Is it fear of looking uninformed? Not wanting to seem difficult? Think about what holds you back from asking, and what it could protect you from if you did.

Q: Think about a commitment you're currently holding. Does it still fit who you are and what you believe? Is there someone in your life, a friend, a mentor, someone at church, who knows you well enough to tell you the truth about your choices? If not, that might be worth thinking about too.

Q: When you pray about a decision, do you actually wait for an answer, or do you pray and then do what you were already going to do? What would it look like to genuinely bring a current decision to God this week and sit with it before moving forward?

PRAYER JOURNAL

 racious God,

Thank You for giving me opportunities to make a difference in the world. I confess that sometimes I have jumped into causes or commitments without fully understanding them. Forgive me for acting without discernment and for not seeking Your direction first.

Please give me wisdom as I consider where to invest my time and energy. Help me to seek understanding, ask the right questions, and follow only what aligns with Your truth and love. Teach me to be bold in saying yes to Your purposes and gentle in saying no when something is not right.

Thank You for guiding me patiently and for redeeming every experience for my growth. May my choices honor You, and may I always be led by Your Spirit.

In Jesus' name, Amen.

Prayer Thoughts for Today: ✦✦✦✦✦

~ END PRAYER JOURNAL "THE SIMPLE ONE" ~

LAUGHING IT UP

THE FOOL

PROVERBS 16:28 (NIV)

"A perverse person stirs up conflict, and a gossip separates close friends."

 laire was the girl everyone wanted at their lunch table. She had a story for everything and somehow always knew what was going on with whom. People gravitated toward her; she was funny, quick, and never let a dull moment breathe. If something was happening at school, Claire knew about it. And if she didn't know the full story, she'd fill in the gaps herself.

Gossip, to Claire, felt like harmless fun. She didn't think twice about passing along something she'd overheard or adding a little flair to a story for effect. She never considered the ripple effects of her words or the trust people placed in her. If anything, she felt it made her more popular, more in-the-know. It gave her a sense of power and belonging.

One afternoon, Claire learned that her close friend, Mateo, was struggling with some family issues. Mateo had confided in another friend, who let it slip to Claire, trusting that she would be discreet. But the secret was too tempting, and before long, Claire was sharing a watered-down version with a few people at lunch. "Don't say anything, but did you hear what's going on with Mateo's family?" she began, as friends leaned in, eager for details.

The next day, Mateo found out. Someone had texted him about it, a screenshot of a group chat. He found Claire between classes, and he didn't yell. That almost made it worse. "I trusted you," he said. His voice was steady, but his jaw was tight. "Why would you do that?"

Claire shrugged, uncomfortable but unwilling to accept blame. "It wasn't a big deal," she muttered. "People would've found out anyway. We were just talking." She tried to brush it off, convincing herself that the gossip hadn't really hurt anyone, that it was all just part of how people interacted at school.

But over the next few weeks, Claire noticed things starting to change. Friends stopped asking her for advice or sharing personal stories. She'd walk up to a group and feel conversations shift, grow guarded, or go quiet altogether. When she asked what was new, people replied with vague answers or changed the subject. The laughter and camaraderie she'd enjoyed began to fade, replaced by a growing sense of isolation. She watched as others formed tighter bonds, sharing inside jokes and secrets without her. There were moments she'd catch a laugh from across the lunchroom and realize she didn't know what it was about. She used to know everything. Now she felt like she was watching her own life from the outside, pressing her face against a window she hadn't noticed she'd closed.

Claire felt left out, confused, and lonely. She missed the closeness she'd once had with friends, especially Mateo, who now barely spoke to her. She couldn't understand what had changed. She felt resentful at first, blaming others for being too sensitive or dramatic. But as the days passed, she began to notice a pattern: she was no longer trusted. People didn't confide in her, didn't invite her to smaller gatherings, didn't treat her as part of their inner circle.

One evening, she saw it: photos from a hangout she hadn't heard about. Everyone was there. No one had texted her. She stared at the screen for a long time. She'd always told herself it was just talking. Just venting. Just being real. But sitting alone in her room, she couldn't sell herself that story anymore.

Claire decided to make a change. She sat with the discomfort for a few days before finally texting Mateo. He didn't respond right away, and she didn't blame him. When he did, it was short: "We can talk." They met after school, and Claire didn't make excuses this time. She apologized sincerely, told him she was wrong, and asked for nothing in return. Mateo didn't forgive her on the spot, and she had to learn to be okay with that. She promised to be more mindful of her words and to respect the privacy of others. Though it took time, and rebuilding trust wasn't easy, Claire learned to listen more and speak less. She found that real friendship was built on honesty, respect, and loyalty, not on knowing secrets or being the life of the party.

Looking back, Claire was grateful for the painful lesson. She realized that the thrill of gossip could never replace the warmth of genuine connection, and that true friends are those who guard each other's hearts, not expose their wounds. From then on, Claire became known not as the biggest talker, but as someone you could trust (a friend who had learned, the hard way, the value of keeping confidence and choosing kindness in every conversation).

Day 1: Q&A:

Q: Why did Claire gossip about others?
A: She acted without thinking, driven by a desire for attention rather than a concern for others. She never paused to consider the weight of her words or the hurt they could leave behind.

Q: What was the result?
A: People stopped confiding in her. Conversations got shorter. She was still around, but she wasn't really included anymore. The loneliness crept in slowly, which almost made it harder, because there was no single moment to point to. Just a gradual quiet where closeness used to be.

Day 2: Explanation: *Proverbs 18:6 says, "A fool's lips walk into a fight, and his mouth invites a beating."* This vivid imagery illustrates how reckless words don't just cause harm to others; they inevitably bring consequences back upon the speaker. Fools often underestimate the power of their words, treating speech as something casual and weightless while remaining unaware of the damage it can inflict. Wisdom, however, teaches us to pause before we speak, to consider the impact our words will have on those around us. Guarding our speech is not a sign of weakness, but of maturity and reverence for the relationships God has placed in our lives.

Day 3: Anecdote: A teacher once shared how repeating a rumor in school destroyed a friendship she had cherished for years, all because of a single careless conversation. The fallout was immediate: her friend felt betrayed and withdrew completely, leaving a painful silence where closeness once existed. It took years of patience and sincere effort to slowly rebuild what had been broken in a moment. Through that experience, she learned one of life's most valuable lessons: be slow to speak about others, especially when the words are not yours to share.

Day 4: Warning: Gossip may seem trivial in the moment, just a passing comment or a whispered secret, but its effects can be devastating and long-lasting. It erodes trust, tarnishes reputations, and quietly dismantles the very friendships we value most. Proverbs 16:28 warns, "A perverse person stirs up conflict, and a gossip separates close friends." This is not a minor caution but a sobering reminder that careless words carry real consequences. What begins as idle talk can end in broken bonds that take years to repair, if they can be repaired at all.

Day 5: Encouragement: If you've hurt others with your words, know that it is never too late to make things right. Seeking forgiveness takes courage, but it is one of the most powerful steps toward healing and restoration. A sincere apology, offered with humility, can open doors that careless words once slammed shut. From that point forward, you have the opportunity to be intentional, choosing words that build up, inspire, and breathe life into the people around you. Every conversation is a new chance to reflect the grace you yourself have received.

Day 6: God's Love and Redemption: No matter how much damage our words have caused, God's love is greater still, capable of reaching into the broken places and bringing restoration where we least expect it. He does not condemn those who come to Him with a repentant heart; instead, He extends grace and the power to change. When we confess our careless speech and turn to Him, He begins the work of healing not only the relationships we have wounded but also the habits of our hearts. In His hands, the very tongue that once tore down can become an instrument of encouragement, truth, and blessing to everyone it touches.

Day 7: Reflection Questions:

Q: Have you ever said something about someone that you later wished you hadn't? What was happening in you in that moment: were you bored, trying to fit in, or just not thinking? And what did it cost you, or the other person, afterward?

Q: Why is it sometimes easy to underestimate the impact of our words on others? Often, we speak from our own perspective without fully considering how the other person will receive what we say, making it easy to dismiss words as harmless when they may actually land with far more weight than we intended. Because we rarely see the full aftermath of our words, whether it is the quiet hurt someone carries home or the way a comment replays in their mind for days, we can mistakenly believe our speech had little effect at all.

Q: What changes can you make to guard your speech and use your words to build others up instead of tearing them down? One practical step is to develop the habit of pausing before you speak, asking yourself whether your words are true, necessary, and kind before letting them leave your lips. Beyond simply avoiding harmful speech, look for daily opportunities to speak life into the people around you, offering genuine encouragement, affirmation, and truth that reminds others of their worth and potential.

Q: How does understanding God's forgiveness help you move forward after you've hurt someone with your words? When we truly grasp that God has already forgiven us for our worst failures, it frees us from the paralyzing weight of guilt and shame that can keep us stuck in regret. That same grace becomes the foundation from which we can humbly seek forgiveness from those we've hurt, not out of obligation, but out of a genuine desire to restore what was broken. And as we experience God's mercy firsthand, we are empowered to extend that same compassion to ourselves, allowing us to grow, change, and move forward with a renewed commitment to using our words wisely.

PRAYER JOURNAL

$\mathcal{M}$erciful Father,

Thank You for Your unfailing love and grace. I admit that I have sometimes used my words carelessly, speaking gossip or negativity that has hurt others. Please forgive me for the pain I have caused and for not honoring others with my speech. Teach me to guard my tongue and to use my words to encourage, heal, and build up those around me. When I am tempted to join in harmful conversations, give me the strength to choose kindness and wisdom instead. Thank You for Your forgiveness and for the chance to make things right. Help me to seek reconciliation where I have caused harm and to become a vessel of Your love and peace.

In Jesus' name, Amen

Prayer Thoughts for Today:

✦✦✦✦✦

~ END PRAYER JOURNAL "THE FOOL" ~

THE SEARCH THAT NEVER ARRIVED

THE SCORNER

PROVERBS 14:6 (NIV)

"The mocker seeks wisdom and finds none, but knowledge comes easily to the discerning."

D iana had spent most of her adult life pursuing wisdom. She read constantly, attended lectures, and filled notebooks with quotations and frameworks she never quite got around to living by. She had a shelf of annotated books that most people had never heard of, and she could speak fluently about nearly all of them. People who met her for the first time were impressed. People who knew her well were troubled.

She worked as a leadership coach, and she was good at it. Her ability to diagnose others' problems was sharp, sometimes uncomfortably so. She could talk about humility and accountability with the kind of clarity that makes people take notes. The trouble was that she had never actually practiced either. She had studied them.

Her life was organized around convictions that no amount of reading had ever been allowed to disturb. She believed she was more perceptive, more committed to truth than people who had not read as widely. That belief was never on the table for examination. It was the table. She sought wisdom the way a collector seeks rare objects: not to be changed by what she found, but to add it to the shelf.

Proverbs 14:6 says that a scoffer seeks wisdom and does not find it. This is not a person who lacks intelligence or access. It is a person whose heart is not in the right posture to receive wisdom. Diana had read the books and engaged with the ideas, but she approached all of it from a position of superiority rather than surrender. At every turn, she took only what confirmed her existing conclusions and set aside the rest. She was not aware she was doing this. That was part of the problem.

Over time, clients began to notice something. Diana was good with frameworks, but her sessions had a strange quality, like being analyzed rather than helped. When a client admitted fault, she would redirect to systemic causes. When someone got vulnerable, she responded with theory. She could not quite be present to what was happening in the room because she was too busy narrating it. She always had a name for what was going on. She rarely sat with it long enough to feel it.

A long-term client named Margaret finally said it out loud. She told Diana that she seemed to know a great deal about wisdom without being shaped by it, and that their sessions felt like watching someone perform insight rather than practice it. It was a careful, honest observation, the kind that costs something to give. Diana received it with composure. She thanked Margaret, gently reframed the concern as a misunderstanding of her methodology, and left the session having let none of it land.

Margaret did not renew her contract. Neither did two other long-term clients that year. Diana attributed the departures to natural turnover, to clients who had simply grown beyond what she could offer. She did not consider the possibility that the departures were telling her something about herself that her reading had never managed to reach.

Diana's knowledge was real. But knowledge and wisdom are not the same thing, and Proverbs has always known the difference. Wisdom is not what you know. It is what has changed you. Diana had taken in an enormous amount of information. None of it had humbled her, because humility requires an openness that pride will not allow.

She kept searching. More seminars, more books, more frameworks added to the collection. The gap between what she knew and who she was kept widening. She could feel it sometimes, late in the evening after a session that had not gone well, a vague sense that something was missing. But she never followed that feeling far enough to find out what it was. Proverbs 14:6 had described her in half a sentence: she sought wisdom and did not find it. Not because it was hidden. Because the heart doing the seeking was closed.

Diana's story does not have to be yours. The same Proverbs that describes the scoffer who seeks and does not find also describes the path that leads to genuine wisdom. Proverbs 9:10 says that the fear of the Lord is the beginning of wisdom. Wisdom does not begin with the right books. It begins with the right posture before God, one marked not by confidence in what you already know, but by honest dependence on the One whose wisdom is not an addition to your own.

Day 1: Q&A

Q: What does Proverbs 14:6 mean when it says that a scoffer seeks wisdom but does not find it?
A: Proverbs 14:6 reveals that the obstacle to wisdom is not a lack of intelligence or effort but a heart condition, one that approaches wisdom as something to be acquired rather than something that must challenge and change the seeker. Diana embodied this precisely. She pursued wisdom diligently by every outward measure, yet her pride made genuine wisdom impossible to receive regardless of how much knowledge she accumulated.

Q: How did the gap between Diana's knowledge and her character affect the people she was supposed to be helping?
A: Diana's clients received analysis without genuine presence, counsel shaped more by her need to demonstrate insight than by their need to be helped. When they expressed vulnerability or named a concern, she responded with theory rather than truth. Several eventually left, not because her knowledge was insufficient, but because knowledge without genuine wisdom cannot produce the kind of transformation that real coaching requires.

Day 2: Explanation: Proverbs 14:6 makes a distinction worth sitting with. The scoffer does not refuse to seek wisdom. She seeks it and does not find it. The problem is not effort. It is posture. Wisdom, as Proverbs presents it, is not a body of knowledge to be accumulated. It is a quality of heart that only grows in genuine humility. Diana had every outward mark of a wisdom seeker. What she lacked was the one thing wisdom requires most: a heart willing to be corrected. Her seeking was real. It was just in the service of pride, and pride is the one condition wisdom cannot enter.

Day 3: Anecdote: A theologian spent thirty years studying grace, writing papers, teaching courses, tracing its development across centuries with real precision. Those who knew her personally found her quick to judge and slow to forgive. A former student once said that studying under her taught everything you could want to know about grace intellectually, and almost nothing about how to extend it. Like Diana, she had pursued wisdom diligently and missed it in the place that mattered most: her own life. The knowledge was real. The transformation had not come.

Day 4: Warning: The danger of seeking wisdom without humility is that the seeking itself becomes a substitute for the transformation it was supposed to produce. A person can develop a convincing impression of wisdom, to others and to herself, while remaining unchanged. Proverbs 14:6 warns that this kind of seeking does not find what it is looking for. The warning is easy to miss because the seeking feels productive. The notebooks fill up. The vocabulary grows. And none of it requires you to actually change. The question is not whether to seek. It is whether your seeking is in the service of transformation, or in the service of the image you have of yourself as someone who seeks.

Day 5: Encouragement: Diana's story does not have to be yours. Proverbs 9:10 says that the fear of the Lord is the beginning of wisdom: not the right books, not the right frameworks, but the right posture before God. Reverence. Honest dependence. A willingness to let his wisdom replace the pride that has been standing in its place. If you have been seeking for a long time without finding that it has changed you, the invitation is not to seek more. It is to seek differently, to bring your searching before God with the honest admission that the heart doing the seeking is part of what needs to change. That kind of prayer is where wisdom actually begins.

Day 6: Why People Become Scorners: Almost no one becomes a scorner on purpose. Most begin with a genuine desire to learn and grow. But somewhere along the way, the seeking gets tangled up with identity. Wisdom stops being something to receive and becomes something to display. The more a person invests in the pursuit of knowledge, the more her sense of self gets tied to being someone who knows. New ideas get quietly filtered: does this confirm what I already believe, or challenge it? Over time, the filtering becomes automatic. Invisible. And the person arrives at the condition described in Proverbs 14:6 without ever having chosen it. The remedy is not more seeking. It is a reorientation of the heart that is doing the seeking.

Day 7: Reflection Questions:

Q: When you engage with wisdom, whether through Scripture, books, teaching, or counsel, are you genuinely open to being changed by what you encounter, or are you primarily looking for confirmation of what you already believe? How would you honestly know the difference?

Q: When someone has named a gap between what you believe and how you live, did you allow their words to reach you? Or did you reframe the feedback in a way that left your existing view of yourself intact?

Q: Is there anyone in your life who might be sensing a gap between your knowledge and how you live, even if they have never said so? What would it take for you to ask them honestly and receive their answer without defending yourself?

Q: Proverbs 14:6 says that wisdom is easily found by a person of understanding. What does the condition of your heart before God look like right now? Is it a heart that is humble and open to being taught, or is it a heart that seeks wisdom on its own terms and in the service of its own image?

PRAYER JOURNAL

*F*ather,

We confess that we have sometimes sought wisdom not to be changed by it but to add it to what we already think of ourselves. We have read the right books, used the right language, and engaged with the right ideas while keeping our hearts carefully protected from the transformation that wisdom is meant to produce. Forgive us for the pride that turned seeking into performance, that filtered every new truth through the question of whether it confirmed our existing self-image rather than whether it challenged it. We ask You to reorient our hearts. Give us the genuine humility that wisdom requires, the kind that does not merely acknowledge its need for instruction but actually opens itself to receive it. Teach us the fear of the Lord that Proverbs says is the beginning of wisdom, the reverent, honest, dependent posture before You that makes real learning possible. Where we have accumulated knowledge without character, convict us. Where we have taught others what we have not ourselves received, correct us. We want to be people who are not merely students of wisdom but people who are genuinely shaped by it, whose lives reflect the truth we have encountered rather than simply the breadth of our reading.

In the name of Jesus, Amen.

Prayer Thoughts for Today:

◆◆◆◆◆

~ **END PRAYER JOURNAL "THE SCORNER"** ~

Wisdom In Rest

THE WISE

Proverbs 3:7–8 (NIV)

"Do not be wise in your own eyes; fear the Lord and depart from evil.

It will be health to your body and nourishment to your bones."

Mary was the kind of person who answered emails at midnight and considered that normal. She was first in the office, last to leave, and somewhere in between she had stopped asking whether any of it was sustainable. Her calendar was packed. Her weekends were packed. Even her lunch breaks were packed, usually with calls she could have skipped. People said she was driven. She told herself the same thing.

For a while, it worked. Promotions came. Her boss trusted her with the hard stuff. She built a reputation as the person who got things done, and she wore that like armor. But somewhere around month eighteen of running at full speed, her body started sending signals she kept ignoring. She was tired in a way that sleep didn't fix. She snapped at people she liked. She sat through meetings and retained almost nothing.

Her solution, predictably, was to work harder. More lists. Earlier alarms. She started treating Saturday mornings like Monday mornings and told herself she'd rest when things slowed down. They never slowed down. She used to paint. Used to hike on weekends, cook big meals for friends on Sunday nights. At some point those things quietly disappeared, and she barely noticed until she realized she was dreading Mondays before the weekend had even started.

The turning point was small, as they usually are. She missed her closest friend's birthday dinner. Not because of an emergency. Because of a deadline that, looking back, could have waited. She sat in her car in the parking lot of her office at 8 p.m. and felt something crack open. That weekend, she finally talked to her pastor. He didn't lecture her. He just listened, then said, "You can't pour out what you haven't received. Rest isn't a reward, Mary. It's a gift God's been trying to give you."

She wasn't convinced, but she was tired enough to try. She blocked off the following Sunday. Laptop in the drawer. Notifications off. She told herself it was just one day. The first hour was uncomfortable in a way she hadn't expected. Her hands kept reaching for her phone out of habit. She made a mental list of everything she was falling behind on. She felt guilty for sitting still.

She went for a walk. Not a productive walk with a podcast in her ears. Just a walk. She noticed things she had stopped noticing, the way afternoon light hits the trees, a dog losing its mind over a squirrel, kids arguing over a soccer ball. She came home and read Scripture slowly, not scanning for something to apply, just reading. She prayed without a list. She ate dinner with her family and actually heard what they were saying. By 9 p.m., she felt something she hadn't felt in a long time. Not accomplished. Just okay. Just rested. She kept the practice going. Sundays became protected. And slowly, things shifted. She slept better. Her mind felt less cluttered. Ideas started coming back.

People at work noticed before she did. A colleague asked if she'd changed something. Her manager commented that her thinking seemed sharper in meetings. She started telling people about the Sabbath, not in a preachy way, just honestly. "I take one day a week completely off. It changed things." She also found that her faith deepened in a way she hadn't expected. Worship felt different when she wasn't half-composing a work email in her head. Prayer felt less like a transaction. Rest had become something she understood differently now, less like a break and more like trust.

Looking back, she could see how close she had come to falling apart. Not dramatically, not all at once, but the slow kind of falling apart that sneaks up on you. She was grateful for the conversation with her pastor, grateful she had been desperate enough to listen. The rest hadn't just helped her work better. It had helped her be a better person to the people she loved.

Friends started coming to her when they felt burned out. She didn't have a formula for them. She just told them what had happened to her and that God's invitation to rest was real and open.

She still honors the Sabbath. Some weeks it's harder than others. But she's learned that rest isn't something you graduate from needing. It's something you keep choosing, and God keeps meeting you there.

Day 1: Q&A:

Q: What wisdom did Mary receive?
A: To honor rest and the Sabbath. Her pastor reminded her that the Sabbath is not merely a suggestion but a gift from God, a sacred rhythm designed to restore the soul. By setting aside one day to disconnect from work and reconnect with God, Mary found the renewal and peace she had been desperately chasing.

Q: What blessing resulted?
A: Renewed strength and joy. As Mary embraced the Sabbath, her exhaustion gave way to a deep, lasting energy that no amount of extra work had ever provided. She discovered a joy rooted not in accomplishment, but in resting in God's presence and trusting His provision.

Day 2: Explanation: Exodus 20:8 "Remember the Sabbath day by keeping it holy." This commandment, given by God to Moses, reminds us that rest is not optional but a sacred act of obedience and worship. By setting apart one day each week, we declare our trust in God as our provider and acknowledge that our lives are sustained by His grace, not our own efforts.

Day 3: Anecdote: A business leader shared how Sabbath rest increased his effectiveness. Despite leading a demanding company, he committed to taking one full day off each week, stepping away from emails, meetings, and decisions entirely. He found that returning to work after a true day of rest made him sharper, more creative, and better equipped to lead his team with wisdom and clarity. Over time, he came to see the Sabbath not as a loss of productivity, but as the very foundation of his success.

Day 4: Blessing and Rewards: Resting wisely brings renewal and delight. When we honor God's design for rest, He replenishes our strength, restores our joy, and refreshes our spirit in ways that no amount of striving can produce. Isaiah 40:31 reminds us that those who wait on the Lord will renew their strength, soaring on wings like eagles. In rest, we find not emptiness, but the fullness of God's presence and the delight of simply being His.

Day 5: Encouragement: Rest is a gift, embrace it as a blessing from God. From the very beginning, God modeled rest on the seventh day, not because He was tired, but to show us that rest is holy, intentional, and good. In a world that glorifies busyness, choosing to rest is a radical act of faith, a declaration that you trust God more than your own striving. He invites you to lay down your burdens, to step away from the noise, and to find your sufficiency in Him alone. Rest is not something you have to earn; it is freely given by a Father who knows your limits and loves you deeply. So receive it with gratitude, protect it with intention, and let it become a sacred space where God renews, restores, and delights in you.

Day 6: God's Love and Redemption: God loves you enough to command rest. Think about that for a moment, the Creator of the universe, who spoke galaxies into existence, looked at you and said, "You need to stop, and that is okay." His command to rest is not a restriction but an expression of His deep, fatherly love for you. He knows you are finite, that your body grows weary, your mind grows heavy, and your spirit needs to be replenished. Rather than leaving you to run yourself into the ground, He built rest into the very rhythm of creation so that you would never have to earn your way to peace. His Son, Jesus, extended that same invitation when He said, "Come to me, all you who are weary and burdened, and I will give you rest" (Matthew 11:28). In resting, you are not being unproductive; you are responding to the love of a God who redeems your weariness and transforms it into wholeness. Let His love be the reason you rest, and let His grace be the peace that meets you there.

Day 7: Reflection Questions:

Q: How do you practice rest? Think about the specific rhythms, habits, or routines you have built, or could build, to honor rest in your daily life. Consider whether those practices are truly restorative or simply a pause before the next rush of activity. Ask God to help you create space that is intentional, unhurried, and rooted in His presence rather than your own comfort or convenience.

Q: What keeps you from embracing Sabbath? Reflect on the fears, habits, or pressures that make it difficult to step away, and ask God to help you release whatever is standing between you and the rest He has designed for you.

Q: How does rest help you serve God better? Consider how stepping away from the demands of life allows you to return to God's work with a renewed spirit, a clearer mind, and a heart more fully surrendered to His purpose.

Q: Where is God inviting you to slow down? Take a moment to reflect on the areas of your life where His gentle nudge toward rest is being drowned out by the noise of busyness.

 reator God,

Thank You for designing me to need rest and for commanding Sabbath as a gift, not a burden. I confess that I have sometimes neglected rest, believing that my worth depends on productivity or that I must do everything myself. Forgive me for ignoring Your invitation to slow down and trust You.

Grant me wisdom to rest well. Teach me to set healthy boundaries and to find delight in the rhythms You created work and rest, giving and receiving. Help me to lay down my worries and find peace in Your presence.

Give me humility to accept my limitations and to trust that You are always working, even when I am still. Restore my body, mind, and spirit as I honor You through rest. Thank You for refreshing my soul and for the joy that comes from Sabbath moments. May I encourage others to rest and to find renewal in You. Let my life be a testimony to Your sufficiency and grace.

In Jesus' name, Amen.

Prayer Thoughts for Today: ✦✦✦✦✦

~ END PRAYER JOURNAL "THE WISE" ~

DON'T WORRY

THE SIMPLE ONE

PROVERBS 27:5: (NIV)

"Better is open rebuke than hidden love."

ora had always thought of herself as someone who just went with the flow. She was the friend who'd brush off inconveniences, the classmate who'd quietly pick up the slack, and the girl who'd smile and say, "It's fine, don't worry about it," even when something was gnawing at her inside. She'd grown up watching her parents sidestep arguments and keep things calm, and she'd taken that lesson to heart. Peace, she believed, was always worth protecting.

When Nora moved into her first apartment with three other college students, she pictured late-night pizza runs and the kind of friendships that stick with you for life. And for a while, things really were good. They divided up the chores, made a schedule, and kept to it for the first few weeks. The apartment wasn't spotless, but it felt like home, and everyone was pulling their weight.

But slowly, things started to slip. Chris left dishes in the sink "just for the night," then forgot about them. Sam kept promising to take the trash out tomorrow while the bag filled until it practically toppled over. Even Alyssa, usually the most dependable of the three, started skipping her bathroom days, citing a busy week or an upcoming exam.

At first, Nora told herself it was no big deal. Everyone has off days, she figured, and she didn't want to be the person who made a fuss over a few dirty dishes. So she grabbed the sponge. She hauled the trash bag down to the dumpster. She told herself it was temporary, that things would even out on their own, and that it was just easier to handle it herself than to make it into something bigger.

But weeks passed and nothing changed. Dishes multiplied, the bathroom grew grimier, and a smell settled into the apartment that Nora couldn't ignore. She found herself scrubbing countertops at midnight while her roommates watched TV or headed out with friends. She'd even started buying cleaning supplies out of her own pocket, too uncomfortable to ask anyone to chip in. The resentment was building, but Nora kept it locked away. She couldn't bring herself to say anything, too afraid of coming across as difficult. So she kept smiling, kept saying "no problem," and even laughed along when her roommates called her a "clean freak," even though it stung a little more each time.

Over time, the weight of it wore her down. She became tired in a way that sleep didn't fix, and she pulled back from her roommates, spending more evenings alone in her room or at the library. She felt invisible and a little used. Worst of all, she started turning it inward, wondering if maybe she was just too sensitive, or simply not built for living with other people.

One evening, after another long stretch of cleaning up on her own, Nora called her older sister. She needed to talk to someone. Her sister listened without interrupting, and when Nora finally ran out of words, she asked one simple question: "Have you ever actually told them how you feel?" Nora went quiet. The honest answer was no. She'd been so focused on avoiding conflict that she'd never once given her roommates the chance to understand what was happening or to do something about it.

That night, Nora sat with that question. She'd been quietly absorbing everything, telling herself it was fine when it clearly wasn't. She hadn't been keeping the peace. She'd just been keeping quiet, and those were two very different things. For the first time, she understood that healthy boundaries aren't walls. They're what make real relationships possible.

The next day, with her heart pounding, Nora asked her roommates to sit down together. She kept her voice steady as she told them how overwhelmed she'd been and how much the chore imbalance had been affecting her. She braced herself for awkwardness. Instead, they looked genuinely surprised and sorry. They hadn't realized how much she'd been carrying. They agreed to a new schedule and offered to pay her back for the supplies.

The conversation hadn't been easy, but walking away from it, Nora felt lighter than she had in months. Silence hadn't protected anything. It had just let the tension pile up, the same way the dishes had. By finally speaking up, she hadn't just fixed the chore situation. She'd done something for herself.

From that point on, Nora made a conscious effort to speak up sooner, to name what she needed before it became something she was quietly carrying. She still cared deeply about harmony. That hadn't changed. But she'd learned that real peace isn't something you protect by going silent. Sometimes it's something you have to be brave enough to go after. Her good nature had always been a strength. She just finally understood that it worked best when she let a little courage stand beside it.

Day 1: Q&A:

Q: Why did Nora keep quiet about the chores?
A: As a simple one, Nora avoided confrontation and hoped the problem would resolve itself, rather than seeking wisdom on how to address it. Instead of speaking up, she quietly absorbed the burden, letting resentment build beneath the surface. Her desire for peace actually prevented the honest conversation that could have restored it.

Q: What can you do if you're tempted to avoid necessary conversations?
A: Ask God for courage and wisdom, trusting that He will give you the right words when you need them. Practice speaking the truth in love, choosing honesty not to wound but to heal and strengthen your relationships. Set healthy boundaries, even if it feels uncomfortable at first, knowing that boundaries are not walls but bridges to deeper respect and understanding. Over time, what once felt difficult will become a natural part of how you walk in wisdom.

Day 2: Explanation: Simple Ones often shy away from difficult conversations, hoping problems will disappear on their own. But Proverbs teaches that wisdom involves addressing issues with honesty and grace, rather than burying them beneath a surface of false peace. True wisdom recognizes that silence can be just as harmful as harsh words, because it allows hurt and misunderstanding to take root. Learning to speak with both truth and gentleness is one of the key marks of a person growing in godly wisdom.

Day 3: Anecdote: A marriage counselor once shared that many of the couples she works with let small problems fester rather than address them early. By the time they sought help, what began as a minor frustration had often turned into years of unspoken hurt and emotional distance. She encourages people to have gentle, honest conversations before issues grow out of control, noting that the sooner a concern is addressed, the easier it is to resolve. A small act of courage early on, she says, can save a relationship from far greater pain down the road.

Day 4: Warning: Avoidance can lead to bigger problems. What starts as a small, unaddressed issue can quietly grow into deep resentment, broken trust, or damaged relationships. Proverbs 27:5 says, "Better is open rebuke than hidden love." Ignoring issues rarely makes them go away; silence may feel safe in the moment, but it often allows wounds to deepen and distance to grow.

Day 5: Encouragement: God wants to help you grow in courage and wisdom. You don't have to face difficult conversations alone. His Spirit equips you with the strength and grace you need in those moments. He will be with you as you learn to speak up, resolve conflicts, and build healthy relationships. Every step of growth you take, no matter how small, is a step toward the life of peace and purpose He has for you.

Day 6: God's Love and Redemption: Even if passivity has caused trouble or pain, God's love is patient and restorative. He does not condemn you for the times you stayed silent or shrank back, but instead gently draws you toward growth and healing. He gives second chances and teaches you how to handle life's challenges in a way that brings lasting peace and renewed strength.

Day 7: Reflection Questions:

Q: Have you ever kept quiet about a problem or unfair situation because you wanted to avoid conflict, even though it continued to bother you? Looking back, what was the outcome, and how did staying silent affect you or the relationship? Is there anything you wish you had handled differently?

Q: Why do you think it can be difficult to address issues or set boundaries with others, even when you know it's the right thing to do? What fears or past experiences might be holding you back from having those honest, necessary conversations?

Q: How can you practice speaking the truth in love, even when it feels uncomfortable or risky? What is one specific relationship or situation in your life where you could take a small, courageous step toward honest, loving communication?

Q: How can you intentionally turn to God's wisdom and strength before and during difficult conversations, rather than relying solely on your own understanding? In what ways has He already shown up for you in challenging situations, giving you the right words or a sense of peace? How might remembering those moments encourage you to trust Him more the next time you face a hard conversation?

PRAYER JOURNAL

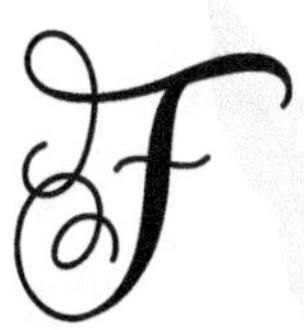 aithful Lord,

Thank You for being my source of peace and strength. I confess that I have sometimes avoided confrontation or necessary conversations out of fear or discomfort. Forgive me for allowing problems to grow instead of seeking Your wisdom to address them with love and honesty.

Grant me the courage to speak the truth with grace. Help me to set healthy boundaries and to resolve conflicts in a way that honors You and brings healing to relationships. Fill my heart with Your love so I may pursue peace, not through silence, but through wisdom and truth.

Thank you for your patience and for teaching me how to handle life's challenges. Guide me in every conversation, and help me to grow in confidence, courage, and understanding.

In Jesus' name, Amen.

Prayer Thoughts for Today: ✦✦✦✦✦

~ END PRAYER JOURNAL "THE SIMPLE ONE" ~

THE THRILL

THE FOOL

PROVERBS 13:18: (NIV)

"Whoever disregards discipline comes to poverty and shame,

but whoever heeds correction is honored."

Ashley blew her first paycheck in four days. A pair of sneakers she didn't need, two rounds of drinks for people she barely knew, and a skincare set she saw on a video at two in the morning. By Friday, her account sat at eleven dollars.   She wasn't worried. There would always be another check.

Her dad sat her down once with a legal pad and a pen, ready to walk her through a budget. She lasted about six minutes before she found a reason to leave the room. Her mom left a book about personal finance on her nightstand. It collected dust for months before Ashley used it to prop up a wobbly lamp. She wasn't trying to be cruel. She just genuinely believed the rules that applied to other people didn't quite apply to her.

She opened her first store credit card to get a 15% discount on a jacket. Then another one, for a free tote bag. Within a year, she had four cards and a rough idea of the balances on maybe two of them. When her checking account got low, she swiped plastic without thinking too hard about the math. Thinking too hard about the math always ruined the mood.

She was the one who always had a plan. Happy hour on Thursday, brunch on Sunday, and a road trip someone had been talking about forever. She loved being that person. She picked up tabs, bought birthday gifts that were a little too nice, and said yes to things she couldn't afford because saying no felt like admitting something she wasn't ready to admit. There was a low hum of dread underneath all of it, but it was easy enough to drown out.

The first collection call came on a Tuesday afternoon. She let it go to voicemail, then deleted the voicemail. The letters she stuffed into the back of her junk drawer, unread. Minimum payments had crept up to the point where she was paying close to three hundred dollars a month just to keep the balances from getting worse, and they were still getting worse. She knew the drawer was full. She just kept not opening it.

She started talking about her job as if it were the problem. Her salary was too low. The cost of living was out of control. Her friends spent money, so what was she supposed to do, sit home alone? She ran through the list often enough that she almost believed it. It was easier than sitting still long enough to trace every charge back to a choice she had made herself.

She stopped sleeping well. She'd lie awake running numbers that never added up and wake up tired and short with everyone around her. She snapped at her mom over nothing. She picked a fight with a friend over something stupid at dinner. Shopping didn't feel fun anymore. She'd add things to her cart and then just stare at them, a knot in her stomach where the excitement used to be.

Her friends got tired of it. Not the debt, exactly, but the complaints that went in circles and never led anywhere. Her parents had stopped offering advice. There was nothing left to say that hadn't already been said and ignored.

The group chat went quiet around her. She told herself people were just busy.

Her dad brought up the idea of a financial counselor one more time. She said she'd think about it. She didn't think about it. She was waiting for something to shift: a raise, a tax refund, some stroke of luck that would level everything out without her having to sit across from a stranger and explain how badly she'd handled things.

She took out a payday loan to cover a credit card payment. Then another one two weeks later. She looked up what her laptop might sell for, then closed the tab. Every fix she came up with just dug the hole a little deeper, and she was running out of ideas. Her card got declined at dinner. Not a nice dinner, just a casual place with friends. She laughed, called it bad luck, and handed over a different card, praying it would go through. It did, barely. She was quiet on the drive home. For the first time, she didn't try to think her way around what was happening. She just let herself feel how tired she was.

She called her mom the next morning. She didn't have a speech ready. She just said she needed help and let the silence sit there until her mom said, " Okay, let's figure it out. It wasn't a clean resolution. There were hard conversations, a spreadsheet she hated looking at, and a lot of months when progress felt invisible. But she kept going. She learned, slowly and without much grace, that asking for help wasn't weakness. It was the only thing that had actually worked.

Day 1: Q&A:

Q: Why did Ashley ignore warnings about her spending?
A: She rejected correction, believing she could manage on her own and resenting any suggestion to change. Pride made it nearly impossible for her to admit that she didn't have all the answers, and she mistook stubbornness for strength. Rather than viewing guidance as a gift, she saw it as an attack on her independence, pushing away the very people who could have helped her most.

Q: What was the result?
A: Her refusal to accept guidance led to debt, stress, and strained relationships, a common outcome for those who despise instruction. The financial pressure bled into every area of her life, eroding her health, her friendships, and her sense of self-worth. Proverbs 13:18 warns that poverty and shame come to those who ignore correction, and Ashley's story was a painful illustration of that truth.

Day 2: Explanation: *Proverbs 21:20 says, "The wise store up choice food and olive oil, but fools gulp theirs down."* Fools squander resources, thinking only of today, while wisdom plans for the future. Ashley embodied this foolishness, consuming every dollar she earned without a thought for tomorrow, leaving nothing in reserve when hardship arrived. True wisdom, by contrast, disciplines present desires in order to secure future stability, recognizing that what we do with what we have today shapes the life we will live tomorrow.

Day 3: Anecdote: A coworker once shared how ignoring budgeting advice in college led to years of financial struggle, mounting credit card debt, a damaged credit score, and the constant weight of financial anxiety that followed him well into his adult years. It wasn't until he swallowed his pride, sought counsel from a financial advisor, and committed to a structured plan that things began to turn around. Slowly but surely, his debts were paid down, his relationships improved, and the peace that had long escaped him was finally restored. His story is a powerful reminder that it is never too late to choose wisdom and that humility opens the door to the help we need.

Day 4: Warning: Ignoring wise financial counsel can lead to long-term hardship, trapping you in a cycle of debt that grows heavier with every passing month. Proverbs 22:7 reminds us, "The borrower is slave to the lender," a sobering truth that reveals how financial carelessness does not simply create inconvenience but can rob you of your freedom. Like Ashley, many people discover too late that the small, seemingly harmless choices of today can become the chains of tomorrow, making it all the more urgent to heed wisdom before the consequences become overwhelming.

Day 5: Encouragement: No matter how far you've fallen into debt or bad habits, God gives wisdom generously to those who ask (James 1:5), and His grace is more than sufficient to cover every financial mistake you've ever made. Like Ashley, you may have spent years ignoring wise counsel, but the moment you choose humility and surrender your situation to God, the path forward begins to clear. Step by step, with His guidance and the support of trusted people in your life, you can rebuild not just your finances but also your peace, your relationships, and your hope for the future.

Day 6: God's Love and Redemption: God's love doesn't depend on your bank account, no matter how deep your debt or how great your regret, His grace reaches further still. He forgives past mistakes completely, washing away the shame and guilt that financial failure so often leaves behind. Through His Word and the wisdom of trusted counselors, He provides practical guidance for wise living, equipping you with the tools you need to make lasting change. When you place your trust in Him, He offers not just hope for financial freedom, but the peace that surpasses all understanding as you walk faithfully through the process.

Day 7: Reflection Questions:

Q: Have you ever ignored financial advice or warnings and regretted it? Reflect on what happened as a result and how those consequences shaped the way you think about money today.

Q: Why do you think it can be difficult to accept guidance about money and spending habits? Consider how pride, fear, or past experiences may contribute to your resistance to change.

Q: What practical steps can you take to seek and apply wisdom in your financial decisions? Think about one specific area, such as budgeting, saving, or seeking counsel, where you can begin making a change this week.

Q: How does knowing that God's love is not based on your financial status encourage you to seek help and make positive changes? Let that assurance free you from shame and motivate you to take the next bold step toward financial healing.

PRAYER JOURNAL

*H*eavenly Father,

Thank You for being my provider and for offering wisdom in every area of life, including my finances. I confess that I have sometimes ignored good advice and made careless decisions with money, leading to stress and difficulty. Please forgive me for not seeking Your guidance and for neglecting the wisdom of those who care about me. Help me to be a good steward of all You've given, to make wise choices, and to ask for help when I need it. Thank You that Your love is not based on my success or failure, but on Your grace. Teach me to trust You with my resources and to walk in freedom and responsibility. Restore what has been lost and lead me into a future of hope and peace.

In Jesus' name, Amen

Prayer Thoughts for Today: ✦✦✦✦✦

~ END PRAYER JOURNAL "THE FOOL" ~

ANSWERED TO NO ONE

THE SCORNER

PROVERBS 1:22: (NIV):

"How long will you who are simple love your simple ways?

How long will mockers delight in mockery and fools hate knowledge?

Petra had never been comfortable with authority. From the time she was a young girl, she bristled at the idea that someone else's position could give them the right to direct her life, correct her behavior, or place limits on what she could do. She grew up in a home where rules were inconsistently enforced and the adults around her were not always worthy of the trust their roles required. From that beginning, she drew a conclusion that felt reasonable at the time. Over the years, it hardened into something she never questioned again: authority was not something to be respected. It was something to be questioned, resisted, and wherever possible, dismantled.

She carried that conclusion into every environment she entered. In school, she challenged teachers not out of curiosity but because it felt like power. In her early career, she cycled through several jobs, leaving each one under roughly the same circumstances. A manager who had overstepped. A policy she found unreasonable. A structure she considered arbitrary. She told the story of each departure with herself as the principled figure who had refused to be controlled. She had told it so many times that she believed it completely.

By her forties, Petra had built a following on a media platform where she critiqued institutional leadership across every sector. She positioned herself as a voice for people silenced by structures that protected the powerful at the expense of everyone else. There was enough truth in some of what she said to make the rest hard to examine carefully. She had figured out that contempt for authority, dressed in the language of justice, could attract a great deal of loyalty.

Petra had long since placed herself beyond the reach of instruction or rebuke. Teachers were instruments of conformity. Rulers were, by definition, self-interested. She had built a worldview in which contempt for authority was not a character flaw but a form of enlightenment, and she had surrounded herself with people who told her she was right.

The platform was real, and the audience was genuinely devoted. But her content was not shaped by honest inquiry. It was shaped by a contempt she had carried since she was a girl. She was not investigating the leaders she criticized. She was prosecuting them, and the verdict was always decided before she started. She took a partial truth, stripped away context, amplified the worst possible interpretation, and presented the result as courageous journalism. Her audience applauded. The people she targeted had little recourse.

A city councilwoman named Aldene became the focus of Petra's most sustained campaign. Aldene had served her district for eleven years. Her record, looked at honestly, was mixed. There were genuine accomplishments, decisions that had not worked out, and areas where criticism was fair. Petra did not look at it honestly. She selected the failures, ignored the accomplishments, attributed the worst possible motives to every decision, and published a series of pieces portraying Aldene as corrupt and contemptuous of the people she served. The campaign worked. Aldene faced a recall effort that, though ultimately unsuccessful, consumed months of her time and cost the district the momentum on several initiatives it had been building.

When the recall failed, independent journalists looked into Petra's claims. Several turned out to be misleading. The sources she had relied on had their own agendas. The context she had stripped away turned out to matter quite a bit. The picture she had painted of Aldene was not a portrait. It was a caricature, and that became clear once people with no stake in the outcome actually looked at the record.

Petra's response was the same one she had always given to any challenge. She dismissed the journalists as defenders of the establishment and called the review an attempt to silence dissent. She produced more content, angrier and more certain than before, and her most devoted followers accepted it without question. But something had shifted in the broader audience. People who had watched her with genuine trust began to drift away. What was left was a smaller group whose loyalty had less to do with her credibility and more to do with a shared contempt for the same targets.

Petra's contempt was not selective. It was total. She had never learned to tell the difference between authority that deserved challenge and authority that deserved respect, because she had decided long ago that no authority deserved respect at all. That decision had made her a compelling voice for people who shared her anger. It had also made her incapable of the honest discernment that genuine accountability requires.

She had answered to no one for so long that she had forgotten what it felt like to be genuinely accountable. And in forgetting that, she had lost the one quality that could have made her voice worth trusting.

Day 1: Q&A

Q: What do Proverbs 1:22 and 13:1 reveal about the person who despises authority and refuses to receive instruction?
A: Together, they reveal that the rejection of authority is not merely a behavioral pattern but a settled disposition of the heart, marked not by what a person believes but by how she responds when her beliefs are challenged. Petra embodied both descriptions, having constructed an entire worldview in which contempt for authority was a virtue, and that worldview made it impossible for any voice of correction, regardless of its source or validity, to reach her.

Q: How did Petra's contempt for authority ultimately undermine the credibility she was trying to build?
A: Petra's contempt undermined her credibility because it removed the one quality genuine accountability requires, which is honest discernment: she was not investigating authority but prosecuting it, with the verdict always determined before the evidence was examined. When independent journalists found her work misleading, the audience that had trusted her recognized that her contempt was not a tool of truth-telling but a substitute for it, and the voice that had positioned itself as the honest alternative to self-serving authority turned out to be serving nothing more than its own settled contempt.

Day 2: Explanation: Proverbs 1:22 and 13:1 describe not someone who has examined authority and found it wanting, but someone who has dismissed the very category of authority as illegitimate, deciding in advance that no one has standing to instruct or rebuke her, as Petra's story illustrates. A person who cannot distinguish between authority that deserves challenge and authority that deserves respect is not a voice for justice but a voice for her own unexamined wound, and the communities that listen to her pay the price.

Day 3: Anecdote: A young attorney joined a public-interest law firm with genuine idealism, and her early work produced real results, but over time her contempt for the legal establishment broadened from specific injustices into a general disdain for the entire legal framework, and she began approaching every case with the assumption that every judge, every opposing counsel, and every institutional actor was operating in bad faith. She stopped listening to the senior partners who counseled her on strategy, dismissed their guidance as accommodation of a corrupt system, and was eventually asked to leave the firm, having allowed something genuine to harden into a contempt so total that it consumed the very capacity for discernment her work required.

Day 4: Warning: Contempt for authority is one of the most socially rewarded forms of pride today, and that is precisely what makes it dangerous: it attracts audiences and generates loyalty that looks like influence, while Proverbs is concerned not with the size of the audience but with the condition of the heart that produces it. A person who has made contempt a settled posture has removed herself from the reach of instruction, and though she may grow louder and gather more followers, she will not grow wiser, and the communities that depend on her will eventually discover that contempt is not a substitute for the honest discernment that wisdom requires.

Day 5: Encouragement: If you recognize in Petra's story a pattern you have carried yourself, Proverbs 13:1 makes clear that the posture of receiving instruction is available at any age and requires only that you remain open to the possibility that someone in authority might have something worth hearing. That single shift, from contempt to discernment, is the beginning of a very different kind of influence, one built on wisdom rather than on the applause of people who share your anger.

Day 6: Why People Become Scorners: People who develop a deep contempt for authority rarely arrive there without cause, and Petra's story is no exception: her contempt began in a home where the adults had not been trustworthy, and the wound that experience left taught her that the distinction between authority deserving challenge and authority deserving respect did not exist. The problem was never that she learned to question authority but that she never learned to distinguish, and healing from that kind of wound does not mean pretending bad authority does not exist but developing the capacity to see clearly enough to tell the difference, a capacity that grows only in the soil of genuine humility and honest self-examination before God.

Day 7: Reflection Questions:

Q: When you encounter someone in authority, is your first response an openness to receive what they might offer, or a reflexive suspicion that prepares you to resist before you have heard them, and what does that reveal about the posture of your heart?

Q: Think about a specific authority figure you have consistently dismissed or resisted. What might your contempt have cost you?

Q: Is there a wound in your own history that has shaped the way you respond to authority, and what would it look like to bring it honestly before God and ask Him to heal it?

Q: Who in your life holds legitimate authority over you, and is what stands between you and their instruction rooted in wisdom or in pride?

PRAYER JOURNAL

ather,

We confess that we have not always honored the authority You have placed in our lives. We have dismissed teachers who had something genuine to offer. We have resisted leaders whose counsel could have protected us. We have wrapped our contempt in the language of justice and called it courage when it was really the unexamined wound of a heart that learned long ago not to trust. Forgive us for the pride that made us answerable to no one and the contempt that closed us off from the instruction we needed. We ask You to heal the wounds that taught us to distrust authority before we had examined it, and to give us the discernment to distinguish between authority that deserves challenge and authority that deserves honor. Teach us to submit where submission is right, to speak where speaking is right, and to do both from a posture of genuine humility rather than settled contempt. We want to be people who are genuinely teachable, who receive instruction as a gift rather than a threat, and who honor the structures You have established while remaining faithful to the truth You have revealed.

In Jesus' name, Amen.

Prayer Thoughts for Today: ✦✦✦✦✦

~ END PRAYER JOURNAL "THE SCORNER" ~

WISDOM IN LEARNING

THE WISE

PROVERBS 1:5: (NIV)

"Let the wise listen and add to their learning, and let the discerning get guidance."

Avery had always struggled in school. The lessons moved too fast, the instructions never quite made sense, and she spent most of class watching her classmates raise their hands while she stared at her desk. Some mornings, she stood outside the front doors for a full minute before walking in. She just needed a second. The hallways were loud, the classroom felt like everyone had gotten a memo she never received, and by October, she had stopped raising her hand altogether. At home, it was worse. She would sit at the kitchen table for an hour, erase the same problem four times, and still get the wrong answer. Her parents told her to keep trying. She smiled and nodded. Then she stuffed her graded tests to the bottom of her backpack where nobody would find them. She was not ready to explain a 58 to anyone, least of all herself. Some nights she just put her head down on her notebook and gave up.

After a math test she barely passed, her teacher pulled her aside and mentioned the school tutor. Avery said thank you and walked straight to her locker. A tutor meant someone else knowing she was behind, and she was not ready for that. She told herself she would figure it out. She did not figure it out. The numbers kept blurring, the reading assignments kept piling up, and two weeks passed with nothing getting better.

She finally signed up for tutoring in November, mostly because she had run out of other options. Ms. Keller's room smelled like dry-erase markers and old coffee. Avery sat down, ready to be talked at, but Ms. Keller just asked her where things stopped making sense. No sighing, no look of surprise. She drew things out on a notepad, explained them differently when the first way didn't land, and waited. Avery asked a question she had been too embarrassed to ask for months. Ms. Keller answered it as if it were a perfectly normal question.

Things did not turn around overnight. But slowly, they turned. Ms. Keller connected her with a classmate's older sister, who had struggled with the same subjects and came out the other side. She showed Avery how to break an assignment into smaller pieces, how to rewrite notes in her own words instead of just highlighting everything, and how to study for 30 minutes and actually retain it, instead of grinding for 2 hours and retaining nothing. Small things. But they added up.

By spring, she was raising her hand in class. She got an answer right one Tuesday morning and felt her face go warm. It sounds small. It was not small. She had spent the better part of a year convinced that school was a place she did not belong, and now she was starting to think that maybe she had just been missing a few tools.

Her mom noticed before Avery even said anything. One evening, she just hugged her and said she was proud, not about the grades specifically, but about the fact that Avery had asked for help when she needed it. That part stuck with her.
She started helping a girl in her math class who reminded her of herself from the fall. She shared the same study tips, explained things the way Ms. Keller had explained them to her. It helped her understand the material better, too. She had spent so long thinking that needing help meant something was wrong with her. Now she mostly thought it meant she was paying attention. School did not become easy. But it became hers. She stopped dreading it and started being curious about it, which felt like a bigger shift than any grade ever could.

Nobody has to do it alone. That was the thing she kept coming back to. She just wished someone had told her that at the beginning.

Day 1: Q&A:

Q: What did Avery do to improve?
A: She asked for help and applied the advice she received. Avery worked with a tutor, connected with older students, and consistently used new study strategies. Over time, her effort and willingness to learn from others led to real improvement in her grades.

Q: What was the reward?
A: Avery earned better grades and discovered a genuine love for learning. She no longer dreaded going to school and began approaching every subject with curiosity and confidence.

Day 2: Explanation: *Proverbs 1:5 "Let the wise listen and add to their learning…"* This verse reminds us that wisdom is not a destination but a continuous journey. No matter how much we know, there is always more to discover, and those who are truly wise remain open to learning from others. Seeking guidance and instruction is not a sign of weakness but a mark of humility and strength.

Day 3: Anecdote: A librarian shared how wise mentors inspired her lifelong growth. Early in her career, she felt overwhelmed by the vast amount of knowledge her job required, but a seasoned colleague took her under his wing and taught her how to find answers, ask better questions, and never stop being curious. His guidance changed the way she approached her work and her life. Years later, she made it her mission to be that same kind of mentor to others, believing that wisdom multiplies when it is passed from one person to the next.

Day 4: Blessing and Rewards: Learning from others brings growth and wisdom. When we humble ourselves and open our hearts to instruction, we gain far more than knowledge. We develop character, build meaningful relationships, and grow into the people we were created to be. God blesses those who seek understanding, and the rewards of a teachable spirit extend far beyond the classroom and into every area of life.

Day 5: Encouragement: Seek out wisdom. There is always more to learn. Do not let pride or fear keep you from asking questions or reaching out to those who know more than you do. Every teacher, mentor, book, or honest conversation is an opportunity to grow into a wiser and stronger version of yourself. The wisest people in the world are not those who believe they have all the answers, but those who remain curious and humble enough to keep seeking them. Make it a habit to learn something new each day, whether it is a skill, a perspective, or a deeper understanding of something you already know. When you commit to a life of continuous learning, you open yourself up to possibilities that you never imagined were within your reach.

Day 6: God's Love and Redemption: God delights in your growth and curiosity. He created you with a mind designed to wonder, question, and discover, and every step you take toward learning is a step toward becoming more of who He made you to be. When you pursue knowledge with an open and humble heart, you are honoring the gifts He placed inside of you. God does not expect you to have everything figured out. He simply invites you to trust Him in the process and to keep moving forward, even when the answers are not yet clear. Just as Avery found courage to ask for help and grew beyond what she thought was possible, God is ready to meet you in your own journey and lead you into a wisdom that is greater than anything you could find on your own.

Day 7: Reflection Questions:

Q: Who can help you grow in knowledge? Think about the teachers, mentors, family members, or friends in your life who have wisdom and experience to share. How can you reach out to them and invite their guidance into your journey?

Q: What new skill do you want to learn? Consider what excites you or what you have always been curious about but never had the chance to explore. What small step could you take this week to begin pursuing it?

Q: How can you share your learning with others? Think about the people around you who might benefit from what you have already discovered and experienced. Sharing knowledge does not require you to be an expert. Sometimes, a kind word of encouragement, a useful tip, or simply being present with someone who is struggling can make all the difference.

Q: What inspires your curiosity? Is it a subject you love, a question you cannot stop thinking about, or a problem in the world that you wish you could help solve? Pay attention to the things that light you up and make you want to know more. Those sparks of interest are not accidental. They are clues to the unique purpose and passion God has placed within you.

All-Knowing God,

Thank you for the gift of learning and for the opportunity to grow in knowledge and understanding. I confess that I have sometimes resisted learning from others or assumed I already knew best. Forgive me for pride, laziness, or fear that keeps me from seeking wisdom. Grant me a teachable heart, eager to listen, ask questions, and learn from others' experiences. Help me to value the wisdom you provide through mentors, teachers, friends, and even challenges. Give me humility to admit when I don't understand and courage to seek help. Show me how to use what I learn for Your glory and the good of others. Thank You for the ways You reveal Yourself through creation, Scripture, and the wisdom of Your people. Restore my desire to learn and grow, and help me to share knowledge generously with others.

In Jesus' name, Amen.

Prayer Thoughts for Today:

♦♦♦♦♦

~ END PRAYER JOURNAL "THE WISE" ~

OVERLY COMMITTED

THE SIMPLE ONE

PROVERBS 19:2: (ESV)

"Desire without knowledge is not good, and whoever makes haste with his feet misses his way."

Jenna had been counting down to college since the eighth grade. Not in a dramatic way, just the quiet kind of certainty that this was where things would finally click. So when move-in day came, she was ready. She'd packed too much, cried a little saying goodbye to her dog, and still managed to feel like the luckiest person on campus by the time she reached her dorm room.

The activity fair during the first week did not help. It was held in the gym, and every table had someone enthusiastic and friendly who made their club sound like the one thing Jenna absolutely could not miss. She picked up a pamphlet for the environmental club because she genuinely cared about that. She signed up for the student newspaper because a girl at the table had a great laugh and Jenna wanted to be around people like that. The debate team was a dare from her roommate. The tutoring program felt like the right thing to do. By the time she left the gym, she had signed up for five things and was considering a sixth.

For a few weeks, it was actually great. She was meeting people in every corner of campus and had something to look forward to almost every day. Her phone had more notifications than she could keep up with, and she liked that. She'd text her mom things like "I have no idea how I'm going to sleep this week" and her mom would send back a laughing emoji, and Jenna would laugh too because it still felt like a good problem to have.

Then October arrived and something shifted. She started eating granola bars for dinner because she didn't have time to go to the dining hall. She was always five minutes late to everything. She'd sit down in class and realize she had no memory of the reading she was supposed to have done, or worse, no memory of doing it even though she had. Her dorm room started to feel less like a home base and more like the place she went to stare at the ceiling before her alarm went off again.

She turned in a paper late for the first time in her life. She'd always been the kind of student who finished things early, who color-coded her notes. Now she was submitting things at 11:58 and hoping the professor had a loose definition of midnight. The worst part was not the grades, though those were slipping too. It was that she stopped caring about the things she used to care about. The environmental club felt like an obligation. Debate practice felt like a punishment. Even the tutoring, which she had genuinely wanted to do, started to feel like one more thing she was failing at.

Her roommate asked if she was okay one night, and Jenna said yes without even looking up from her laptop. She missed a newspaper deadline and didn't tell anyone until the editor texted her. She started leaving her phone on do not disturb because the group chat notifications felt like accusations. She'd gone from someone who wanted to be everywhere to someone who was hiding.

The breaking point came on a Tuesday. She had missed a review session for her hardest exam because she had forgotten to write it down, and when she finally looked at her planner that night she just sat there. The pages were a mess of crossed-out times and arrows pointing to things she had already missed. She closed it and cried, not dramatically, just the tired kind of crying where you're not even sure what you're most upset about.

She thought about why she had said yes to everything in the first place. Some of it was genuine interest. But a lot of it was just not wanting to be the person who sat alone in the dining hall. She had been so afraid of missing out that she had missed out on having any actual margin in her life. Something had to change.

She went to see her academic advisor the next morning, half expecting to be told she was behind and needed to catch up. Instead, her advisor just listened. She asked Jenna what she actually wanted her college experience to look like, and Jenna realized she had not thought about that since the first week. They talked through what to keep and what to let go. Writing the emails to step back from a few clubs was uncomfortable, but the moment she hit send on the last one, she felt something loosen in her chest.

With more time and mental space, Jenna's grades improved, and she found herself actually enjoying the activities she chose to continue. She learned to schedule downtime and recognized the value of rest. Over time, she discovered that being discerning about her commitments led to deeper friendships, better grades, and a healthier, happier college life.

By spring semester, Jenna had a system. Before she said yes to anything new, she gave herself at least a day to think about it. She asked herself whether she actually wanted to do it or whether she just didn't want to say no. It wasn't a perfect system, but it was hers. And it turned out that doing fewer things with her whole attention felt a lot more like the college experience she had imagined than doing everything ever had.

Day 1: Q&A:

Q: Why did Jenna overcommit herself?

A: Jenna's eagerness to belong and her fear of missing out made it nearly impossible for her to pause and evaluate each opportunity before saying yes. Her inexperience meant she had no framework for counting the cost or recognizing her own limits. Without that discernment, she found herself overcommitted, overwhelmed, and far from the fulfilling college experience she had imagined.

Q: How can you avoid overcommitting?

A: Before saying yes to anything, take time to pray and seek wise counsel to ensure it aligns with God's purpose for your season of life. Learning to say no is not a failure; it's a form of wisdom. Setting clear priorities and guarding your time allows you to show up fully for what truly matters.

Day 2: Explanation: Proverbs warns that the Simple One is easily swayed, saying yes to every opportunity without pausing to discern whether it is truly good or aligned with God's will. Not every open door is meant to be walked through. God calls us to be intentional stewards of our time and energy, choosing depth over busyness and purpose over pressure.

Day 3: Anecdote: A pastor once shared that early in his ministry, he said yes to everything, convinced that being available to everyone was the same as being faithful to God. The relentless pace left him burned out, ineffective, and disconnected from the very calling he was trying to fulfill. It was only when he learned to focus on what God specifically called him to do and release the rest that his ministry truly flourished.

Day 4: Warning: Overcommitment is not just a scheduling problem, it is a spiritual one, quietly robbing you of the focus, rest, and depth that God intends for your life. Proverbs 19:2 warns, "Desire without knowledge is not good, and whoever makes haste with his feet misses his way," reminding us that enthusiasm without discernment leads us off course. When we say yes to too much, we risk doing many things poorly rather than a few things well, and we can miss the very growth God has prepared for us in the quiet, unhurried spaces of life. Guard your commitments carefully, because what you give your time to shapes who you are becoming.

Day 5: Encouragement: You don't have to do everything, and God never asked you to. He knows your limits better than you do, and He promises to guide you toward the commitments that are truly meant for you. In Matthew 11:28, Jesus invites the weary to come to Him for rest, a reminder that a life of frantic busyness is not the abundant life He designed for you. God values your wholeness, and He wants you to show up fully present and rooted, not scattered and depleted. Trust that saying no to the wrong things creates space for the right ones to flourish.

Day 6: God's Love and Redemption: Even if you've stretched yourself too thin and feel like you've lost your way, God's love meets you right where you are, not in your perfection, but in your exhaustion. He is not disappointed in you; He is inviting you to return to Him for rest, renewal, and a fresh sense of direction. Like a shepherd who gently leads the sheep that are with young, God will not drive you beyond what you can bear, but will tenderly guide you back to a pace that is sustainable and life-giving. As you surrender your overloaded schedule to Him, He brings clarity about what truly deserves your time and energy. It is in that place of surrender that you will find not just relief, but genuine joy in serving Him wisely and well.

Day 7: Reflection Questions:

Q: Have you ever said yes to too many commitments and found yourself overwhelmed or exhausted? What did that season teach you about your limits and God's design for rest?

Q: What helps you determine which opportunities or activities are truly aligned with God's purpose for your life? How do prayer, wise counsel, or past experience shape the way you make those decisions

Q: How can you set healthy boundaries to protect your time, energy, and well-being? What is one practical step you can take this week to guard the space God has given you?

Q: In what ways can you seek God's guidance when deciding what to commit to and what to let go? Is there a current commitment you are unsure about, and have you brought it to God in prayer? What would it look like to fully trust Him with the outcome?

Prayer Journal

Heavenly Father,

Thank You for giving me opportunities and gifts to use for Your glory. I confess that I have sometimes said yes to too many things, trying to please others or not wanting to miss out. Forgive me for not seeking Your priorities or guarding my time and energy well.

Give me wisdom to know when to say yes and when to say no. Teach me to set healthy boundaries, to seek Your direction, and to focus on what matters most. Help me to rest in Your guidance and to trust that You will lead me to the right commitments.

Thank You for restoring my soul when I am weary and for giving me clarity and balance. May my life reflect Your wisdom, peace, and joy.

In Jesus' name, Amen.

Prayer Thoughts for Today:

✦✦✦✦✦

~ END PRAYER JOURNAL "THE SIMPLE ONE" ~

THE NON-PLANNER

THE FOOL

PROVERBS 6:6–8: (NIV)

"Go to the ant, you sluggard; consider its ways and be wise! It has no commander, no overseer or ruler, yet it stores its provisions in summer and gathers its food at harvest."

lla had a saying she used so often it became a kind of personal motto: "I'll figure it out when I get there." College? Later. Career? Later. Savings account? Please. She was seventeen, and the sun was out, and her friends were texting her about going to Riverside Park. Whatever "later" held could wait.

Junior year, she missed so many Monday classes that her homeroom teacher, Mr. Okafor, started marking her absent before she even had a chance to show up late. She'd laugh it off. Her friends would cover for her when they could. There were always assignments she meant to finish, but she just never quite got around to them. There was always next week.

Mr. Okafor pulled her aside twice. The school counselor, Ms. Reyes, left two voicemails for her mom. Ella sat through one mandatory check-in where Ms. Reyes slid a printed list of scholarship deadlines across the desk and said, "Ella, these doors don't stay open forever." Ella folded the paper in half, shoved it in her backpack, and forgot about it by the time she got to the parking lot.

Her mom started asking about grades at dinner every night, which Ella found exhausting. "You're always on me," she told her once, pushing back from the table. "I'm handling it." She wasn't handling it. But saying it out loud made it feel true enough. By senior year, her friend Dani had already been accepted to two schools and was stressing over financial aid forms. Ella teased her about it ("You're literally doing homework on a Saturday"), but something about watching Dani's excitement made her stomach feel funny. She pushed the feeling down and suggested they go get food instead.

February came fast. The hallways were full of people comparing acceptance letters and talking about dorms. Ella didn't have any letters. She hadn't applied anywhere. She kept telling herself she still had time, but even she wasn't sure she believed it anymore. She finally sat down in March and Googled "college applications still open" at eleven o'clock on a Tuesday night. Most deadlines had passed. The scholarships Ms. Reyes had printed out, the ones she'd stuffed in her backpack, were long gone. She found the crumpled paper that same night, wedged under a textbook she'd never opened.

Her first instinct was to be angry. The school should have done more. Her parents should have pushed harder. Dani should have dragged her to the counselor's office instead of just going by herself. The anger felt better than the alternative: sitting with the fact that she'd had every warning and ignored every single one.

She spent a few weeks in that anger. It was easier to stay there. Admitting the truth meant admitting she had wasted something real, and she wasn't ready for that yet.

Dani stopped texting as much. Ella's mom stopped asking about grades, not because things were better, but because she didn't know what else to say. The house got quieter. Ella told herself she liked it that way.

Graduation was a Saturday in June. She walked across the stage, shook a hand, got her diploma. Dani's family threw a party that afternoon, and Ella went, and she smiled when she was supposed to. But watching everyone talk about move-in dates and roommates, she felt like she was standing on the outside of a window, looking in at something she could have had.

That summer was long and uncomfortable. She got a job at a coffee shop, started looking into community college programs, and called Ms. Reyes once, just to ask where to start. It wasn't a dramatic turnaround. It was slow and a little embarrassing and full of moments where she wanted to quit before she'd really begun. But she kept going. And somewhere in the middle of all that ordinary, unglamorous effort, she started to understand what everyone had been trying to tell her all along.

Day 1: Q&A:

Q: Why did Ella avoid planning ahead?

A: She saw no value in preparation, believing things would work out on their own. Advice from teachers, parents, and mentors felt like noise, well-meaning interference from people who didn't understand her. She had convinced herself that life would naturally fall into place and that those who planned were just too afraid to live freely. It never occurred to her that the very freedom she prized was being quietly undermined by her refusal to take responsibility for her own future.

Q: What resulted from this attitude?

A: Ella's lack of foresight brought anxiety, missed opportunities, and regret, which are typical outcomes for those who reject wisdom. Without a plan or sense of direction, she found herself overwhelmed when the future she had ignored finally arrived at her door. The very freedom she thought she was protecting slowly unraveled into uncertainty, isolation, and a deep sense of loss. Her story is a sobering reminder that wisdom ignored is not simply delayed; its absence leaves a mark on every area of life it was meant to guide.

Day 2: Explanation: *Proverbs 6:6-8 encourages us to learn from the ant, a small creature that needs no overseer yet diligently gathers and stores for the season ahead.* This passage reminds us that wisdom is not passive; it takes initiative, plans ahead, and works consistently even when no one is watching. Fools, on the other hand, ignore such wisdom, convincing themselves they can coast through life and still avoid the consequences of their inaction. They mistake comfort for safety, unaware that every season of neglect draws them closer to hardship. True wisdom calls us to be like the ant: intentional, disciplined, and always preparing for what lies ahead.

Day 3: Anecdote: A young man once shared that he never studied for exams, assuming he could rely on natural ability and good luck to carry him through. He walked into test after test unprepared, brushing off the warnings of teachers and classmates who urged him to take his studies more seriously. It wasn't until repeated failures began closing doors that he finally stopped and took an honest look at his habits. The wake-up call was painful, but it became the turning point he needed. Through that season of struggle, he discovered that discipline and preparation are not burdens to be avoided, but gifts from God that equip us to walk confidently into the opportunities He places before us.

Day 4: Warning: Neglecting responsibilities may feel freeing now, but the weight of avoidance grows heavier with every passing season. What seems like freedom today quietly becomes a trap tomorrow, as missed deadlines, unprepared moments, and unmet obligations begin to stack up. Proverbs 13:16 says, "Every prudent man acts with knowledge, but a fool flaunts his folly." The prudent person understands that every decision carries consequences and acts accordingly, with intention and care. The fool, however, mistakes recklessness for confidence and avoidance for ease, never realizing that folly always reveals itself in the end. The warning is clear: what you neglect today, you will be forced to face tomorrow, often at a much greater cost.

Day 5: Encouragement: If you've ignored responsibility, you can start fresh. It's never too late to turn around, refocus, and begin making choices that align with the future God has in mind for you. He doesn't withhold His grace because of past carelessness; instead, He extends it freely to those who are willing to change. God gives new chances, renewed direction, and the wisdom needed to live an intentional, meaningful, and purposeful life. Every new day is an invitation to step forward with greater discipline and trust that He will guide your steps as you do.

Day 6: God's Love and Redemption: God doesn't define you by past neglect. Your failures, missed opportunities, and seasons of irresponsibility do not have the final word over your life. His mercies are new every morning, and His grace reaches back into every regret to redeem what was lost. He offers strength to rebuild what has been broken, wisdom to make better decisions, and hope to carry you forward with purpose. No matter how much time has been wasted or how heavy the weight of past choices feels, God's plan for your life is not finished. What is behind you does not have to determine what is ahead, because in His hands, even your setbacks can become the foundation for something greater.

Day 7: Reflection Questions:

Q: Have you ever put off responsibilities or avoided planning for the future? What were the results of those choices? Reflecting honestly on those moments can reveal patterns that God may be calling you to surrender and change.

Q: Why do you think some people choose to live only for the moment instead of preparing for what is ahead? Sometimes the future feels too distant or uncertain, making it easier to focus on what feels good right now rather than what is truly needed later.

Q: What are some practical ways you can start taking responsibility and making wise plans for your future? Consider starting small by setting daily goals, seeking wise counsel, and asking God for direction as you take each step forward.

Q: How does God's offer of new beginnings give you hope when you feel unprepared or regretful about past choices? His grace meets you exactly where you are, no matter how far behind you feel. With God, no mistake is too great to be redeemed or too late to be turned around.

Prayer Journal

*L*oving Father,

Thank You for Your patience and for the opportunities You give me to prepare for the future. I confess that I have sometimes avoided responsibility and lived only for the moment, missing out on the blessings that come from wise planning. Please forgive me for neglecting the gifts and responsibilities You've entrusted to me. Give me a heart that seeks wisdom, discipline, and foresight. Help me to make choices today that will honor You and build a better tomorrow. Thank You for offering new beginnings and for guiding me back when I get off track. Lead me in Your ways and fill me with hope and purpose as I trust in Your plans.

In Jesus' name, Amen.

Prayer Thoughts for Today:

✦✦✦✦✦

~ End Prayer Journal "The Fool" ~

The Company Kept

THE SCORNER

PROVERBS 15:12: (NIV)

"Mockers resent correction, so they avoid the wise."

Madelyn had a gift for surrounding herself with people who made her feel good about herself. Over the years, she had cultivated a circle of friends, colleagues, and acquaintances who were uniformly enthusiastic about her ideas, supportive of her decisions, and reliably absent when it came to honest engagement that might have required her to reconsider anything. It had formed gradually, through the quiet and consistent removal of anyone who made her uncomfortable, and the equally quiet retention of everyone who did not.

She worked as a creative director at a marketing agency in Fenwick, a role that suited her considerable talent for visual storytelling and brand development. In the early years of her career, her gifts had been sharpened by the friction of working alongside people who challenged her thinking, including a demanding creative director whose rigor felt harsh at the time and proved invaluable in retrospect. Those years had produced her best work.

But as she rose through the agency and eventually took on the creative director role herself, something shifted. The friction that had once sharpened her began to feel like interference, and the mentors who had once spoken plainly to her began to feel like people who did not fully appreciate what she was trying to accomplish. One by one, without any formal decision or dramatic rupture, she had moved away from those who challenged her and toward those who affirmed her, and she only noticed, much later, what it had cost her.

Proverbs 15:12 says that a scoffer does not like to be reproved and will not go to the wise. Madelyn had not stopped valuing wisdom in any conscious sense. She still spoke about the importance of honest feedback and considered herself open to input. But her actions told a different story. The people she spent time with were the people who agreed with her, and the relationships she invested in were the relationships that cost her nothing in terms of self-examination.

There was a senior creative strategist at the agency named Doris, a woman of considerable experience and uncommon perceptiveness, who had tried on several occasions to offer Madelyn the kind of feedback that genuine mentorship requires. Madelyn had received each conversation with a surface politeness that masked a deeper resistance, thanking Doris, acknowledging the input, and returning to her office without having allowed any of it to change a single decision. Over time, Doris had stopped trying, recognizing that the door Madelyn presented as open was, in practice, firmly closed.

The creative team that formed around Madelyn reflected the preferences she had established. She hired people who were talented but deferential, and she ran brainstorming sessions that felt collaborative but were organized around the refinement of directions she had already chosen. The team produced work that was competent, consistent, and increasingly safe, and Madelyn told herself that consistency was a virtue and safety was a form of respect for the client. The agency began to lose pitches it had previously won, and clients who had once been loyal to her team began to move toward a newer agency producing work that was bolder and more resonant. The agency's leadership commissioned an independent creative review, and the consultant's report noted that the work had become internally consistent in ways that suggested a team no longer being genuinely challenged, operating in a closed loop without the benefit of meaningful dissent or outside influence.

Madelyn read the report and felt the particular discomfort of someone who recognizes the truth of something she has been carefully avoiding. The consultant had named, with professional precision, the exact condition that Proverbs 15:12 had described in the language of wisdom. She had organized her professional life around the avoidance of people who might correct her, and the work had become exactly as small as that avoidance had made it.

She thought about Doris, who had retired the previous year. She thought about the colleagues she had quietly moved away from, the mentors whose calls she had returned less and less frequently, the voices she had filtered out because they complicated what she wanted to do. Madelyn had kept the company that felt good, and lost the company that could have made her great. And the distance between those two things was visible now in every piece of work her team had produced in the last three years.

Proverbs 15:12 had known what she had not been willing to know. The scoffer does not go to the wise. And the life built without the wise is always smaller than it needed to be.

Day 1: Q&A

Q: What does Proverbs 15:12 reveal about the scoffer's relationship with wise and correcting voices?
A: Proverbs 15:12 reveals that the scoffer's avoidance of wise people is not accidental but deliberate; she has organized her relational life around protecting her existing beliefs, surrounding herself with those who affirm rather than challenge her. Madelyn's story illustrates this pattern precisely: she did not reject wisdom dramatically, but simply moved away from it quietly and consistently, until her life had grown smaller and less fruitful with every wise voice she had removed.

Q: How did Madelyn's avoidance of correcting voices affect the quality of her work and the health of her team? **A:** Madelyn's avoidance of correcting voices created a closed creative environment where her own perspective was the only one that genuinely shaped the work, producing output that was competent and consistent but increasingly predictable and stagnant. The independent review that eventually named this condition confirmed what the losing pitches had already signaled: the avoidance of wise voices had cost the team the very quality that made creative work worth producing.

Day 2: Explanation: Proverbs 15:12 identifies a pattern that is easy to miss because it develops gradually and feels, at each stage, like a reasonable preference rather than a dangerous avoidance: the scoffer does not drive wise voices away, she simply never seeks them out, gravitating without conscious decision toward the company of people who make her comfortable. This reveals the true condition of her heart, because a person who genuinely loves wisdom seeks it out even when it is uncomfortable, and a person who has placed her own comfort above growth will, without ever intending to, construct a life from which wisdom has been quietly excluded. Madelyn's story is a portrait of that construction, built one comfortable relationship at a time.

Day 3: Anecdote: A pastor led a growing congregation for many years with considerable skill, and in the early years of her ministry she maintained a small group of trusted advisors who knew her well enough to speak plainly when she was heading in the wrong direction. But as her platform expanded, she gradually stopped seeking them out, spending more time with those who celebrated her ministry without reservation, until the meetings became effectively nonexistent. Years later, a series of decisions that those advisors might have caught led to a painful season of conflict, and a trusted elder reflected afterward that the warning signs had been visible long before the crisis but that by then there was no one in her inner circle close enough to speak and trusted enough to be heard. Like Madelyn, she had not lost her love for wisdom. She had simply stopped going where wisdom lived.

Day 4: Warning: The warning of Proverbs 15:12 is not directed at people who openly reject wisdom but at those who avoid it quietly, describing themselves as open to correction while organizing their lives in ways that make receiving it impossible. The person caught in this pattern does not experience herself as avoiding wisdom; she experiences herself as choosing healthy relationships, establishing good boundaries, and exercising discernment, and all of those framings can feel true while being entirely false. The test is not how the relationships feel but what they produce, and if the people around you never challenge you, never correct you, and never make you genuinely uncomfortable, Proverbs is giving you a clear and urgent warning about the condition of your circle and the direction of your life.

Day 5: Encouragement: If Madelyn's story has stirred something in you, the path back begins with a single honest question: who in my life is positioned to tell me what I need to hear rather than what I want to hear, and am I actually going to them? Proverbs 15:31 promises that the one who listens to life-giving reproof will dwell among the wise, and that invitation is always open. Seek out one wise voice and let what they offer reach the place in you where growth actually happens.

Day 6: Why People Become Scorners: People rarely choose to avoid the wise in any conscious or deliberate sense; the pattern develops through the accumulation of small, individually reasonable choices that add up, over time, to a life from which correction has been quietly excluded. The causes vary: a person harshly corrected in a formative context may have learned that correcting voices signal danger rather than care, while a person who followed affirming relationships because they felt better may have simply never examined where that feeling was leading. Each of these paths is understandable, and none of them leads anywhere good. The only way forward is the honest recognition that the comfort being protected has been costing something far more valuable than the discomfort being avoided.

Day 7: Reflection Questions:

Q: Look honestly at the people you spend the most time with and seek out most consistently. Do any of them regularly challenge your thinking, correct your blind spots, or offer you reproof that is genuinely difficult to receive? If not, what does that reveal about the circle you have built and the kind of growth it can produce?

Q: Think about a wise person in your life, a mentor, a trusted friend, or a spiritual leader, from whom you have gradually drifted. What was it about their presence that made you uncomfortable, and is it possible that the discomfort was not a sign that the relationship was unhealthy but a sign that it was genuinely valuable?

Q: Madelyn told herself she was open to feedback while consistently organizing her work in ways that made genuine challenge impossible. In what ways might you be doing the same thing, using the language of openness while building structures, habits, or relationships that protect you from the correction you claim to welcome?

Q: Proverbs 15:31 says that the one who listens to life-giving reproof will dwell among the wise. Who is one specific wise person you could seek out this week, not for affirmation, but for the kind of honest input that has the power to make you genuinely better? What is stopping you from going to them?

Father,

We confess that we have sometimes chosen comfort over correction and affirmation over truth. We have moved away from the people who could have made us wise and toward the people who made us feel good about staying exactly as we are. Forgive us for the quiet avoidance that dressed itself as discernment, for the narrowing of our circles that felt like growth but was actually the removal of every voice that might have helped us grow. We ask You to restore in us a genuine love for the wise, a love that is willing to seek out correction even when it is uncomfortable, to remain in the presence of people who challenge us even when it would be easier to leave, and to receive reproof as the gift that Proverbs says it is. Show us the wise voices we have been avoiding, and give us the humility to return to them. Build around us the kind of community that sharpens rather than merely soothes, that loves us enough to tell us the truth, and that walks with us toward genuine wisdom rather than simply toward the feeling of being understood. We want to dwell among the wise. Teach us to go where they are.

In Jesus' name, Amen.

Prayer Thoughts for Today:

♦♦♦♦♦

~END PRAYER JOURNAL "THE SCORNER" ~

WISDOM IN FORGIVENESS

THE WISE

PROVERBS 17:9: (ESV)

"Whoever covers an offense seeks love, but he who repeats a matter separates close friends."

Jenna and her closest friend had been inseparable for years. They knew each other's families, finished each other's sentences, and had talked each other through some of the hardest seasons of their lives. So when her friend made a careless, cutting remark at a birthday party one Saturday afternoon, Jenna wasn't just embarrassed. She was blindsided. A few people laughed. Jenna laughed too, because what else do you do? She drove home with her hands tight on the wheel and spent the rest of the night replaying it, wondering how someone who knew her so well could say something like that so easily.

She told herself she was fine. She stayed busy, kept her head down at work, and answered her friend's texts with short, polite replies that said nothing. But the hurt didn't fade. It settled in. She started leaving her friend on read for hours, then days. When her friend tagged her in something funny online, Jenna scrolled past it without reacting. She wasn't trying to be cold. She just didn't know how to act normal when she felt anything but.

A mutual friend pulled her aside one Sunday and said, "You know she misses you, right?" Jenna nodded and changed the subject. She knew she should say something, but every time she got close to picking up the phone, she stopped herself. It wasn't stubbornness exactly. It was more like she didn't trust herself not to say something she'd regret, or worse, cry before she could get a word out. So she waited. Weeks passed. The silence between them started to feel permanent.

One night, Jenna sat on the edge of her bed and just started talking to God. Not a polished prayer, just honest words about how tired she was of carrying the whole thing around. She admitted she didn't really want to forgive her friend yet. She was still hurt. But she asked God to help her want to. That was the most she could offer that night, and somehow it was enough to get her to open her Bible.

She read through the parable of the unmerciful servant and sat with it for a long time. The servant had been forgiven an enormous debt and then turned around and refused to forgive someone who owed him almost nothing. Jenna didn't like how much she recognized herself in that. She thought about how many times God had extended grace to her without condition, and she started to wonder if holding on to this was really worth what it was costing her.

She prayed for her friend that night. Not a big, sweeping prayer, just a quiet ask that God would be good to her. It felt strange at first, praying for someone she was still upset with. But by the time she said amen, something in her chest had loosened just a little. Not gone, but lighter.

The next morning, she typed out a message, deleted it twice, and finally sent three words: "Can we talk?" Her friend replied in under a minute. They met that afternoon at the coffee shop on Maple where they used to split pastries and stay until closing. Jenna got there early and ordered something she didn't drink. When her friend walked in, they hugged before either of them said a word, and Jenna nearly lost it right there. The conversation was slow and awkward and honest. Jenna told her how much the comment had hurt, not to punish her, just because it was true and she needed her to know.

Her friend didn't make excuses. She put her face in her hands and said she had known something was wrong for weeks and had been too scared to ask. She apologized, and it was the kind of apology that didn't try to explain itself into nothing. Jenna believed her. The wall didn't come down all at once, but there was a crack in it now, and that felt like a start.

By the time they left, the afternoon had turned gray and cold, and neither of them had noticed. Jenna sat in her car for a minute before starting the engine. She didn't feel like everything was fixed. But she felt free in a way she hadn't in weeks, like she had put down something heavy she had been carrying for so long she had forgotten it wasn't supposed to be there.

Over the months that followed, their friendship settled into something steadier than it had been before. Not perfect, but more honest. Jenna noticed she had more patience with people in general. She was quicker to give others the benefit of the doubt, slower to assume the worst. The hurt had changed her, but not the way she feared it would.

She started sharing pieces of the story when it came up, not as a lesson, just as something that had happened to her. She told people the part she found most true: that forgiveness didn't mean pretending it didn't hurt. It just meant she stopped letting the hurt have the last word.

Looking back, Jenna was grateful she had sent that message, even when everything in her said to wait. God had met her in the middle of something messy and helped her find her way through. Her friendship was still standing, and so was she.

Day 1: Q&A:

Q: What did Jenna choose to do?
A: She forgave her friend, seeking God's wisdom through prayer and time in His Word. Rather than holding on to hurt and pride, Jenna chose to trust God's guidance and take the courageous step toward reconciliation.

Q: What blessing came?
A: Restored friendship and inner peace. Jenna's willingness to forgive opened the door to reconciliation, and in letting go of her hurt, she found a peace in her heart that she had not felt in weeks. What once seemed like an irreparable break became a bond made stronger by honesty, humility, and the grace of God.

Day 2: Explanation: James 3:17 "Wisdom from above is...full of mercy and good fruit." This verse reminds us that true wisdom does not come from our own pride or emotions, but from God, and it is always marked by mercy, humility, and a willingness to make peace. When we tap into His wisdom, we are equipped to respond to hurt not with retaliation, but with grace. The good fruit of that wisdom is seen in healed hearts, restored relationships, and a spirit set free from the grip of bitterness.

Day 3: Anecdote: A counselor shared how forgiveness healed decades-old wounds in a family. For nearly thirty years, two brothers had refused to speak after a bitter dispute over their late father's estate, and the silence had fractured the entire family around them. One brother, after seeking Christian counseling, made the courageous decision to reach out with a letter asking for forgiveness and offering it in return. What followed was a tearful reunion that neither brother thought possible, and the ripple effect of their reconciliation brought healing to children, grandchildren, and extended family members who had only ever known division. The counselor often used their story as a reminder that it is never too late for God to restore what bitterness has broken.

Day 4: Blessings and Rewards: Forgiveness brings freedom and restored relationships. When we release the weight of bitterness, we make room for joy, peace, and the fullness of life God intended for us. Forgiveness does not excuse the wrong done, but it breaks the chains that bind us to pain. As we walk in forgiveness, God honors our obedience by mending what was broken and drawing people closer together.

Day 5: Encouragement: God's wisdom empowers you to forgive and heal. When you feel too weak to let go of hurt, His wisdom steps in and gives you the strength you cannot find on your own. Through prayer and time in His Word, He guides your heart away from bitterness and toward wholeness. Trust that the same God who forgave you is working in you to bring healing to every broken place.

Day 6: God's Love and Redemption: His love covers all offenses and brings reconciliation. God's love is not conditional on our perfection but is poured out freely, even in the middle of our failures and pain. When we choose to forgive, we reflect His heart and open the door to the healing He alone can bring. His love is the foundation of every restored relationship, reminding us that no offense is too great for His grace to cover.

Day 7: Reflection Questions:

Q: Who do you need to forgive? Take a moment to sit quietly before God and ask Him to bring to mind anyone you may be holding resentment toward, whether a friend, a family member, or even yourself. Ask God for the courage and wisdom to take the first step toward forgiveness, trusting that He will meet you in that moment.

Q: How has forgiveness blessed you? Think about a time when you chose to let go of hurt and consider the peace, freedom, and restored relationships that followed as a result of that decision. Recognizing the blessings of forgiveness can strengthen your faith and encourage you to keep choosing grace, even when it is difficult.

Q: What wisdom have you gained from past hurts? Think about the painful seasons you have walked through and consider how God used those experiences to grow your faith, deepen your compassion, and shape your character. The hurts that once felt like setbacks were often the very moments God was preparing you to walk in greater wisdom and grace.

Q: How does God's forgiveness inspire you? Reflect on the countless times God has extended grace and mercy to you, despite your shortcomings, and consider how that same love can move you to offer forgiveness to those who have wronged you. Let His example be the motivation that pushes you beyond your own limitations and into a life marked by compassion and grace.

PRAYER JOURNAL

Merciful Father,

Thank You for the boundless forgiveness You offer me through Jesus. I confess that I have sometimes withheld forgiveness from others, holding onto grudges or letting hurt define my relationships. Forgive me for my stubbornness and for failing to reflect Your mercy. Please grant me wisdom and strength to forgive as You have forgiven me. Help me to let go of bitterness and to trust that healing comes through Your love. Give me humility to seek reconciliation, even when it is difficult, and to extend grace to those who have wronged me. Restore broken relationships, Lord, and bring peace where there has been pain. Teach me to forgive quickly and completely, and to remember how much I have been forgiven. Thank You for the freedom and joy that come from releasing others and myself from the burden of unforgiveness. May my life be marked by mercy, compassion, and the wisdom that comes from walking closely with You.

In Jesus' name, Amen.

Prayer Thoughts for Today:

✦✦✦✦✦

~ END PRAYER JOURNAL "THE WISE" ~

Always Seeing The Best In People

THE SIMPLE ONE

Proverbs 14:15: (ESV)

"The simple believes every word, but the prudent gives thought to his steps."

Bella had always seen the best in people. She grew up in a small town where neighbors dropped off casseroles when someone got sick and left their doors unlocked at night. Her parents settled disputes over fences and property lines with a handshake, and nobody thought much of it. That was just how things worked. Bella carried all of that with her when she moved to the city at twenty-two, not as a philosophy exactly, just as the only way she knew how to be.

The city was louder and faster than she'd expected, and her apartment was a forty-minute bus ride from the office. She needed a car. After a week of searching online listings between shifts, she found one that looked right: a silver sedan, clean in the photos, priced just under what she'd saved. She called the number, and the man who answered was easy to talk to, the kind of person who laughed at his own jokes and remembered her name by the end of the call. "One owner, low miles, never been in a wreck," he told her. "Honestly, I hate to let it go." She believed him without a second thought.

They met the next morning in a grocery store parking lot. The car had been freshly washed and smelled like a pine tree air freshener hanging from the mirror. The engine started on the first try. The man shook her hand, asked about her job, and said he was glad the car was going to someone who would take care of it. At one point, he glanced across the lot and said, "I've had two other people reach out this morning, so I can't promise it'll still be here this afternoon." Bella heard that and felt her chest tighten. She didn't want to lose it.

She didn't call her dad. She thought about it. Her hand even went to her phone, but she put it back in her pocket. She didn't want to seem like she couldn't handle things on her own. She didn't ask about a mechanic's inspection or request a vehicle history report, partly because she didn't know those were things she could ask for. She handed over almost every dollar she had saved since graduation, signed where he pointed, and drove back to her apartment feeling like she had finally figured something out.

For three weeks, the car was fine. She drove to work, found a grocery store she liked, and took a long route home on Fridays just because she could. Then one Tuesday morning it wouldn't start. The engine turned over twice, made a sound like something scraping, and quit. She sat in the parking lot turning the key for longer than made sense before she called a tow truck. At the shop, the mechanic pulled up a vehicle history report and set it on the counter in front of her. The car had been in two accidents. He listed what needed fixing and the total came to more than she had in her checking account.

She called the man's number from the repair shop's parking lot. It rang twice and went to a generic voicemail. She called again. Same thing. That night, she searched for the listing and found it had been removed. There was no name, no address, nothing she could trace. She sat in her car, which was now back at her apartment and not going anywhere, and stared at her phone for a while. She called her dad that night. She hadn't planned to, but she did, and when he picked up, she started crying before she could get a sentence out. He didn't say "I told you so" because she hadn't told him anything. He just listened. When she finished, he was quiet for a moment and then said, "You'll know better next time. That's nothing." It didn't fix anything. But she wrote it down anyway.

She kept the car and paid for the repairs in installments over four months. A coworker helped her find a mechanic she could trust, and that same coworker explained what a vehicle history report was and how to read one. Bella filed it away. Not as a lesson she'd been taught, but as something she'd earned the hard way.

She still saw the good in people. She didn't think that was wrong. But she had started asking more questions, slowing down when something felt rushed, and calling her dad before making big decisions, rather than after. It wasn't a transformation. It was more like a small adjustment, the kind you make when something costs you enough that you don't want to pay for it twice.

Day 1: Q&A:

Q: Why did Bella fall for a bad deal?

A: As a simple one, Bella's trusting nature and lack of experience made her vulnerable to being misled by someone with more knowledge or fewer scruples. She had never been taught to question the motives of others, so when the salesperson spoke with confidence, she accepted his words at face value. Without wise counsel or careful research, her good heart became an open door for deception.

Q: How can you protect yourself from being taken advantage of?

A: Seek advice from wise, experienced people before making big decisions. Take time to verify information, check reputations, and never let urgency rush you into a choice you haven't fully considered. Do your research, and pray for discernment.

Day 2: Explanation: Proverbs warns that Simple Ones are easily deceived because they lack experience and caution. They tend to believe everything they hear without questioning the source or motive. This does not mean they are foolish; it simply means they have not yet learned to look deeper. God wants us to be innocent, but also wise and careful in our dealings with others. Just as a shepherd protects his flock, God equips us with discernment so we are not left defenseless in a world that does not always have our best interests at heart.

Day 3: Anecdote: A friend once shared how he bought a laptop online without checking the seller's reputation. It never arrived. The loss was frustrating, but it became one of the most valuable lessons he ever learned. Now, he always investigates before spending money or trusting a new source.

Day 4: Warning: If you don't learn to ask questions and seek wisdom, others may take advantage of your good nature. Proverbs 14:15 says, "The simple believes everything, but the prudent gives thought to his steps."

Day 5: Encouragement: God wants to protect you and give you wisdom! He does not want you to walk through life afraid but equipped. He will teach you to balance trust with discernment so you can enjoy honest relationships and avoid unnecessary trouble.

Day 6: God's Love and Redemption: Even when you're deceived, God's love never fails. He sees every hurt, every loss, and every moment you felt foolish or alone. He is your defender and teacher, and He will use every experience to grow you in wisdom and grace.

Day 7: Reflection Questions:

Q: Have you ever trusted someone or something too quickly and ended up disappointed or taken advantage of? What did that teach you?

Q: What steps can you take to seek wise counsel or do your own research before making important decisions? Start by identifying two or three trusted people in your life, whether a mentor, pastor, or experienced friend, who you can turn to when facing significant choices. Make it a habit to slow down, gather information, and ask questions before committing, knowing that a little patience upfront can save a great deal of pain later.

Q: How do you balance being trusted and open-hearted with being cautious and discerning? Being trusting and discerning are not opposites; they work together when you choose to love people freely while still paying attention to their actions and patterns. Ask God to help you extend grace without abandoning wisdom, so your open heart remains a strength rather than a weakness.

Q: In what ways can you invite God into your decision-making process to help you avoid unnecessary trouble? Begin by bringing your decisions to God in prayer before acting on impulse or outside pressure. When you pause to seek His guidance through Scripture, wise counsel, and a quiet heart, you open yourself to the clarity and protection only He can provide.

PRAYER JOURNAL

Gracious God,

Thank you for being my protector and guide. I confess that at times I have trusted too quickly or acted without caution, leading to disappointment or trouble. Forgive me for not seeking Your wisdom or asking for help from those You've placed in my life.

Please give me discernment and a cautious heart. Help me to seek wise counsel, to do my research, and to wait for Your direction before making decisions. Teach me to balance trust with prudence, so I may walk in safety and peace.

Thank You for turning every experience into a lesson and for covering me with Your love and grace. May I grow in wisdom and become a blessing to others through what I learn.

In Jesus' name, Amen.

Prayer Thoughts for Today:

✦✦✦✦✦

~ END PRAYER JOURNAL "THE SIMPLE ONE" ~

THE POT STIRRER

THE FOOL

PROVERBS 18:2: (NIV):

"Fools find no pleasure in understanding but delight in airing their own opinions."

ora liked to start things. From the time she was young, she figured out that a single well-placed comment could crack open a room, and she never really lost the taste for it. It was not about being mean, at least not at first. She just liked to see what happened when she poked at something. The look on someone's face right after she said the thing no one else would say gave her a little rush she did not know how to explain.

She turned friendly arguments into something messier without much effort. In a group, she always knew which opinion would land wrong, and she would drop it right in the middle of things just to watch people scramble. She told herself it was wit. She was quick, she was sharp, and most of the time nobody could prove she had done it on purpose.

Her friends tried to keep up at first. They laughed when they could and changed the subject when they had to. But after a while, the group chat got quieter, and the hangouts felt less easy. Nora read that as boredom or sensitivity. She never considered that what she thought was honesty had started to feel like something else to everyone else in the room.

When people started pulling back, she noticed but did not understand it. The group chat went quiet. Invitations stopped. She told herself they were too sensitive, too wrapped up in their own feelings to handle a real conversation. She was just being herself. If that was too much for them, that was their problem.

She convinced herself she was the one being wronged. People were jealous, or they could not handle someone who actually said what she thought. So she doubled down. The more people pulled away, the louder she got, as if she could prove something to them by not needing them at all.

When someone actually tried to say something to her face, she laughed. She made a joke out of it or turned it back on them. "You are so sensitive. You cannot take a joke." Any doubt that crept in got buried fast, because being wrong was not something she was willing to sit with.

Her circle got smaller. The people who stuck around either did not push back or had learned it was easier not to. Nora told herself that was fine, that she preferred a smaller group anyway. People who could actually keep up. She believed that right up until the remaining friendships started feeling hollow too.

It crept into family, too. People stopped bringing up anything that might set her off. Relatives who used to look forward to seeing her started finding reasons to miss the same gatherings she was at. The conversations she used to love got replaced with small talk and short goodbyes nobody meant.

At work and school, it was the same story. People did not want to be partnered with her on projects. She stopped getting invited to things that were not required. She told herself she did not care, but being left out had a sting she could not quite shake.

Still, she would not budge. It was easier to believe she was smarter than everyone else, more honest, more real. Their discomfort was their problem. Anytime a thought crept in that maybe she had something to do with all of it, she pushed it back down. Being misunderstood was a much easier story to live with.

Then one afternoon, she heard them before she saw them. A group of people she used to know were laughing in a way she recognized, easy and loose. She caught enough to understand they were talking about how much calmer things had been. She stood just outside the doorway and did not go in. For the first time in a long time, the quiet on her end felt like something. Change did not come quickly. She still caught herself reaching for the old habits, the sharp word, the well-timed jab. But the emptiness was getting harder to argue with. Slowly, she started listening more than she talked. She started thinking about what she was about to say before she said it. Rebuilding the trust she had burned through took longer than she expected, and she did not always get it back. But she was starting to understand that getting a reaction and actually being known were two very different things.

Day 1: Q&A:

Q: Why did Nora keep provoking others?
A: She rejected correction, finding amusement in chaos and ignoring the pain she caused. Every attempt to reason with her was met with laughter or deflection, as if accountability were a joke only others had to face. She had mastered the art of avoiding consequences, never pausing long enough to consider the wounds she left behind.

Q: What did this lead to?
A: Nora's actions brought isolation and broken friendships, a result often seen in those who delight in foolishness rather than wisdom. The people she once called friends quietly slipped away, unwilling to keep paying the emotional cost of her chaos. In the end, her need to stir up trouble left her with nothing but the silence she had created.

Day 2: Explanation: *Proverbs 18:2 says, "A fool takes no pleasure in understanding, but only in expressing his opinion."* This kind of foolishness is not simply ignorance; it is a deliberate choice to value self-expression and amusement above genuine connection and truth. Fools prize their own entertainment over the well-being of others, using words as weapons rather than tools for understanding. When we refuse to listen and only seek to be heard, we close the door on wisdom and open it wide to conflict.

Day 3: Anecdote: A youth volunteer once shared how teasing a classmate drove that person away, never imagining at the time how deep the wound truly went. What began as harmless fun quickly became a pattern of mockery that chipped away at the classmate's confidence and sense of belonging. It took years of distance and a long, sincere apology to begin restoring the friendship, and even then, the trust had to be rebuilt piece by piece. Through that painful experience, the volunteer learned that words and actions carry real weight, long after the moment has passed. He now uses that story to remind young people that what feels like a joke to one person can feel like a wound to another.

Day 4: Warning: Seeking entertainment at others' expense destroys trust and community, eroding the very bonds that hold relationships together. When we treat conflict as sport, we wound people who deserve dignity and respect, often without realizing the lasting damage we leave behind. Proverbs 20:3 teaches, "It is to one's honor to avoid strife, but every fool is quick to quarrel."

Those who ignore this warning will find themselves surrounded by broken bridges and closed doors, reaping the bitter fruit of a life lived at others' expense.

Day 5: Encouragement: You can choose to be a peacemaker instead of a troublemaker, and that choice begins with a single decision to value people over conflict. God's wisdom brings unity and joy to those who pursue peace, replacing the empty thrill of strife with something far more lasting. When you commit to building up rather than tearing down, you reflect the very heart of God. The path of peace is not always easy, but it leads to the kind of relationships and community that truly flourish.

Day 6: God's Love and Redemption: God calls us out of foolish conflict and into His peace, inviting us to lay down pride and embrace the stillness only He can give. His love restores what strife has broken, healing wounds that bitterness and discord have left behind. When we seek His way, He empowers us to build healthy, loving relationships rooted not in self-interest, but in grace and truth.

Day 7: Reflection Questions:

Q: Have you ever stirred up conflict or provoked arguments just for fun or out of habit? Take an honest look at those moments and consider how they affected the trust, closeness, and health of the relationships involved.

Q: Why do you think some people find it entertaining or satisfying to create drama or discord among others? Reflect on whether you have ever been drawn to that same pull, and consider what it reveals about the deeper needs or insecurities that conflict can temporarily mask.

Q: What steps can you take to become a peacemaker instead of a troublemaker in your community or relationships? Think about one practical habit, such as choosing words carefully, listening before responding, or seeking reconciliation, that you could begin practicing this week to reflect God's peace in your interactions.

Q: How does God's call to peace and His power to restore relationships encourage you to change your approach? Consider a specific relationship or situation where conflict has taken root. How might surrendering that strife to God open the door to healing and restoration?

PRAYER JOURNAL

*H*eavenly Father,

Thank You for being the God of peace and unity. I confess that I have sometimes stirred up conflict or provoked arguments, caring more about my own amusement than the feelings of others. Forgive me for the hurt I have caused and the relationships I have damaged by my foolish actions. Please give me a heart that seeks understanding and reconciliation. Teach me to be a peacemaker, to use my words and actions to build trust and harmony instead of discord. Thank You for Your love that restores what has been broken and for Your power to bring healing where there is strife. Guide me to reflect Your peace in all my relationships.

In Jesus' name, Amen.

Prayer Thoughts for Today:

♦♦♦♦♦

~ END PRAYER JOURNAL "THE FOOL" ~

BROKEN PEACE

THE SCORNER

PROVERBS 22:10: (NIV):

"Drive out the mocker, and out goes strife; quarrels and insults are ended."

Whenever Daphne entered a room, something shifted. Not always loudly. Sometimes it was a comment just quiet enough to walk back if she had to, a slight edge in a greeting, a question that was really a test. The effect was hard to name at first but impossible to ignore once you had felt it a few times. People left her conversations unsettled in ways they could not quite explain, and the communities she joined developed fault lines that had not been there before she showed up.

She had lived in the Crestwood neighborhood for six years and had been present for nearly every conflict the community had seen in that time. There was a fence dispute with the homeowners' association. There was the falling-out between two families who had been close for over a decade, a friendship that came apart after Daphne retold a garden misunderstanding in a way that made forgiveness seem naive. There was the community meeting about the neighborhood park that turned into a two-hour argument about money and fairness and who really belonged there. Several long-time residents later said that meeting was the moment they stopped believing the neighborhood could work together.

Disputes involve more than one party, and communities carry tensions that go back long before any single person arrives. That is worth saying plainly. But there was a pattern, and once you had seen it enough times it was hard to unsee. She knew where people were most exposed and she pressed there. She framed things so that backing down felt like losing. She repeated what people told her in confidence, always in the right room, always at the wrong time. She asked questions that were not really questions.

Proverbs 22:10 says that when the scoffer is driven out, strife goes out, and quarreling and abuse cease. The verse is not describing someone who occasionally says the wrong thing. It describes someone whose presence is the source, not just the backdrop, of conflict. The strife that followed Daphne was not accidental. She generated it steadily, the way a fire generates heat, and she had lived inside it long enough that peace, when she encountered it, felt like something was wrong.

The Crestwood Community Center had been something the neighborhood was genuinely proud of. It ran a weekly gathering for elderly residents, an after-school program for kids, and a monthly community dinner that had become one of the few occasions when people from different parts of the neighborhood reliably showed up for each other. When Daphne joined the volunteer planning committee, the atmosphere changed within two meetings. She went after the committee chair, a steady and capable woman named Sylvia, not with better ideas but with questions about her motives. She raised alarms about the youth program without anything solid to back them up. She turned the monthly dinner into a debate about who was really being included and who was really in charge.

Sylvia tried to address it directly, the way a good leader does, with honesty and without cruelty. Daphne received the conversation as an injury. Every observation became an attack in her retelling, and she left with a story about Sylvia as a defensive, controlling person who could not handle being questioned. She told that story to enough people, and it found an audience. There were people who had small, manageable frustrations with Sylvia, and Daphne gave those frustrations a shape and a voice.
Three of the committee's best volunteers were gone within a month. The youth program coordinator stepped back because she was tired of the tension and did not see it ending. The monthly dinner, which had run without interruption for eleven years, was cancelled because the committee could not agree on the basics. The elderly residents' weekly gathering was scaled back because the people who had run it were no longer willing to show up somewhere that felt like a minefield.

The community center did not collapse. But it was smaller than it had been, and anyone paying attention knew when the shrinking had started. The people who stayed after Daphne moved on to other things described what changed in words that would have fit Proverbs exactly, though none of them would have known that. When she was no longer in the room, the arguing stopped. When she was off the committee, people who had not spoken to each other in months began, slowly, to try again. Daphne moved through all of it without ever seeming to notice that she was the one thing every conflict had in common. She thought of herself as someone who cared about fairness, who would not look away from a problem, who had the nerve to say what everyone else was too afraid to say. She had no way of seeing that the problems she named were often problems she had made, and that what she called courage looked, from the outside, exactly like what Proverbs had been warning about for thousands of years.

The peace she broke had taken years to build. It took years more to come back. She was not around for any of that. She had already moved on, to the next neighborhood or the next committee or the next room full of people who did not yet know what she carried with her.

Day 1: Q&A

Q: What does Proverbs 22:10 reveal about the connection between the scoffer and the strife that surrounds her?

A: Proverbs 22:10 reveals that the scoffer is not simply present when conflict occurs but is its active source. When she is removed, strife, quarreling, and abuse cease with her. Daphne's story illustrates this exactly. The conflicts around her followed a pattern directly connected to her presence and her gift for finding the fault lines in a community and pressing on them until they broke. When she moved on, the peace she had disrupted began to return.

Q: How did Daphne's disruption of the community center affect people who had no direct conflict with her?

A: Daphne's disruption affected people far beyond those directly involved in her conflicts. The elderly residents found their program reduced in size. The youth program lost its coordinator. The community dinner was canceled. None of these people had a conflict with Daphne. They simply paid the cost of her presence without ever being party to it. The damage a disruptor causes is never limited to those she is directly in conflict with. It radiates outward and touches everyone who depends on the community she has destabilized.

Day 2: Explanation: Proverbs 22:10 identifies the source of communal strife and prescribes the remedy with striking directness: drive out the scoffer and the strife goes with her. The scoffer is not simply someone who argues but someone whose presence makes argument inevitable and unresolvable. She is the catalyst, not merely a participant. Daphne's story illustrates this precisely: the tensions she exploited were real, but she processed them into something the community could not contain. Proverbs points to the person rather than the symptoms, knowing that when the source is removed, the conflict resolves.

Day 3: Anecdote: A neighborhood book club had met monthly for eight years with a warmth its members described as one of the reliable pleasures of their lives. When a new member joined who had a talent for turning literary discussions into personal confrontations, members who had spoken freely for years began choosing their words with care, draining the joy from every gathering. Two founding members stopped attending. When the new member eventually left, the original members described the return of the old atmosphere as immediate and unmistakable. She had not manufactured conflict from nothing but had simply brought to every gathering a quality of presence that made peace impossible to sustain.

Day 4: Warning: The person who disrupts communal peace rarely presents herself as a disruptor. She presents herself as someone who cares, who pays attention when others do not, who is willing to name what everyone else pretends does not exist. This presentation is often persuasive in communities with real and unresolved tensions. The warning of Proverbs 22:10 is not that every person who raises concerns is a scoffer. It is that the scoffer can be identified by the pattern of what her presence consistently produces. If conflict follows her arrivals and peace follows her departures, the question is not whether she raises real concerns but whether her presence makes the community capable of addressing them.

Day 5: Encouragement: If you are part of a community shaped by a chronic disruptor, the promise of Proverbs 22:10 is genuinely encouraging. The verse does not describe a situation beyond remedy; it describes a specific remedy and promises that it works. The strife a scoffer generates is not the permanent condition of your community. It is the condition of a community that has not yet addressed its source of disruption. Communities can recover. Relationships can be restored. Traditions that were derailed can be restarted. None of this is easy or instant, but all of it is possible. The first step is always honest recognition of the source, and the courage to act on what you see.

Day 6: Why People Become Scorners: Chronic disruptors rarely set out to cause harm. Most developed their patterns in environments where conflict was the primary form of engagement, and the skills that produce harmony were never modeled or taught. They arrived at their patterns through a logic that once made sense. Daphne did not experience herself as a disruptor but as someone who cared enough to speak. The tragedy was that her caring had become so entangled with conflict that she could no longer tell the difference between naming a real problem and creating one.

Day 7: Reflection Questions:

Q: Think honestly about the communities you are part of. Is there a pattern in which tension tends to increase after your involvement and decrease in your absence? What would it mean to take that pattern seriously rather than explaining it away?

Q: Daphne reframed every honest observation about her behavior as an attack on her character. When someone raises concerns about the way you engage in community, what is your first response? Do you receive it with genuine openness?

Q: Think about a specific community that was healthier before a particular person joined it and recovered after that person left. What did that experience teach you about the relationship between individual behavior and communal peace, and how does that lesson apply to your own presence in the communities you are part of?

Q: Proverbs 22:10 says that when the scoffer is driven out, quarreling and abuse cease. Is there a community in your life right now that is suffering under the weight of ongoing conflict? What would honest discernment about the source of that conflict require you to see, and what would it require you to do?

PRAYER JOURNAL

Father,

We ask You to search our hearts and show us honestly whether we have been sources of disruption in the communities You have placed us in. Forgive us for the times we have pressed on the fault lines of other people's relationships for reasons that served us rather than them. Forgive us for the arguments we have started in the name of honesty, the grievances we have amplified in the name of justice, and the peace we have broken in the name of courage. We confess that we have not always known the difference between naming a real problem and creating one, and we ask You to give us that discernment. We want to be people whose presence brings peace rather than disruption, whose words build up rather than tear down, and whose involvement in community makes it stronger rather than more fragile. Where we have caused damage, give us the humility to acknowledge it and the courage to repair it. Where we carry patterns that produce conflict without our awareness, bring those patterns into the light and give us the grace to change them. Teach us to love peace the way You love it, actively, sacrificially, and with a patience that outlasts the temptation to stir things up.

In Jesus' name, Amen.

Prayer Thoughts for Today:

✦✦✦✦✦

~ END PRAYER JOURNAL "THE SCORNER" ~

SERVING THE POOR

THE WISE

PROVERBS 19:17: (NIV)

"Whoever is kind to the poor lends to the Lord, and he will reward them for what they have done."

Ella could not shake the feeling that she was supposed to do something. It started small, a heaviness she felt whenever she passed someone sleeping on a bench or noticed a man standing at a busy intersection holding a cardboard sign. She would drive home and still see their faces. The feeling did not go away. If anything, it grew louder with each passing week. But every time she thought about actually doing something, the same questions crept in. Where would she even start? What could one person possibly do when the need was this big?

So she prayed. Not a one-time prayer, but the kind she kept coming back to every morning, asking God to show her where to go and what to do. A few weeks later, a friend casually mentioned a local ministry that served meals and provided resources to people experiencing homelessness. It was a brief comment, almost an afterthought, but Ella could not stop thinking about it. She looked up the ministry that same night. Nervous and unsure of herself, she signed up to volunteer.

Her first day was not what she expected. She had braced herself to feel awkward and out of place, but the team welcomed her like she had been there before. She told them upfront that she was new and honestly had no idea what she was doing. They laughed warmly and told her that was perfectly fine. Just watch, they said. Listen. Ask questions. Nobody expected her to have it all figured out on day one. She left that afternoon feeling something she had not anticipated: like she belonged.

For the first few weeks, Ella mostly watched. She noticed how the experienced volunteers greeted people by name, made eye contact, and never seemed to be in a hurry. Nobody was brushed off or treated like a problem to be managed. Even a simple hello carried something in it, a kind of warmth that said you matter. She also picked up on the practical things, like keeping extra socks on hand or knowing which shelters had available beds on a given night. Small details, but they made a real difference. One volunteer, Mr. Lee, took Ella under his wing. He had been serving with the ministry for over a decade, and there was a quiet steadiness about him that she found reassuring. He showed her the small things that went a long way, like handing someone a hot cup of coffee on a cold morning, or remembering a person's birthday. He taught her how to ask open-ended questions and how to simply sit with someone when there was nothing useful left to say. "It is not about fixing every problem," he told her one afternoon. "It is about showing up and letting people know they are not invisible."

Ella started bringing homemade cookies on Saturdays. It was a small thing, but people remembered. She began learning names and hearing stories she never would have expected. Thomas had worked as an engineer for years before everything fell apart. Priya was in her mid-twenties and quietly determined to rebuild her life after a stretch of circumstances that had knocked her sideways. The more Ella listened, the looser her assumptions grew. These were not strangers to be pitied. They were people with histories, humor, and hope.

There were hard days, too. Some nights, Ella drove home in tears, feeling the weight of how much need there was and how little she could actually fix. She would wonder if any of it was making a difference. During one of those moments, a woman on the team put a hand on her shoulder and said, "God multiplies what we offer. We are just called to show up and love." Ella held onto those words. They did not make the hard days disappear, but they made them easier to carry.

As the months went on, something in Ella shifted. She started taking on more, helping organize clothing drives and stepping in to coordinate volunteers for larger events. She realized that her knack for planning and logistics was genuinely useful, not just a background skill but something the ministry actually needed. Eventually, she found herself leading orientation sessions for new volunteers, offering the same reassurance that had steadied her on her very first day.

Over time, Ella watched lives begin to shift. Thomas landed a part-time job. Priya moved into a small apartment. Others found something harder to measure but just as real, a sense of belonging, a reason to keep going. Ella learned to celebrate every one of those moments, big or small, because she had seen firsthand that change rarely arrives all at once. What surprised her most, though, was how much she had changed. Her faith felt more grounded, more honest. She had seen God show up in unexpected places and through people she never would have thought to look for Him. She came to understand that serving well had less to do with having the right answers and everything to do with humility, patience, and staying open to learning. She was grateful for Mr. Lee and the others who had walked alongside her, and for the friendships she had built with the people she served.

Looking back, Ella could hardly believe how far she had come from that woman who had sat in her car outside the ministry building, too nervous to go in. What had started as a restless feeling and a lot of uncertainty had grown into something she could only describe as a calling. She saw the world differently now, and she was glad for it.

Her story became an encouragement to others who felt the same pull she once had but did not know what to do with it. She always told them the same thing: you do not need to have it all figured out before you start. Wisdom comes in the doing. It grows through listening, learning, and choosing to love, one small act at a time.

Day 1: Q&A:

Q: How did Ella approach serving?
A: She sought wisdom from experienced volunteers, humbly admitting she was new and willing to learn. She observed how they treated each person with dignity and listened closely to their guidance. Their example taught her that effective service begins with humility and a teachable heart.

Q: What blessing followed?
A: She witnessed people find jobs, housing, and renewed hope, watching lives slowly change through consistent acts of love and service. At the same time, her own faith deepened, and her assumptions gave way to compassion and humility. Serving others transformed Ella just as much as it transformed those she served.

Day 2: Explanation: *Proverbs 19:17 "Whoever is kind to the poor lends to the Lord…"* This verse reveals a profound truth: acts of kindness toward the poor are not merely human gestures but a direct transaction with God Himself. When we serve those in need, God takes it personally, as if we are lending to Him, and He promises to repay. This means no act of generosity goes unnoticed or unrewarded in His eyes. Serving the poor is therefore not just a moral duty but a sacred privilege, one that draws us into a deeper relationship with a God who sees and honors every sacrifice made in love.

Day 3: Anecdote: After leading his church in a weekly outreach to its local homeless community, the pastor noticed a remarkable shift in his congregation's spiritual life. Members who had once struggled with apathy began showing up with renewed purpose, deeper prayer lives, and a hunger for Scripture they had not experienced before. He became convinced that proximity to the poor had opened his people's hearts to God in a way that no sermon alone ever could.

Day 4: Blessing and Rewards: Serving with wisdom multiplies compassion and impact.
When we serve others with intentionality and wisdom, our efforts reach far beyond what we can see or measure in the moment. A

single act of kindness, offered thoughtfully, can restore someone's dignity, inspire another volunteer, and ripple outward in ways only God can trace. Wisdom in service also protects us from burnout, helping us give sustainably and joyfully rather than out of obligation. As we grow in discernment, our capacity to love deepens, and the impact of our service multiplies in ways that reflect God's abundance.

Day 5: Encouragement: God guides every act of service. Trust His wisdom.

When you feel uncertain about how or where to serve, you can rest in the assurance that God is already at work ahead of you. He does not call us to have all the answers but to take the next faithful step, trusting that His wisdom will illuminate the path. As you surrender each act of service to Him, He will direct your steps and multiply your efforts in ways you could never accomplish on your own.

Day 6: God's Love and Redemption: His love meets us as we serve others.

When we step out to serve others, we do not go alone. God's love shows up in the spaces between us and those we serve, softening hearts, bridging divides, and making His presence known in tangible ways. It is often in the act of giving that we most clearly receive His love in return.

Day 7: Reflection Questions:

Q: Where is God calling you to serve?

Take a moment to reflect on the people or places that stir compassion in your heart. That stirring is often God's way of pointing you toward your purpose. Ask Him to make the path clear and give you the courage to take the first step.

Q: Who can teach you how to serve well?

Think about the experienced, faithful people in your life or community who have already walked the path of service, as their wisdom and example can save you years of uncertainty. Ask God to connect you with a mentor who can guide, encourage, and challenge you to grow in your calling.

Q: How has serving changed your perspective? Reflect on moments when being around those in need shifted how you see the world, other people, or even yourself. Consider how those shifts have drawn you closer to God and shaped the person He is calling you to become.

Q: What blessings have you seen through service?

Pause to recall the specific moments when God showed up in your service, whether through a life changed, a friendship formed, or a quiet sense of His presence. Recognizing these blessings builds gratitude and strengthens your faith to keep serving with an open and expectant heart.

PRAYER JOURNAL

Compassionate Father,

Thank You for Your heart for the poor and for inviting me to share in Your care for those in need. I confess that I have sometimes turned away from opportunities to serve or acted without wisdom, failing to see the dignity and value in each person. Forgive me for my indifference, my busyness, or my reluctance to step outside my comfort zone. Grant me wisdom as I serve the poor and vulnerable. Open my eyes to see the needs around me and to respond with humility, generosity, and discernment. Teach me to listen well, to learn from those I serve, and to partner with others in ways that bring lasting hope and transformation. Guard me against pride or the temptation to serve for recognition. Instead, let my acts of service flow from a heart shaped by Your love and compassion. Thank You for the blessings that come when I share Your resources, time, and kindness with others. Restore my vision to see people as You see them, and fill me with a spirit of joy as I give. May my service point others to Your goodness and bring glory to Your name.

In Jesus' name, Amen.

Prayer Thoughts for Today:

✦✦✦✦✦

~ END PRAYER JOURNAL "THE WISE" ~

Keeping The Peace

THE SIMPLE ONE

PROVERBS 24:11-12: (NIV)

"Rescue those being led away to death; hold back those staggering toward slaughter. If you say, 'But we knew nothing about this,' does not He who weighs the heart perceive it? Does not He who guards your life know it? Will He not repay everyone according to what they have done?"

Eva had always been the kind of person who made things easier for everyone around her. Her colleagues knew her as warm, steady, and easy to talk to. She had a gift for reading a room, for sensing when tension was rising and quietly steering things back toward calm before anyone even noticed there had been a problem. Her supervisors appreciated her for it. Her coworkers trusted her with the kinds of things people don't usually say out loud. She listened well, never judged, and never made anyone feel small. Keeping the peace wasn't just something Eva did. It was something she believed in.

When Eva was assigned to a new project team at the manufacturing plant, she felt a quiet mix of excitement and nerves. The team had a reputation for being fast and capable, and on her first day, she could see why. They moved through their work with the kind of ease that only comes from years of doing the same thing. But it didn't take long for Eva to notice something that made her stomach tighten. They were cutting corners. Safety checks were skipped. Required paperwork went untouched. Lockout procedures before equipment repairs were treated more like suggestions than rules. "It saves time," one coworker told her with a shrug. "We've been doing it this way for years. Nothing's ever happened."

Eva felt uneasy in a way she couldn't shake. She had taken every training seriously and understood exactly why the protocols existed. But she was the newest person on the team, and that mattered to her more than she wanted to admit. She didn't want to come across as difficult or overly cautious. She didn't want to be the person who slowed everyone down or made things awkward on her first week. The others were experienced and confident, and Eva told herself that maybe they knew something she didn't. She stayed quiet and tried to focus on fitting in.

Weeks passed, and what had once felt alarming started to feel familiar. The shortcuts became part of the rhythm, and Eva's silence became part of it too. She thought about saying something more than once. She rehearsed the words in her head, imagined finding the right moment, the right tone. But every time she got close, she pulled back. She pictured the awkward pause, the sideways glances, the quiet shift in how people would see her. She told herself that as long as no one got hurt, it was better to leave it alone.

Then one rainy afternoon, everything changed. The team was pushing to finish before the shift ended when a machine malfunctioned. A coworker, not wanting to lose time, skipped the lockout procedure and reached in to fix it. The scream that followed stopped everyone cold. His hand was caught in the gears. People shouted. Someone ran for help. The whole floor came to a standstill.

Eva stood there, heart pounding, watching it all unfold. The worker was rushed to the hospital. Production stopped. An investigation began. When the plant manager gathered the team and started walking through the safety violations that had led to the accident, Eva couldn't look away from the floor. The guilt she felt wasn't abstract. It was specific and heavy. She had seen the shortcuts. She had known better. And she had said nothing. Someone was seriously hurt, and her silence had played a part in that. That night, Eva lay awake going over every moment she had let slide. Every skipped check. Every time she had felt that knot in her stomach and swallowed it down anyway. She kept coming back to the same thought: she had known. She had known, and she had chosen comfort over courage.

She realized that keeping the peace wasn't always the same as doing what was right. Sometimes real care for the people around you looked like disruption. It looked like saying the uncomfortable thing, asking the hard question, and risking the awkward moment so that something far worse didn't happen later.

The next morning, Eva asked to meet with her supervisor. Her voice shook as she laid it all out: the habits she had witnessed, the silence she had kept, and the regret she was carrying. She wasn't sure what to expect. But her supervisor listened without interrupting, thanked her for coming forward, and took it seriously. The company followed up with mandatory safety training for every team and made it clear that reporting concerns was not just allowed but expected.

Eva learned something she would never forget: silence isn't neutral. It has weight. It has consequences. She made a promise to herself that she would never again let her need to be liked outweigh her responsibility to do what was right. She had always thought of herself as someone who cared about people. She understood now that caring sometimes meant saying the thing no one wanted to hear.

Over time, something shifted in how her coworkers saw her. They still came to her when they needed someone to listen. But now they also came to her when they needed someone to be straight with them. She became the kind of person people looked to, not because she always made things comfortable, but because they knew she genuinely cared. She encouraged others to speak up and made sure that doing the right thing was never treated as optional. Looking back, Eva was grateful for the lesson, even though it came at a cost. It had made her braver, steadier, and far more certain that her voice was worth using.

Day 1: Q&A:

Q: Why did Eva stay silent?
A. Eva's deep-seated need to be liked and keep the peace made it nearly impossible for her to speak up, even when she knew something was wrong. Rather than risk the discomfort of conflict, she stayed silent, convincing herself that going along with others was the same as doing right.

Q: How can you find the courage to speak up?
A: Start by asking God for boldness and wisdom, trusting that He equips you to do what feels hard. Remember that genuine love for others isn't just about keeping them comfortable. It sometimes means speaking a difficult truth that could protect or save them. When you speak from a place of care rather than judgment, honesty becomes an act of love.

Day 2: Explanation: Proverbs teaches that wisdom is not just about knowing what is right, but having the courage to act on it, even when doing so is costly. The Simple One is easily swayed by the crowd, choosing silence over confrontation to avoid discomfort or disapproval. But Scripture makes clear that God calls us to something higher: to be voices of protection and truth for those around us. Proverbs 31:8-9 urges us to "speak up for those who cannot speak for themselves," a charge that requires boldness over comfort. God does not ask us to be popular; He asks us to be faithful, and that faithfulness sometimes means standing alone for what is right.

Day 3: Anecdote: A supervisor once recalled how, as a new employee, she noticed a recurring safety hazard on the floor but said nothing, not wanting to seem difficult or overstep her role. Weeks later, a coworker was injured in an incident directly tied to that same hazard, and the guilt of her silence stayed with her long after the wound healed. The experience became a turning point. She realized that staying quiet had not protected the peace. It had only delayed harm. From that moment on, she committed to speaking up whenever she saw something wrong, regardless of how uncomfortable it made her feel. Today, she makes it a priority to remind those she leads that their voices are not just permitted, but needed.

Day 4: Warning: Silence in the face of wrong can have serious consequences, not just for those who are harmed, but for those who choose to say nothing. When we witness injustice or danger and do nothing, we become passive participants in the outcome. Proverbs 24:11-12 is a sobering reminder that God sees our inaction and holds us accountable for the help we withheld. He does not accept the excuse that we simply did not know, for He who weighs the heart understands what we saw and chose to ignore.

Day 5: Encouragement: God knows how hard it is to speak up, and He does not ask you to do it in your own strength. He promises to equip you for every good work. He honors your gentle spirit and your desire for peace, but He also calls you to be brave and wise when the moment demands it. Do not underestimate the power of your voice. A single word spoken with courage and love can protect someone from harm, change the course of a situation, or give others the permission they need to speak up. Your willingness to be used by God, even in uncomfortable moments, is itself an act of worship.

Day 6: God's Love and Redemption: If your silence has ever caused regret, know this: God's grace is greater than your mistakes, and His forgiveness is not conditional on how perfectly you have spoken up in the past. He does not hold your fear against you. Instead, He meets you right where you are and offers you a fresh start. Just as Eva found the courage to go to her supervisor and make things right, God invites you to take that same step, trusting that it is never too late to do what is right. He is actively at work in you, shaping your character, renewing your mind, and building the wisdom and courage you need for the moments ahead. His love does not just cover your past. It empowers your future. Every day is a new opportunity to grow, to speak up, and to be the voice that someone else desperately needs to hear.

Day 7: Reflection Questions:

Q: Is there someone in your life right now who needs you to speak up on their behalf? What is holding you back, and what would it look like to take one small, courageous step toward using your voice for them this week?

Q: Think about a time when you witnessed something wrong but chose to stay quiet. What held you back? What did that silence cost you or someone else, and what would you do differently today?

Q: What fears or concerns keep you from speaking up in difficult situations? Are you afraid of rejection, conflict, or being misunderstood? How might surrendering those fears to God free you to act with greater courage and conviction?

Q: As you look ahead, what is one specific area of your life where God might be calling you to use your voice more boldly? What would it look like to respond to that call this week, and who in your life could help hold you accountable?

PRAYER JOURNAL

Dear Lord,

Thank You for Your patience and mercy toward me. I confess that sometimes I have stayed silent when I should have spoken up, especially when something was wrong or unsafe. Forgive me for allowing fear or a desire to keep peace to silence my voice.

Grant me the courage to stand for what is right and to speak truth with love and humility. Help me to recognize when my words are needed to protect others or honor You. Fill me with Your wisdom so I can be gentle yet bold and use my voice for good.

Thank you for redeeming my past mistakes and giving me new opportunities to make a difference. May I always rely on Your strength as I grow in wisdom and courage.

In Jesus' name, Amen.

Prayer Thoughts for Today:　　　　　✦✦✦✦✦

~ END PRAYER JOURNAL "THE SIMPLE ONE" ~

ON MY OWN TERMS

THE FOOL

PROVERBS 19:20: (NIV)

"Listen to advice and accept discipline, and at the end you will be counted among the wise."

Bella never saw much point in learning from other people's experiences. She took pride in figuring things out for herself, and she genuinely believed she could handle whatever life threw at her without anyone's help. When someone tried to share a lesson they had learned the hard way, Bella would drift off, change the subject, or offer a polite but dismissive smile. In her mind, those conversations were just people projecting their own mistakes onto her, and she wasn't interested.

At family gatherings, the older relatives would tell their stories. They talked about the chances they had missed, the decisions they wished they could take back, and the things they had eventually learned from all of it. Bella would sit there half-listening, quietly convinced that she was built differently. "That might have happened to you," she'd say with a shrug, "but I'll be fine." She meant it. It never really occurred to her that those warnings were meant for her too.

Her friendships were no different. When a close friend opened up about how cutting corners had cost her a job, or how not speaking up had ruined a relationship, Bella would listen just long enough to respond. "You just had bad luck," she'd say. "That's not going to happen to me." She wasn't trying to be cold about it. She just genuinely believed that her drive and her instincts would carry her past the places where others had stumbled.

At work, it was the same story. Coworkers who had been around longer would pull her aside and flag things they had learned the hard way. Bella appreciated the gesture, but she rarely took it seriously. She skipped trainings she thought were redundant, glossed over checklists that felt like overkill, and filed away deadline warnings under things that probably wouldn't matter. She had her own way of doing things, and it had worked well enough so far.

Then things started going sideways. Deadlines slipped. Important steps got missed. Projects that should have gone smoothly fell apart in ways that felt random and unfair. Each time something went wrong, Bella was genuinely caught off guard. She couldn't figure out where all these problems were coming from, and the frustration started to build.

The consequences she had heard about in other people's stories were now showing up in her own life, and she still didn't make the connection. A project collapsed because she had skipped the steps everyone told her mattered. A friendship went cold after she brushed off something her friend had really needed her to hear. Both times, Bella was blindsided. It didn't register that these were the exact outcomes she had been warned about.

Instead of sitting with what had happened, Bella looked outward. The circumstances were unusual. The timing was bad. Other people had dropped the ball. She cycled through every explanation except the most obvious one: that she had been told, more than once, exactly how to avoid what had just happened to her.

What Bella kept missing was the gift right in front of her. Every story, every warning, every honest conversation had been an offering from someone who genuinely wanted her to do well. She hadn't seen it that way. She had seen it as noise, as people underestimating her. But it was never that. It was care, and she had been walking past it for years.

Over time, people quietly stopped trying. Friends who used to share things with her started keeping more to themselves around her. Coworkers stopped pulling her aside. Her family, who had once been so eager to pass things down, learned that it wasn't worth the effort. Nobody made a big announcement about it. They just slowly stopped offering, and Bella barely noticed.

Even then, Bella held onto her confidence. She figured life was just harder than it should be, that she had been dealt a rougher hand than most. If she pushed a little harder, if the timing finally broke her way, things would turn around. She was sure of it. It took losing her job, watching a close friendship fall apart, and missing an opportunity she had been working toward for a long time before something finally shifted in her. Sitting alone with all of it, she started replaying conversations she had tuned out years ago. Warnings she had shrugged off. Stories she had half-listened to. For the first time, she let herself wonder if those people had actually known something she didn't.

It didn't happen overnight, but Bella began to change. She started asking questions instead of deflecting them. She listened in conversations without already forming her response. She began to understand that accepting someone else's wisdom didn't make her less capable. It made her smarter. And slowly, the same people who had stopped offering began to open up again, because they could tell she was finally ready to receive what they had always wanted to give her.

Day 1: Q&A:

Q: Why did Bella ignore the lessons of others?

A: She rejected instruction, convinced that the mistakes and consequences others had faced simply didn't apply to her. Her pride led her to believe she was above the need for guidance, making her blind to the very wisdom that could have protected her.

Q: What can happen when someone ignores advice and insists on doing things their own way, even when others try to help?

A: Bella repeated the same failures, experiencing avoidable hardship that wiser choices could have spared her. By dismissing the counsel of others, she forfeited the growth and progress that come from simply being willing to listen.

Day 2: Explanation: *Proverbs 26:11 says, "As a dog returns to its vomit, so fools repeat their folly."* This vivid image captures the senselessness of returning to the same destructive patterns when wisdom and warning have already been made available. Fools are not simply those who lack intelligence, but those who refuse to receive instruction, choosing familiar failure over the discomfort of change. By ignoring the wisdom freely offered through others' experiences and God's Word, they suffer hardship that was never meant for them.

Day 3: Anecdote: A camp counselor once shared that he ignored repeated warnings about fire safety during an outdoor trip, convinced he knew better than the required precautions. One careless moment near the campfire resulted in a minor but painful burn that left a lasting mark. As he treated the wound, he thought back to every warning he had brushed aside, realizing each one had been offered to protect him. The experience humbled him, and he committed to listening more carefully to those with wisdom and experience. He later told his campers that the burn taught him more about pride than it did about fire.

Day 4: Warning: Refusing to learn from others guarantees repeated mistakes, locking you into a cycle of pain that wisdom could have broken. Proverbs 19:20 urges, "Listen to advice and accept discipline, and at the end you will be counted among the wise." The path to wisdom is not paved with stubborn self-reliance, but with the humility to receive what God and others are offering you.

Day 5: Encouragement: You don't have to learn every lesson the hard way, because God has already placed wisdom within your reach. He provides wise people in your life whose experiences are meant to spare you from avoidable pain. His Word is filled with real stories of triumph and failure, each one offering a lesson you can apply before you ever make the mistake yourself. Receiving this wisdom is not a sign of weakness; it is one of the greatest gifts God offers to those who are willing to listen.

Day 6: God's Love and Redemption: God's love provides wisdom through His Word and His people, ensuring that guidance is always within reach. Even if you've refused it before, He is patient and ready to offer instruction again, extending second chances to all who are willing to receive them. His desire is not to condemn your past choices, but to lead you toward a wiser, fuller life rooted in His grace.

Day 7: Reflection Questions:

Q: Have you ever ignored advice or lessons from others, believing their experiences didn't apply to you? What was the outcome, and looking back, can you see the wisdom that was being offered to you at the time? How might things have been different if you had chosen to listen?

Q: Why do you think it's sometimes hard to learn from other people's mistakes instead of making our own? Is it pride, a belief that your situation is unique, or simply the human desire to experience things firsthand? What does your answer reveal about areas where God may be calling you to grow in humility and trust?

Q: How can you become more open to receiving wisdom from those around you? What practical steps can you take, such as seeking out a mentor, spending more time in God's Word, or simply choosing to listen more before responding?

Q: In what ways does God provide you with opportunities to learn and grow, even after you've made repeated mistakes? Think about the people He has placed in your life, the experiences He has allowed, and the wisdom found in His Word. How has He used these to redirect your path?

eavenly Father,

Thank You for surrounding me with people who share wisdom and lessons from their own journeys. I confess that I have sometimes ignored advice, believing I had nothing to learn from others' experiences. Please forgive my pride and stubbornness. Open my heart and mind to receive instruction and to learn from both the successes and failures of those around me. Help me to recognize that Your wisdom comes in many forms and through many voices. Thank You for second chances and for Your patient love that guides me toward growth. Teach me to be humble and eager to learn, so I can avoid needless mistakes and walk in the path You've prepared for me.

In Jesus' name, Amen.

Prayer Thoughts for Today:

✦✦✦✦✦

~ END PRAYER JOURNAL "THE FOOL" ~

THE LOUDEST VOICE

PROVERBS 14:3: (NIV)

"A fool's mouth lashes out with pride, but the lips of the wise protect them."

Meredith had never learned the art of silence. Growing up in the small river town of Dellwood, she had always believed that the person who spoke the most knew the most. Her mother tried to teach her otherwise. Her teachers tried. Even her childhood friends drifted away one by one, worn down by the relentless current of her words. But Meredith always found a way to make their leaving their problem, never her own.

By her mid-thirties, Meredith had built a modest career as a community organizer in Hargrove. She was loud and visible, and she mistook those two things for leadership. She sat on three neighborhood committees and made sure her voice rose above everyone else's. Her words came fast and sharp, delivered with the kind of confidence that only comes from never once stopping to wonder if you might be wrong.

The women around her noticed. They noticed the way she laughed at quieter women, brushing careful thoughts aside with a wave of her hand. She mocked anyone who paused to think, as if taking your time was a sign of weakness rather than wisdom. She called them slow. She called them timid. She never once called them right, even on the days when they clearly were.

There was a woman named Clara Osei who served on the same housing committee. Clara was soft-spoken and methodical, the kind of person who showed up to every meeting with a folder full of annotated documents. When she spoke, you could feel the weight of preparation behind her words. Meredith found her insufferable. She would cut Clara off mid-sentence, finish her thoughts with the wrong conclusion, and say it all so loudly that others just went along with it. Clara never fought back. She simply waited.

The housing committee had been asked to review a proposal for a new development on the east side of Hargrove. Meredith had skimmed the summary document and declared herself ready. She pushed the committee toward a quick approval, mocked anyone who asked for more time to review it, and publicly embarrassed a younger member who raised questions about the flood risk data, calling her concerns overblown and dramatic.

The vote passed. The development was approved. Meredith celebrated loudly.

Fourteen months later, the first reports came in. The environmental assessment had missed a critical drainage issue. The eastern parcels sat on land that had been quietly flooding for decades, a fact documented in a county report from eleven years earlier, a report that Clara had cited in her notes, notes that Meredith had never read. The development stalled. Lawsuits followed. Three families were left in financial ruin. The story made regional news.

Meredith's name appeared in the coverage. Not favorably.

In the weeks that followed, she found herself in a strange and unfamiliar quiet. The calls she expected from allies never came. The meetings she had always dominated started happening without her. The room had stopped waiting for her to fill it.

She began, slowly and painfully, to sit with herself in a way she never had before. One evening she picked up the old committee notes and read through Clara's careful documentation. She saw the flood data. She saw the county report. She saw the questions that had been raised and dismissed, many of them dismissed by her own loud and careless words. The scorner's tongue, Proverbs warned, carried a rod for her own back. Meredith had never believed that. She believed it now.

What hit her hardest was not the embarrassment, though that was real and it stayed. It was realizing that her foolishness had never been hidden. She had put it on display at every meeting, in every room, every time she mistook volume for wisdom. At least a silent fool conceals what she does not know. Meredith had been announcing hers from the front of every room she had ever walked into.

Restoration came slowly and without any fanfare. Meredith started showing up to meetings without speaking first. She sought out Clara, not to make a grand apology, but to genuinely listen to the kind of thinking she had spent years dismissing. Clara welcomed her without ceremony and without resentment, and that quiet grace humbled Meredith more than any confrontation ever could have.

She never became a quiet woman. But she learned the difference between a voice that serves and a voice that performs. She learned that wisdom does not rush to be heard, and that the fool who speaks before she thinks does not just embarrass herself. She wounds others, and the damage does not always stop when the talking does.

Dellwood, the little river town where she grew up, had a saying her mother used to repeat: A full pitcher makes no sound. Meredith had spent thirty-five years being very, very loud. She spent the next thirty learning what it meant to finally be full.

Day 1: Q&A

Q: What is the difference between a fool and a scorner?
A: A fool acts without thinking, but a scorner goes further. She not only rejects wisdom but mocks those who pursue it. Proverbs 14:3 warns that her words carry a self-inflicted consequence. The scorner does not hide her ignorance. She broadcasts it and calls it confidence.

Q: Can a scorner change?
A: Yes, though Scripture warns she is difficult to reach. Proverbs 9:7 cautions that correcting a scorner invites insult, but Proverbs 21:11 notes that when a scorner is punished, the simple are made wise. Consequences open ears that words could not. It was not a sermon that reached Meredith. It was the weight of what her pride had cost.

Day 2: Explanation: Proverbs 14:3 says, "In the mouth of the foolish is a rod of pride, but the lips of the wise will preserve them." A rod was an instrument of punishment. The fool's own words become the very thing that beats her. She does not need an enemy to bring her low. Her tongue does the work.
The scorner is not simply ignorant. She is aggressively ignorant, convinced that her way of seeing the world requires no refinement. She speaks to dominate, to dismiss, and to protect herself from the discomfort of being wrong. Every word she uses to silence others is another swing of the rod against her own back.
Speech is never neutral. The scorner's words reveal exactly what she has refused to become.

Day 3: Anecdote: Researchers call it the illusion of explanatory depth. People consistently overestimate how well they understand complex systems until they are asked to explain them. The moment they try, the gap between what they assumed they knew and what they actually know becomes undeniable. The scorner lives permanently inside that illusion. Meredith's reckoning came when she sat alone with a document she had never read and realized the answers had always been there. She simply had not been willing to be the kind of person who looked for them.
The illusion of competence is loudest in those who have never been truly tested. Wisdom waits quietly for the test to come.

Day 4: Warning: The scorner's greatest danger is not that others will stop listening to her, though they will. It is that she will stop hearing herself. Pride builds a wall that grows thicker with every dismissal, until she can no longer receive correction because she has trained herself to experience it as an attack.

Proverbs 13:1 warns that a scorner does not listen to rebuke. This is not stubbornness alone. It is a condition that hardens with use. She has made herself an island. She may be loud on that island, but she is alone.

The warning is this: do not wait for a consequence as large as the one Meredith faced before you examine your words. The rod is already in the mouth. Every proud and careless sentence is another swing.

Day 5: Encouragement: There is grace available for the woman who recognizes herself in this story. Recognition itself is evidence that the heart has not fully hardened. James 1:5 promises that God gives wisdom generously and without reproach. He does not remind the seeker of all the years she spent without it. He gives it cleanly and without a lecture.

She does not have to earn her way back. She simply has to begin, choosing in the next conversation to listen before she speaks. The mouth that once carried a rod can become a mouth that carries life.

Day 6: Why People Become Scorners: No one becomes a scorner overnight. The pattern develops over time, often rooted in experiences that made vulnerability feel dangerous. Controlling the room felt safer than being at its mercy, and mockery became a habit before it was ever recognized as one.

Fear is often at the root. Fear of being wrong, of being seen as less than, of the silence that might reveal something she is not ready to face. The scorner fills every quiet space with noise because quiet is where the questions live.

Understanding this does not excuse the harm. It does, however, invite compassion alongside accountability. Healing begins not just with behavioral change but with the honest work of addressing what the noise was always covering.

Day 7: Reflection Questions:

Q: In what areas of your life do you speak most confidently? When did you last genuinely examine whether that confidence is rooted in knowledge or in habit?

Q: Think of a person in your life who speaks less but often proves to be right. What has your response to that person revealed about your own relationship with pride?

Q: Has there been a moment, like Meredith's, when your words caused harm that you later had to face? What did that experience teach you, and have you fully received the lesson?

Q: What would it look like, practically and specifically, for you to become a woman whose words preserve rather than wound, beginning in the very next conversation you have?

PRAYER JOURNAL

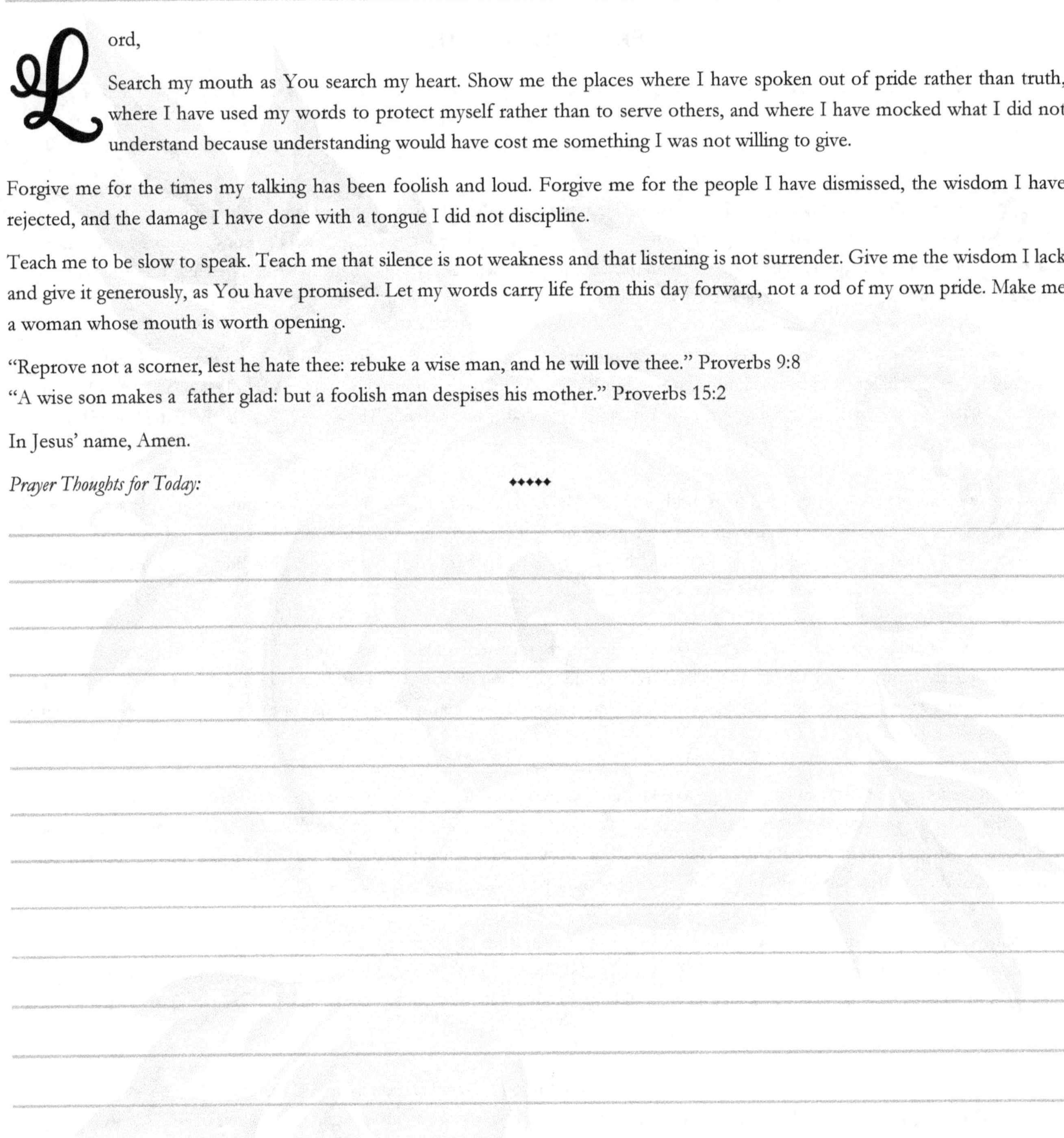

L ord,

Search my mouth as You search my heart. Show me the places where I have spoken out of pride rather than truth, where I have used my words to protect myself rather than to serve others, and where I have mocked what I did not understand because understanding would have cost me something I was not willing to give.

Forgive me for the times my talking has been foolish and loud. Forgive me for the people I have dismissed, the wisdom I have rejected, and the damage I have done with a tongue I did not discipline.

Teach me to be slow to speak. Teach me that silence is not weakness and that listening is not surrender. Give me the wisdom I lack and give it generously, as You have promised. Let my words carry life from this day forward, not a rod of my own pride. Make me a woman whose mouth is worth opening.

"Reprove not a scorner, lest he hate thee: rebuke a wise man, and he will love thee." Proverbs 9:8
"A wise son makes a father glad: but a foolish man despises his mother." Proverbs 15:2

In Jesus' name, Amen.

Prayer Thoughts for Today:

＋＋＋＋＋

WISDOM IN MARRIAGE

THE WISE

PROVERBS 24:3-4: (ESV)

"By wisdom a house is built, and by understanding it is established; by knowledge the rooms are filled with all precious and pleasant riches."

David and Maria had always loved each other. That was never the question. But somewhere along the way, the closeness they once shared started slipping through their fingers. Small misunderstandings piled up, conversations turned into arguments, and the silences between them grew longer and heavier. Both of them felt frustrated and unheard, and neither quite knew how to find their way back to each other.

The tension had a way of bleeding into everything. Even simple things, like deciding what to do on a weekend or dividing up household responsibilities, could spiral into an argument. Rather than working through it, they each pulled away. David buried himself in work. Maria poured her energy into the kids and her social commitments. They were living in the same house but growing further apart.

Then one evening, after a fight that left them both drained, Maria sat alone in the kitchen and cried. She wasn't just sad. She was scared. She wondered if this was just how things were going to be. Later that night, David found her there, and something in him softened. For the first time in a long while, they talked, really talked. Neither had all the answers, but they both admitted they were hurting, and they both agreed they didn't want to give up.

A week later, Maria brought up an idea. There was a couple at their church, older, steady, the kind of couple whose marriage Maria had quietly admired for years. She asked if David would be willing to sit down with them. He wasn't exactly eager, but he said yes. When they met, the couple didn't lecture. They just listened, then gently shared some of their own hard seasons and what had helped them come through.

That conversation gave them enough courage to take the next step. They signed up for marriage counseling. It felt awkward at first, sitting across from someone they barely knew and talking about their most private struggles. But their counselor was patient, and the tools she gave them were practical. They learned to say what they felt without it turning into an attack, to listen without jumping in, and to address small tensions before they grew into something bigger.

Forgiveness kept coming up in their sessions, and for good reason. Both of them had been carrying things, old hurts, unspoken expectations, quiet disappointments they had never voiced. Letting go of those things wasn't easy, but as they did, something shifted. Apologies started coming more naturally. So did forgiveness. Old wounds began to heal, and slowly, trust started to rebuild.

Maria started noticing the things David did right and saying so out loud. David started asking Maria about her day and actually listening. The small gestures they had stopped making, a thank you, a word of encouragement, a moment of real attention, began to reappear. The tension that used to hang over their conversations started to lift.
Slowly, their marriage began to feel like something good again. They laughed together more. They started going on date nights. Some mornings, they would sit with their coffee before the house woke up, just the two of them, and it felt easy. Their kids noticed too. The home had a different feel, lighter and warmer, and that mattered.

Their marriage wasn't perfect. Disagreements still happened. But now when they did, David and Maria faced them differently, with more humility, more patience, and a genuine desire to work it out rather than win. The wisdom they had received gave them something to stand on when things got hard.

They also began praying together, something they had let go of years before. Inviting God back into their marriage brought a kind of closeness they hadn't expected. It helped them keep perspective, especially in the stressful moments when it would have been easy to snap at each other.

Looking back, they were grateful, not just for where they had landed, but for the courage it took to ask for help in the first place. Their story spread quietly through their community, and before long, they found themselves sitting across from other couples who were struggling, listening and sharing the same way that older couple had once done for them.

Their marriage became a quiet testimony to what is possible when two people choose to keep going. Through listening, forgiveness, and a lot of grace, David and Maria found their way back to each other, and in doing so, reminded everyone around them that even the hardest seasons don't have to be the last word.

Day 1: Q&A:

Q: What steps did David and Maria take to turn things around?
A: They started by being honest with each other, which took more courage than either expected. From there, they reached out to trusted mentors and eventually a counselor. They didn't just listen to the advice they received; they put it into practice, even when it felt uncomfortable. They chose humility over pride, and consistency over perfection. Over time, those small and intentional steps transformed their marriage from one filled with silence and tension into one rooted in love and renewed trust.

Q: What was the blessing that came from their willingness to seek help?
A: The blessing was a stronger, more joyful marriage, one built on honesty, forgiveness, and genuine encouragement. David and Maria found themselves laughing together again, growing spiritually as a couple, and facing life's challenges as a united team rather than opponents. Their home became a place of peace rather than tension. What had once felt broken was not only restored but made more beautiful through the wisdom and grace they had chosen to embrace together.

Day 2: Explanation: Ecclesiastes 4:9 "Two are better than one... If either of them falls down, one can help the other up." In this passage, Solomon reminds us that marriage is not meant to be walked alone. God designed the relationship between husband and wife to be one of mutual support, where each partner lifts the other in moments of weakness or struggle. When David and Maria hit their lowest point, it was their commitment to each other and to seeking help together that kept them from giving up. Rather than retreating into isolation, they chose to lean in, reaching out to mentors, a counselor, and ultimately to God. That willingness to be vulnerable and interdependent is exactly what Solomon describes: two lives intertwined, stronger together than either could ever be apart.

Day 3: Anecdote: James and Renee had been married for eleven years when a sudden job loss and financial strain pushed their relationship to the breaking point. Resentment and fear had replaced the warmth they once shared, and both quietly wondered if they had reached the end. It was then that an older couple from their church, married for over forty years, stepped in and offered to walk alongside them. Week after week, they listened, prayed with them, and shared hard-won lessons about perseverance, trust, and choosing love even when it felt impossible. Slowly, James and Renee found their footing again, and today they credit those wise mentors as the turning point that saved their marriage.

Day 4: Blessing and Rewards: Wisdom brings unity, joy, and lasting love.
When a couple chooses to pursue wisdom together, they invite God's blessing into the very foundation of their marriage. Unity grows as two hearts align around shared values, honest communication, and a willingness to serve one another. Joy follows

naturally, not because life becomes perfect, but because they face every season with grace, gratitude, and the assurance that they are not alone. And lasting love is not simply a feeling that fades with time, but a daily choice rooted in commitment, forgiveness, and trust. This is the reward God promises to those who seek His wisdom: a marriage that reflects His faithfulness and endures through every storm.

Day 5: Encouragement: God's wisdom together. He delights in blessing marriages.
No matter where your marriage stands today, God invites you to bring it to Him and seek His wisdom together. He is not a distant observer but a loving Father who takes joy in seeing husbands and wives grow closer to Him and to each other. When you open His Word, pray side by side, and pursue wise counsel, you are not just solving problems; you are building something eternal. Trust that every step taken in faith, no matter how small, is seen and honored by a God who delights in blessing the marriages surrendered to Him.

Day 6: God's Love and Redemption: God heals, restores, and strengthens every relationship surrendered to Him.
No matter how broken or strained a relationship may feel, nothing is beyond the reach of God's healing love. He does not simply patch what is damaged. He restores it to something whole, new, and more resilient than before. When a couple surrenders their marriage to Him, they open the door to a redemption that only He can provide, one that goes far deeper than any human effort alone. His strength becomes their strength, sustaining them through seasons of doubt, conflict, and change. This is the promise of a God who is in the business of redemption, turning broken things into testimonies of His grace.

Day 7: Reflection Questions:

Q: Where do you need wisdom in your relationships? Is there an area where you have been relying on your own understanding rather than seeking guidance from God or someone wiser?

Q: Who can you learn from? Think of a couple or a person whose relationship you genuinely admire. What is one step you could take to invite their wisdom into your life?

Q: How can you encourage your spouse or close friend this week? What is one specific thing you can say or do to remind them that they are seen, valued, and not alone?

Q: What blessings have come from seeking wisdom together? Take a moment to reflect on the ways your relationships have grown when you chose humility, honesty, or the courage to ask for help.

PRAYER JOURNAL

aithful Lord,

Thank You for the gift of marriage and for Your loving presence in our relationship. I confess that I have not always acted with wisdom, patience, or grace toward my spouse. Please forgive me for harsh words, selfish actions, or for drifting away from the unity You desire for us. Grant me wisdom to love, serve, and encourage my spouse as You have loved me. Teach me to listen deeply, to communicate kindly, and to seek understanding even when we disagree. Give us both humility to admit when we are wrong, and the willingness to forgive quickly and completely. Help us seek Your guidance together in every decision, pray for one another, and build a marriage that honors You. Thank You for the blessings that come from walking in unity and for the ways You use our relationship to shape and refine us. Restore areas where we have grown distant, and renew our commitment to one another and to You. Fill our home with Your peace, joy, and love, and make our marriage a testimony of Your faithfulness.

In Jesus' name, Amen.

Prayer Thoughts for Today:

✦✦✦✦✦

~ END PRAYER JOURNAL "THE WISE" ~

BEING LED

THE SIMPLE ONE

PROVERBS 14:15: (NIV)

"The simple believe anything, but the prudent give thought to their steps."

ucy had always found it easier to let someone else take the wheel. She was the youngest of four in a loud, lively household, and somewhere along the way she figured out that going along with her siblings was just simpler than pushing back. They picked the games, they picked the shows, and she went with it. By the time she got to school, that pattern had already settled into her bones. She had a good group of friends, and she genuinely loved being part of it. She just never felt the need to be the one deciding where they were all headed.

That habit followed her right into high school. When it was time to pick classes, she looked at what her friends were signing up for and did the same. Clubs were no different. She joined them without really asking herself whether she cared about any of it. When someone asked what she thought, she'd shrug and say, "I'm good with whatever," and she meant it. Going with the flow felt natural to her, almost like a skill she had quietly perfected.

Relationships worked the same way. If her friends liked someone, Lucy found a way to like them too. When her friends started dating, she felt a quiet pull to keep up, even though she wasn't sure she was ready or even what she was looking for. She borrowed their preferences, their patterns, their inside jokes. It was never calculated. It was just easier than figuring out her own. Her faith, if you could call it that, worked the same way. She went to church because her parents expected it. She joined the youth group because her friends were there. She said the right things in Sunday school without really sitting with what any of it meant. She never dug deeper, never asked hard questions, never brought her real thoughts to God. She just accepted what was handed to her and moved on.

But as graduation got closer, something started to feel off. Her friends were talking about college, career plans, what they believed about God and life and the future. Lucy would nod and agree, but inside she felt strangely empty. The more she tried to match their excitement and certainty, the more she realized she didn't have any of her own. Their dreams were not necessarily her dreams. Their convictions did not quite land for her. But she kept drifting along because she did not know what else to do, and the last thing she wanted was to disappoint anyone.

The turning point came during an ordinary afternoon in class. Her teacher asked everyone to write an essay titled "What Do You Believe?" Lucy opened her notebook and stared at the blank page for a long time. Her mind filled with fragments of things she had heard from other people, but nothing that felt like her own. The longer she sat there, the more a quiet dread settled in. She genuinely did not know what she believed. She felt like she had been floating for years without ever noticing there was no anchor. That night she sat on the edge of her bed, turning it all over in her mind. She thought about all the years she had spent nodding along and going with the crowd, and she felt the weight of it in a way she never had before. She had never really asked God what He thought. She had never brought her questions to Him or asked for direction. She had been chasing comfort and approval for so long that she had never stopped to ask what she actually needed.

She felt the sting of regret, but underneath it something else stirred too. It was not too late. She picked up her Bible, not out of obligation this time, but because she genuinely wanted to hear from God for herself. Her first prayers were clumsy and uncertain, but they were honest. She started writing in a journal, putting her questions on paper, pressing into the parts of her faith she had always glossed over.

She also reached out to a mentor from her youth group, someone she had always admired but never really talked to. That woman listened well and pushed Lucy to seek God's voice in the everyday, not just the big moments. They started meeting regularly, and slowly, Lucy began to find her footing. It was not always comfortable. Some of those conversations were hard. But something real was growing in her, something that felt like peace and purpose all at once.

Over time, Lucy learned what it actually meant to seek wisdom. She learned to sit with decisions before making them, to listen for God's voice instead of just the loudest opinion in the room. She understood now that real faith was not about having all the answers. It was about wrestling with the questions, owning your mistakes, and trusting that God was present through all of it. She found that He was. And she found that her own voice, shaped slowly by prayer and Scripture and honest reflection, was worth listening to.

Looking back, she wished she had started sooner. But she was grateful. She had learned something that could not be borrowed or inherited, only discovered. The easiest road is not always the right one, and real fulfillment does not come from blending in. It comes from knowing who you are, what you believe, and whose you are. From that point on, Lucy resolved to seek God first, trusting that He would give her the wisdom and courage she needed for wherever life was headed.

Day 1: Q&A:

Q: Why did Lucy struggle to make decisions on her own?
A: As a simple person, Lucy never developed her own convictions or discernment, so she depended on others instead of seeking God's guidance. Without a personal faith to anchor her, she drifted wherever the opinions of those around her led, never pausing to ask God what He wanted for her life.

Q: How can you develop your own sense of direction and conviction?
A: Spend time in God's Word, pray for discernment, and ask wise mentors for help. Practice making small decisions thoughtfully, paying attention to how God speaks through Scripture, peace, and godly counsel. As you build this habit, you will grow in confidence and learn to let God lead you step by step.

Day 2: Explanation: Proverbs teaches that the Simple Ones can drift through life without an anchor, easily swayed by whoever or whatever is nearest. Without a foundation of wisdom, every new voice becomes a compass, and every passing pressure shapes the next decision. God wants us to grow in understanding so we can make choices based on His truth, not just convenience or pressure. When we pursue wisdom intentionally, we begin to live with the kind of clarity and purpose that only comes from being rooted in Him.

Day 3: Anecdote: A youth leader once shared that he spent years agreeing with others just to keep the peace, never wanting to cause tension or stand out. He admitted that while it felt safe on the surface, he secretly felt empty and unsure of who he really was. When he began reading Proverbs and journaling his prayers, something began to shift. He heard God's voice more clearly and recognized his own values and convictions. Over time, that daily discipline transformed him from someone who simply went along with the crowd into a leader who could guide others with wisdom, confidence, and grace.

Day 4: Warning: If you never learn to make decisions for yourself, you may miss out on God's best for your life. Drifting through life on the opinions of others can slowly pull you away from the unique calling and purpose God has specifically designed for you. When we fail to seek Him, we risk settling for a life shaped by crowd opinion rather than divine intention. Proverbs 3:5-6 encourages us to "trust in the Lord with all your heart…and He will make straight your paths." This promise is personal. God wants to be your guide, not just a background voice, and He is faithful to lead those who genuinely seek Him.

Day 5: Encouragement: God delights in guiding you personally, and He is never too busy or too distant to speak into the details of your life. You don't have to have everything figured out before coming to Him; He meets you right where you are, in the questions and the uncertainty. As you seek Him through prayer, Scripture, and quiet reflection, He will give you clarity, courage, and a sense of purpose that can't be shaken by other people's opinions. The more you lean into His guidance, the more confident you will become in the unique path He has laid out for you. Trust that He who began a good work in you is faithful to carry it through to completion.

Day 6: God's Love and Redemption: God's love meets you even in your confusion and uncertainty, and He is never disappointed by your need for guidance. He sees every moment you have drifted, every decision made out of fear or people-pleasing, and He responds not with condemnation but with compassion. His grace is the very thing that makes transformation possible, drawing you gently back to Him no matter how far you may have wandered. He patiently leads you into wisdom and confidence, teaching you to hear His voice more clearly with each passing day. As you surrender your need for outside approval and place your trust fully in Him, He gives you a firm foundation for every step ahead, one that no opinion, pressure, or circumstance can shake.

Day 7: Reflection Questions:

Q: Have you ever let others make decisions for you without considering what you truly believe or want? How did that affect you?

Q: What steps can you take to develop your own convictions and seek God's direction in your life? Begin by spending daily time in Scripture and prayer, asking God to reveal His will and shape your understanding of who He has called you to be. As you grow in that discipline, pay attention to the values that stir within you, seek counsel from a trusted mentor, and allow God to confirm your convictions through His Word and the peace He places in your heart.

Q: Who can you turn to for wise counsel and support as you learn to make decisions rooted in your faith and values?

Q: How does trusting in God's plan help you find clarity and confidence when facing important choices? When you trust that God already knows the outcome, it frees you from the pressure of having to figure everything out on your own. His peace guards your heart and guides your steps, giving you the confidence to move forward even when the path is not yet fully clear.

*H*eavenly Father,

Thank You for being my anchor and guide. I confess that I have sometimes let others make decisions for me, instead of seeking Your will and learning to think for myself. Forgive me for lacking conviction and for drifting through important moments without prayer or reflection.

Please help me to develop discernment and a heart that longs for Your truth. Teach me to seek You first in every decision and to build my life on Your wisdom, not on the shifting opinions of others. Give me the courage to trust Your direction and to grow in confidence as I follow You.

Thank You for meeting me in my uncertainty and for patiently guiding me into Your purpose. Help me to walk each day with clarity, strength, and faith in Your loving plan.

In Jesus' name, Amen.

Prayer Thoughts for Today:

~ END PRAYER JOURNAL "THE SIMPLE ONE" ~

FIERCELY INDEPENDENT

THE FOOL

PROVERBS 12:15: (NIV)

"The way of fools seems right to them, but the wise listen to advice."

Maya prided herself on being fiercely independent. Growing up, she had watched her mother work two jobs without complaint, never asking anyone for a favor, and Maya had taken that quiet resilience as the highest form of strength. She carried that belief with her to college, convinced that asking for help was a sign of weakness and that every challenge was hers alone to conquer. When her college offered study groups, Maya declined without hesitation, certain she could master the material on her own. During group projects, she brushed off her teammates' suggestions and pushed forward with her own ideas, unwilling to admit when she was struggling or unsure.

As deadlines approached, Maya found herself overwhelmed. She spent sleepless nights hunched over her laptop, rereading the same paragraphs until the words blurred. Coffee cups lined her desk like a row of small surrenders. Her grades began to slip, and a quiet panic settled in her chest that she refused to name. Still, she rejected her classmates' offers to share study notes and ignored the flyers for free tutoring posted outside the library. "I don't need anyone," she told herself, even as anxiety gnawed steadily at her confidence.

Her friends noticed her stress and gently encouraged her to talk to professors or join tutoring sessions. Her roommate, Destiny, once sat beside her and said, "Maya, there's no trophy for suffering alone." Maya laughed it off and changed the subject. She feared that accepting help would make her look incapable, not just to others, but to herself. When she failed her first major exam, she blamed the test's unfairness and the professor's unclear instructions rather than face the harder truth.

Instead of learning from this setback, Maya doubled down on her isolation. She skipped group meetings and ignored classmates' emails, telling herself she simply didn't have time for distractions. She stayed in her room on Friday nights while laughter drifted down the hallway from Destiny's study group. Her relationships suffered quietly. Friends grew weary of her closed-off attitude and eventually stopped knocking on her door or saving her a seat in the dining hall.

The more Maya withdrew, the harder school became. She missed important announcements shared only in study groups and misunderstood assignments she was too proud to ask about. When her biology professor offered a voluntary review session specifically for students who were struggling, Maya packed up her bag and walked out, telling herself she would figure it out at home. She never did.

By the end of the semester, Maya was exhausted and deeply discouraged. Her grades were the lowest they had ever been, and the campus that had once felt full of possibility now felt vast and indifferent. She watched from a distance as classmates celebrated exam results together, hugging in the hallways and posting photos of study sessions that had clearly paid off. They had built something she hadn't had a community, and she faced her disappointments entirely alone.

Maya finally reached a breaking point when she received an official warning letter about her academic standing. She sat on her bed and read it three times, her hands trembling slightly. For the first time, she stopped deflecting and asked herself a hard question: What if the problem wasn't the tests, or the professors, or the workload? What if the problem was her? She thought about Destiny's words. She thought about the study groups she had turned down, the office hours she had avoided, the notes she had refused. Help had been available at every turn. She simply hadn't been willing to receive it.

That evening, Maya sent Destiny a short, awkward text: "Hey. Is there still room in your study group?" The reply came in seconds, a string of enthusiastic emojis and a meeting time. When Maya showed up the next afternoon, she half-expected pity or judgment. Instead, she was handed a highlighter and pulled into a conversation about the very chapter she'd been stuck on for two weeks. Working together, the material clicked in ways it never had alone. The encouragement and accountability of her peers reignited something in her that isolation had nearly extinguished.

As Maya began to accept support, her confidence steadily returned, and her grades improved. She visited her professor's office hours and discovered that what had seemed like a cold, unapproachable authority was actually a person who genuinely wanted her to succeed. She realized that true strength wasn't about doing everything alone; it was about knowing when to seek help and having the humility to value others' wisdom. Her relationships deepened, and she found unexpected joy in both giving and receiving support.

Looking back, Maya regretted how much time and energy she'd wasted trying to prove herself. She now understood that pride and isolation had only held her back. By opening herself to community, she discovered the blessing of shared growth and mutual encouragement.

Maya's story became a powerful testimony to her friends and younger students. She encouraged others not to let pride keep them from the help they needed. Her journey showed that wisdom and strength are found in humility, teachability, and connection with others.

Through her experience, Maya learned that God places people in our lives for a reason, not to make us feel weak, but to remind us that we are never meant to walk alone.

Day 1: Q&A:

Q: Why did Maya refuse to accept help from others?
A: She believed that independence was the highest form of strength, shaped by watching her mother handle hardship without ever asking for help. To Maya, reaching out to others felt like an admission of failure, a sign that she was incapable or weak.

Q: What was the result of her attitude?
A: Maya became increasingly isolated and overwhelmed, and her grades dropped to the lowest they had ever been. In clinging to her independence, she missed out on the support, encouragement, and wisdom that had been available to her all along.

Day 2: Explanation: *Proverbs 12:15 says, "The way of fools seems right to them, but the wise listen to advice."* Like Maya, we can become so convinced that our own way is right that we shut out the very people God has placed in our lives to guide and support us. Rejecting help and isolating ourselves from wisdom leads to unnecessary struggle, while choosing humility opens the door to growth, community, and lasting support.

Day 3: Anecdote: A teacher once shared that, early in her career, she tried to handle every classroom problem entirely on her own, convinced that asking for help would make her seem inexperienced or unqualified. For months, she struggled in silence, spending long hours after school trying to solve challenges that her colleagues had already solved. It wasn't until a veteran teacher noticed her frustration and gently offered guidance that she began to open up. She eventually realized that seeking advice from experienced colleagues not only made her job easier but also helped her students thrive in ways she never could have achieved alone.

Day 4: Warning: Turning away from help and community leads to burnout and missed opportunities, leaving us to carry burdens that were never meant to be carried alone. Proverbs 11:14 teaches, "Where there is no guidance, a person falls, but in an abundance of counselors there is safety." Pride may feel like protection, but it is often the very thing that leaves us most vulnerable.

Day 5: Encouragement: You don't have to face challenges alone; God has already placed people around you who are equipped to help carry what feels too heavy to bear by yourself. Just as He used Destiny to reach Maya, He uses mentors, friends, and community to speak wisdom and encouragement into our lives. When we humble ourselves to receive that support, we don't become weaker; we become more of who God created us to be.

Day 6: God's Love and Redemption: God's love invites us to lay down our pride and receive His help, often given through others, because He knows we were never designed to carry life's burdens in isolation. Just as a loving Father runs to meet the returning prodigal, He meets us right where our self-sufficiency has run out, with open arms and no condemnation. Even if we've spent months or years resisting support, His grace does not grow impatient; it simply waits, ready to welcome us back into fellowship and shared wisdom. He redeems the time we lost to pride and uses our restored humility as a testimony that encourages others to do the same.

Day 7: Reflection Questions:

Q: Have you ever avoided asking for help because you feared looking weak? What happened as a result? There was a time I struggled in silence rather than risk being seen as incapable, and it only made things harder. Looking back, the cost of my pride far outweighed any discomfort I would have caused by asking for help.

Q: How can letting go of pride open you to new opportunities for growth? When we release pride, we become teachable, and teachability is where real growth begins. Humility creates space for God to work through others in ways our self-reliance never could.

Q: Who in your life offers support and wisdom you've been hesitant to receive?

Q: How does God's loving invitation to community encourage you to accept help when you need it? God designed us for relationships, not isolation, which means accepting help is not weakness but obedience to His design. His open arms remind us that receiving support is part of walking in His love.

*L*oving Father, Thank You for the people You've placed in my life to encourage and support me. Forgive me for the times I let pride and fear keep me from accepting help or advice. Teach me the humility to ask for guidance and the wisdom to learn from others. Help me to build relationships that honor You and to grow in community, not isolation. Thank You for Your patient, gracious love that invites me to walk alongside others.

In Jesus' name, Amen.

Prayer Thoughts for Today:

✦✦✦✦✦

~ END PRAYER JOURNAL "THE FOOL" ~

THE WEIGHT THAT WAS BUILT

Proverbs 19:29: (NIV)

"Penalties are prepared for mockers, and beatings for the backs of fools."

Vanessa had spent twenty years building a reputation in the coastal town of Sunshine Coast, and most of what she built was ruin. Not her own, at least not at first. She had always told herself she was too smart for that. The ruin she left behind belonged to other people: neighbors whose names she quietly poisoned, colleagues whose careers she chipped away at with carefully placed half-truths, and anyone careless enough to get between her and something she had decided was hers. She had grown up watching her grandmother run the most respected dry goods store in Sunshine Coast and inherited the building when the old woman passed. Her grandmother had treated that corner property as a place of honest work and fair dealing. Vanessa had other ideas. She opened a boutique on the ground floor and rented the space above it to short-term visitors, using both to collect information and plant herself at the center of every conversation that mattered in town.

She sat on the tourism board, the historic preservation committee, and the merchant association. She showed up everywhere and answered to no one. When a new restaurant started drawing foot traffic away from her boutique, she filed noise complaints and let rumors about health violations circulate until people started believing them. When a woman named Priscilla Hanes was nominated to chair the merchant association, Vanessa worked behind the scenes to undermine her, planting doubts about Priscilla's finances and her past. None of it was true. All of it worked.

The people of Sunshine Coast were not blind. They had seen what Vanessa was for years. But she had made herself useful in enough places that pushing back felt like too great a risk. She understood that perfectly well, and she used it. If you needed something done in this town, you needed Vanessa. And if you needed Vanessa, you did not dare cross her.

For years, the pattern held. Vanessa collected favors, properties, and influence the way some people collect debts. She bought the vacant lot next to her boutique and pushed through a zoning variance in six months that should have taken two years. Construction on a small inn broke ground. She allowed herself the quiet satisfaction of someone who had never once stopped to wonder whether any of this would eventually come back around.

The first sign came as a state audit. A regional oversight body had received an anonymous complaint about the zoning variance, and whoever filed it had included documents that could only have come from someone on the inside. Vanessa convinced herself she knew who was responsible and went after them. She was wrong. Her retaliation fell on someone who had nothing to do with it, and that mistake drew more attention, which brought two more complaints.

The audit grew. Investigators pulled records from the tourism board and the preservation committee. What they turned up was not always technically criminal, but it painted a clear picture: procedural manipulation, conflicts of interest, years of abusing the trust people had placed in her. A local journalist picked up the story and ran a series of reports over four consecutive weeks. Each one landed harder than the last.

The merchant association voted to remove her. The tourism board suspended her while the audit played out. Her rental bookings dried up as the coverage spread, and three business relationships she had counted on for years quietly dissolved within a single month. The zoning variance for the inn was pulled pending a full review, and construction stopped. The lot sat there, open and idle, a concrete foundation with nothing rising above it, visible from the main road through the center of Sunshine Coast. Priscilla Hanes was elected chair of the merchant association the same month Vanessa was removed. She did not gloat or make a point of it. She simply went to work, quietly rebuilding the trust that had been wearing away for years.

Vanessa did not take any of it with grace. She told anyone who would still listen that she was the victim here, that jealousy was behind it, that small-minded people had always resented a woman who actually knew how to get things done. She filed a defamation claim against the journalist. It was dismissed within weeks. She tried to pull together a counter-campaign, but the allies she had assumed were loyal turned out to be far fewer than she had imagined, and the ones who remained were no longer willing to be seen standing next to her.

Proverbs 19:29 does not describe punishment as something that drops from the sky without warning. It speaks of judgment as the inevitable destination of a path already chosen. The language is not of surprise but of consequence, not of accident but of arrival. Vanessa had been walking toward this place for twenty years. The road had simply, finally, run out.

What made her story worth sitting with was not how dramatic the collapse was but how complete. She had built everything she had on the suffering of other people, and when it came down, it came down all the way. There was no partial accounting, no soft landing. The same care she had taken in dismantling others was, in the end, applied to her. What came was not disproportionate. It was exact.

The concrete foundation sat for two years before the property was sold to cover outstanding debts. The buyers were a young couple who knew nothing of its history. They cleared the lot, put in a small community garden, and opened it to anyone who wanted to come. Neighbors who had once given that corner of town a wide berth began stopping there on their morning walks. The place where so much of Vanessa's scheming had been staged became, over time, somewhere people simply gathered without a second thought.

Sunshine Coast did not forget what had happened. But it healed. The people who had been quieted for years found their voices again. The relationships that had been poisoned by suspicion slowly came back to life. The healing began, as it so often does, right where the damage had gone deepest.

Day 1: Q&A

Q: What does Proverbs 19:29 mean when it says penalties are prepared for mockers?
A: The word "prepared" is significant. It declares that punishment is already in place, already waiting. The mocker does not stumble into judgment accidentally. She walks toward it with every act of contempt. Vanessa's story illustrates this not as a dramatic intervention from outside but as the natural arrival point of a road she had been building for decades.

Q: Is the judgment described in this proverb always public and visible, or can it be internal?
A: The verse pairs mockers with fools, penalties with beatings. The doubling communicates certainty through repetition. The preparation of penalties is not a threat. It is a description of how the world works. Vanessa did not need an enemy to bring her down. She built the instrument of her own collapse with the same hands she used to dismantle others.

Day 2: Explanation: Proverbs 19:29 reads, "Penalties are prepared for mockers, and beatings for the backs of fools." The parallelism is deliberate: doubling communicates certainty through repetition. The mocker is not simply someone who laughs at the wrong things but someone who has made contempt a way of life, scorning correction and treating the suffering she causes as proof of her own superiority. The preparation of penalties is not a threat issued in anger. It is a description of how the world works, and Vanessa did not need an enemy to bring her down.

Day 3: Anecdote: Historians who study corrupt systems note a pattern called the credibility trap. Power built through deception must be sustained through more deception, and the structure grows larger while its foundation grows weaker. Vanessa's collapse followed this pattern exactly. The anonymous complaint was not the cause of her downfall. It was simply the moment the foundation gave way under a weight that had been building for twenty years. The credibility trap has no exit that does not require honesty, and honesty is the one thing the scorner has trained herself never to offer.

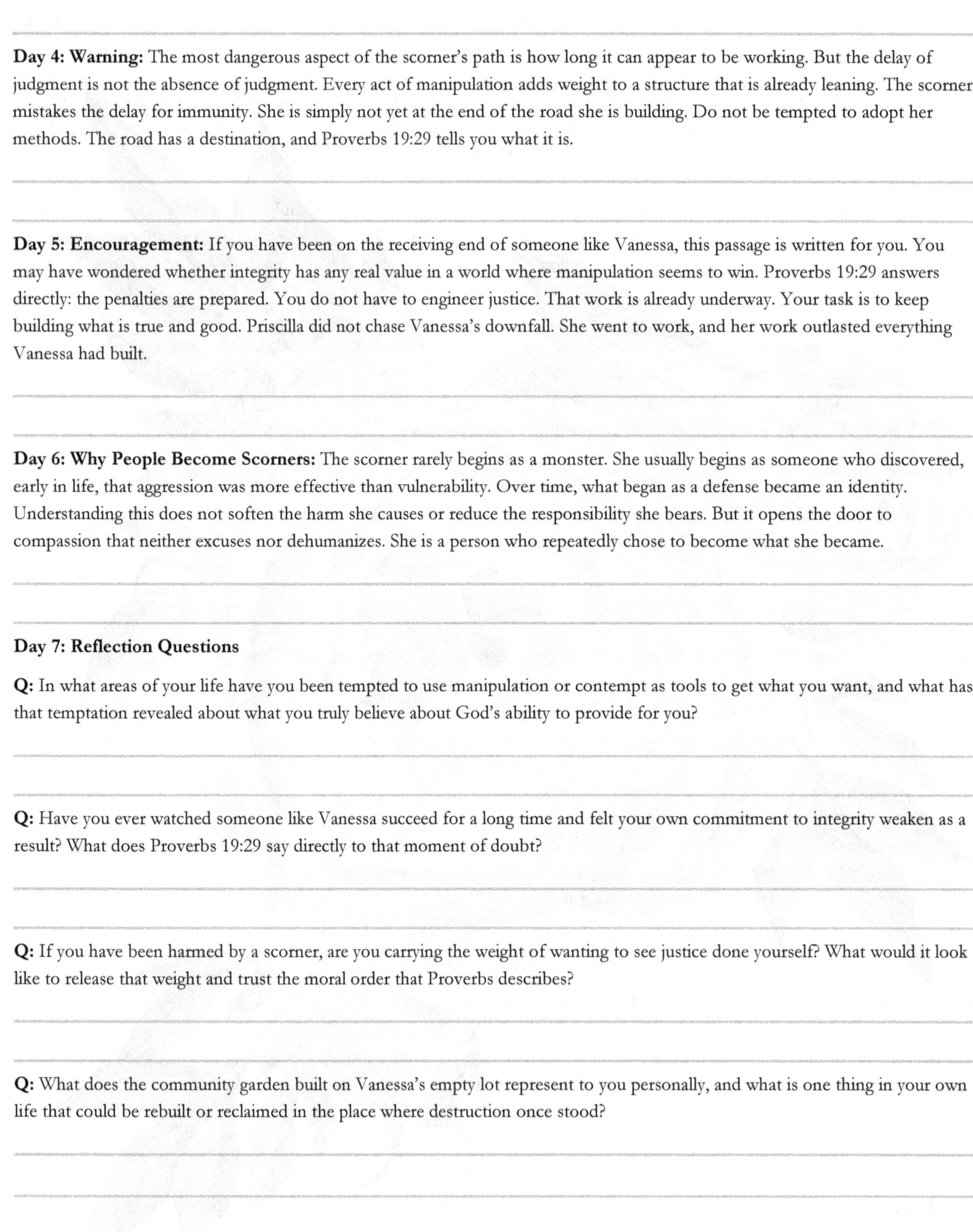

Day 4: Warning: The most dangerous aspect of the scorner's path is how long it can appear to be working. But the delay of judgment is not the absence of judgment. Every act of manipulation adds weight to a structure that is already leaning. The scorner mistakes the delay for immunity. She is simply not yet at the end of the road she is building. Do not be tempted to adopt her methods. The road has a destination, and Proverbs 19:29 tells you what it is.

Day 5: Encouragement: If you have been on the receiving end of someone like Vanessa, this passage is written for you. You may have wondered whether integrity has any real value in a world where manipulation seems to win. Proverbs 19:29 answers directly: the penalties are prepared. You do not have to engineer justice. That work is already underway. Your task is to keep building what is true and good. Priscilla did not chase Vanessa's downfall. She went to work, and her work outlasted everything Vanessa had built.

Day 6: Why People Become Scorners: The scorner rarely begins as a monster. She usually begins as someone who discovered, early in life, that aggression was more effective than vulnerability. Over time, what began as a defense became an identity. Understanding this does not soften the harm she causes or reduce the responsibility she bears. But it opens the door to compassion that neither excuses nor dehumanizes. She is a person who repeatedly chose to become what she became.

Day 7: Reflection Questions

Q: In what areas of your life have you been tempted to use manipulation or contempt as tools to get what you want, and what has that temptation revealed about what you truly believe about God's ability to provide for you?

Q: Have you ever watched someone like Vanessa succeed for a long time and felt your own commitment to integrity weaken as a result? What does Proverbs 19:29 say directly to that moment of doubt?

Q: If you have been harmed by a scorner, are you carrying the weight of wanting to see justice done yourself? What would it look like to release that weight and trust the moral order that Proverbs describes?

Q: What does the community garden built on Vanessa's empty lot represent to you personally, and what is one thing in your own life that could be rebuilt or reclaimed in the place where destruction once stood?

Prayer Journal

eavenly Father,

You see every motive, every word, and every consequence that flows from my actions. Thank You for Your justice and for the ways You warn, correct, and guide me back from paths that lead to harm. Forgive me for any way I have spread hurt, acted out of pride, or used others to get ahead. I confess the times I have justified small wrongs and ignored the warnings You placed before me. Lord, give me the courage to face the truth about myself and to make restitution where I have caused harm. Place people in my life who will speak truth with kindness and give me humility to receive correction without defensiveness or blame.

Teach me to trust Your timing when I see injustice and to resist the temptation to take matters into my own hands. Let my words build up instead of tear down. Fill my heart with a longing for what is right and good, and help me to walk in integrity even when it costs me. Restore what has been broken in me and through me. Guard my steps so that my life becomes a place of healing and not harm. Thank You for the grace that meets me in my failures and for the hope that change is possible. May Your justice and mercy shape my life so that I bring blessing, not destruction, to those around me.

In Jesus' name, Amen.

Prayer Thoughts for Today: In Jesus' name, Amen.

Prayer Thoughts for Today:

✦✦✦✦✦

~ End Prayer Journal "The Wise" ~

THE BEGINNING OF WISDOM

THE WISE

PROVERBS 3:13: (NIV)

"Blessed is the one who finds wisdom, the one who gains understanding."

Emma had always been drawn to people who just seemed to know what to do. A friend who left a dead-end job and landed somewhere better. A neighbor whose kids were genuinely kind. She would watch them and wonder what they had figured out that she hadn't. It wasn't that Emma made terrible decisions, but she often second-guessed herself, circled back, and wished she had a clearer sense of direction. She wanted that kind of steadiness for her own life. She just didn't know where to look for it.

The answer started to take shape on an ordinary Sunday morning. Emma's pastor was preaching through the book of Proverbs, and something he said stopped her mid-thought. Wisdom, he explained, isn't just about being smart or having enough life experience. It starts with reverence for God. "The fear of the Lord is the beginning of knowledge; fools despise wisdom and instruction" (Proverbs 1:7). Emma turned the verse over in her mind on the drive home. That week, she started reading one chapter of Proverbs each morning. The writing was direct, sometimes blunt, and surprisingly practical. She kept coming back to the same themes: humility, honesty, the courage to take correction, the value of surrounding yourself with people wiser than you. It felt less like reading an ancient text and more like a conversation she had needed to have for a long time.

What struck Emma most was that wisdom wasn't something that just happened to you. It had to be sought. Proverbs 2:2-6 put it plainly: "Turn your ear to wisdom...call out for insight...search for it as for hidden treasure...For the Lord gives wisdom; from his mouth come knowledge and understanding." She started praying about it every morning, not in a vague, hopeful way, but specifically, asking God to guide her thinking in her relationships, her work, and the decisions that kept her up at night.

She also started reaching out to people she respected and asking if she could buy them coffee. She came with real questions, not small talk. What she heard surprised her. One woman talked about how swallowing her pride and asking for help had saved her marriage. A man she admired at church described a moment when he chose honesty at work, even when it cost him. Another friend talked about the slow, painful work of letting go of friendships that were pulling her in the wrong direction. These weren't polished testimonies. They were honest stories from people still figuring it out.

Gradually, Emma began to notice a shift. When a coworker snapped at her over something small, she felt the familiar pull to snap back. But Proverbs 15:1 came to mind: "A gentle answer turns away wrath." She took a breath and chose differently. When a shortcut at work tempted her, she thought of Proverbs 13:11: "Dishonest money dwindles away, but whoever gathers money little by little makes it grow." She passed it on. These weren't dramatic moments. They were quiet, everyday choices that added up. She still made mistakes. But she stopped being so defensive about them. Proverbs 12:1 had a way of cutting through her pride:

"Whoever loves discipline loves knowledge, but whoever hates correction is stupid." She laughed the first time she read it. Then she let it sink in. Admitting she was wrong started to feel less like defeat and more like relief.

She also got more comfortable saying the words she used to avoid: "I don't know." Proverbs had a lot to say about pride, and Emma had to admit that some of it landed uncomfortably close to home. She had spent years projecting confidence she didn't always feel. Letting that go was harder than she expected, but also freeing. People didn't trust her less for it. If anything, they trusted her more. Over time, Emma's relationships deepened. Her sister mentioned that she seemed different, calmer somehow. Friends started calling her when things got hard. She wasn't always sure what to say, but she had learned to listen first and talk second, and it turned out that mattered more than having the right answer.

When a job offer came in from a company in another city, Emma felt the old anxiety creep back in. It was a good opportunity, but it would mean leaving everything familiar behind. This time, though, she knew what to do. She prayed. She wrote out the pros and cons. She called two people whose judgment she trusted and listened carefully to what they had to say. Then she waited, not passively, but with a kind of attentive patience she was still learning. The peace she felt wasn't a guarantee that everything would go smoothly. But it was enough to take the next step.

Looking back, Emma could see how much had changed, not all at once, but slowly, the way most real things change. Wisdom wasn't a destination she had arrived at. It was more like a direction she had chosen, one she had to keep choosing every day. Some mornings she still opened Proverbs and felt like she was reading it for the first time. Other mornings a verse she had passed over a dozen times finally made sense. She was grateful for both.

When friends asked what had changed in her, she didn't have a tidy answer. She would tell them about Proverbs, about the morning routine, about the coffee conversations with people she respected. She would tell them it wasn't complicated, just consistent. And she meant it. She had learned that God's wisdom isn't reserved for people who already have it together. It's available to anyone who asks. "Blessed is the one who finds wisdom, the one who gains understanding" (Proverbs 3:13). Emma had found that to be true, and she wanted everyone around her to find it too.

Day 1: Q&A:
Q: How did Emma pursue wisdom?
A: She committed to reading a chapter of Proverbs every morning, letting its timeless truths shape her thinking. Each day, she brought her decisions and struggles before God in prayer, asking for wisdom she knew she couldn't find on her own. She also sought out trusted mentors, sitting with them over coffee to learn how they applied biblical principles to real life. Then, with humility, she put it all into practice, choosing patience, honesty, and discernment even when it was hard.

Q: What blessings did Emma experience?
A: As Emma applied biblical wisdom, her choices became more thoughtful and intentional, and the people around her took notice. Colleagues and friends began to trust her more, knowing she would respond with honesty and grace rather than impulse or self-interest. Her relationships grew deeper, too, as she became a better listener, a peacemaker, and someone others felt safe turning to in hard times. Most of all, Emma found a quiet, steady peace, knowing that her life was anchored in God's guidance rather than her own understanding.

Day 2: Explanation: Proverbs teaches that wisdom is not something we manufacture on our own; it is a gift from God, freely given to all who humbly seek it. It begins with the fear of the Lord, a deep reverence that positions the heart to receive what only He can give. From there, wisdom grows through a teachable spirit, a willingness to be corrected and shaped by God's Word rather than clinging to our own understanding. Prayer, consistent time in Scripture, and learning from wise and godly people are the daily practices that keep that growth alive.

Day 3: Anecdote: A teacher decided to spend one month reading a chapter of Proverbs every morning before heading into her classroom. At first, it was simply a personal discipline, but she quickly noticed that the wisdom she was absorbing began to shape how she handled conflict, communicated with students, and responded to difficult parents. Where she once reacted with frustration, she now pauses, chooses gentler words, and seeks understanding first. By the end of the month, she told her small group that she hadn't just read Proverbs, she felt like Proverbs had read her.

Day 4: Blessing and Rewards: Proverbs paints a breathtaking picture of what wisdom produces in a life fully surrendered to God: clarity in the midst of confusion, peace that steadies the soul, and favor that opens doors no amount of striving could. These are not small rewards; they are the fruit of a life aligned with the Creator of all things. Proverbs 3:15 captures it beautifully: "She is more precious than rubies; nothing you desire can compare with her." When we choose wisdom, we are not settling for less; we are gaining far more than anything the world has to offer.

Day 5: Encouragement: If you find yourself at a crossroads, overwhelmed by a decision, or simply longing for greater clarity and direction, the invitation is simple: ask God for wisdom. James 1:5 promises that He gives generously to all who ask, without finding fault or making us feel foolish for not already knowing. You don't have to have it all figured out before you come to Him; in fact, your need is exactly what draws you to the One who has every answer. Start today with an honest prayer, open your Bible to Proverbs, and trust that the God who created wisdom is more than willing to share it with you.

Day 6: God's Love and Redemption: One of the most comforting truths in Proverbs is that God is not a distant judge waiting for us to fail. He is a loving Father who delights in teaching His children. He does not withhold wisdom from those who have stumbled; in fact, some of the richest lessons come from our moments of greatest failure. No matter how foolish a decision we've made or how far off course we've wandered, His wisdom is always available, ready to meet us where we are. With God, there is always a fresh start, always a hand extended, always a clear path forward for those willing to seek it.

Day 7: Reflection Questions:

Q: In what area of your life do you most need God's wisdom today? Consider the decisions, relationships, or struggles that feel heaviest right now. Bring those specific areas honestly before God, trusting that He already knows and is ready to guide you.

Q: Who can you invite to speak wisdom into your life? Why would you choose this person? Think about someone whose faith, character, and experience you genuinely respect. Reaching out to them could be one of the most meaningful steps you take toward growth.

Q: How can you make seeking wisdom from God's Word a daily habit? Even a few focused minutes each morning in Proverbs can begin to reshape the way you think and respond throughout the day. Small, consistent steps of faithfulness are what turn a good intention into a life-changing rhythm.

Q: What blessings have you seen from following God's guidance in the past? Pausing to remember His faithfulness builds confidence that He will guide you again. Let those moments of past grace fuel your trust in Him today.

PRAYER JOURNAL

Heavenly Father,

You are the source of all wisdom, knowledge, and understanding. Thank You for inviting me to seek Your guidance and for the priceless treasure of Your Word, especially the book of Proverbs. Forgive me for the times I have relied on my own insight or ignored Your gentle correction. I confess that, apart from You, I am prone to folly, pride, and confusion. Lord, I ask for Your wisdom in every area of my life (my work, my relationships, my decisions, and my character). Open my ears to hear Your voice and my heart to receive Your instruction, even when it challenges my comfort or pride. Place-wise mentors and friends around me, and give me the humility to learn from their experiences. Help me to value correction and to welcome advice, knowing that You often speak through others.

Teach me to search for wisdom as for hidden treasure, to meditate on Your Word daily, and to pray for discernment in every choice. Fill my mouth with gentle answers, my mind with discernment, and my actions with integrity. Let Your wisdom guards my steps and shape my life to honor You. Thank You for Your patience and for the promise that You give wisdom generously to all who ask. Restore my heart where I have made foolish choices and lead me forward with confidence and peace. May my life reflect the beauty and power of Your wisdom, bringing blessing to others and glory to Your name.

In Jesus' name, Amen.

Prayer Thoughts for Today:

~ End Prayer Journal "The Wise" ~

A Prayer For You

With a heart overflowing with gratitude and humility, I come before You Lord Jesus, acknowledging Your boundless love and unending grace. You are the giver of all good things, the Author of every beautiful story, the One who breathes purpose into ordinary moments and transforms them into something eternal. You are the One who sees into the depths of every soul and knows our needs before we even speak. How grateful we are that You are not a distant God, but a near and faithful Father who draws close to the brokenhearted and lifts the weary by name.

Thank you to every precious reader who has opened these pages with a spirit of willingness to learn and grow. What a gift it is simply to seek, to hunger for something deeper, truer, and more lasting than what the world offers. I lift each beloved one before You now, asking that You wrap them in Your tender embrace. Pour out Your Spirit of wisdom upon them: illuminate their minds with truth, soften their hearts with compassion, and guide their steps into the fullness of life You have prepared for them. When they face decisions, grant them discernment and the quiet assurance that You are near. When they encounter failure, gently remind them that Your mercies are new every morning and that Your grace covers every misstep. When doubt creeps in and questions linger, meet them there with Your gentle, unwavering truth. When relationships are strained, fill them with humility to forgive, courage to seek peace, and the wisdom to mend what is broken. When the world feels overwhelming, hold them close and be their refuge. Let them find in You a deep wellspring of comfort, rest, and strength that never runs dry.

Shape their lives, moment by moment, by the truth and beauty of Your Word. Let Your Scripture be not merely something they read, but something they live, a lamp for their feet and a light for every uncertain path. Let their words be gentle and uplifting, their actions overflow with compassion, and their presence become a beacon of hope and blessing to everyone they encounter. Surround them with wise mentors, steadfast friends, and a community that reflects Your love. Help them to become encouragers, peacemakers, and living testaments of Your kindness in a world that deeply needs it. May they never underestimate the quiet, lasting power of a single act of grace offered in Your name.

Above all, draw them ever closer to You, that their hearts may beat in rhythm with Yours. May they walk daily in the light of Your unfailing love, discovering in You a wellspring of purpose, hope, and unshakable joy. Bless them with a peace that surpasses all understanding and fill them with the quiet confidence that comes from knowing they are cherished, redeemed, and never, ever alone, held always in the palm of Your loving hand. May the legacy of wisdom, grace, and love take root and flourish in their lives, growing deeper with each passing day. Let it ripple out with ever-widening circles to bless their families, friends, and generations yet to come, so that Your light continues to shine through them long after these words are read.

In Jesus' beautiful name, Amen.

Thank you, from the depths of my heart, for letting me be part of your story. It is a sacred honor to walk even a small stretch of your journey with you. These pages were written with you in mind, with the hope that somewhere within them, you found a word that met you exactly where you needed to be met. May you carry forward not just what you have learned, but who you are becoming. May you walk the path of wisdom with courage and compassion, trusting always in the gentle guidance of God's love. And on the days when the path feels unclear, or the weight feels heavy, may you remember that you do not walk it alone. Wherever life leads, may you feel deeply known, unconditionally loved, and forever held by the One who calls you His own.

Sherri Sullivan

www.ingramcontent.com/pod-product-compliance
Lightning Source LLC
Chambersburg PA
CBHW080339030726
47594CB00012B/4080